The *Iliad* of Homer

Professor Elizabeth Vandiver

THE TEACHING COMPANY ®

PUBLISHED BY:

THE TEACHING COMPANY
4840 Westfields Boulevard, Suite 500
Chantilly, Virginia 20151-2299
1-800-TEACH-12
Fax—703-378-3819
www.teach12.com

Printed in the United States of America

ISBN 1-56585-841-7

Elizabeth Vandiver, Ph.D.

Visiting Assistant Professor of Classics, University of Maryland

Elizabeth Vandiver did her undergraduate work at Shimer College, Mt. Carroll, Illinois, where she matriculated in 1972 as a sixteen-year-old "early entrant." After receiving her B.A. in 1975, she spent several years working as a librarian before deciding to pursue graduate work in Classics at the University of Texas at Austin. She received her M.A. in 1984 and her Ph.D. in 1990.

In addition to her current position at the University of Maryland (flagship campus at College Park), Professor Vandiver has held visiting professorships at Northwestern University, the University of Georgia, The Intercollegiate Center for Classical Studies (Rome, Italy), Loyola University (New Orleans) and Utah State University.

In 1998 Dr. Vandiver received the American Philological Association's Excellence in Teaching Award, the most prestigious teaching award available to American classicists. Other awards include the Northwestern University Department of Classics Excellence in Teaching award for 1998 and the University of Georgia's Outstanding Honors Professor award in 1993 and 1994.

Dr. Vandiver has published a book, *Heroes in Herodotus: The Interaction of Myth and History*, and several articles, as well as delivering numerous papers at national and international conferences. She is currently working on a second book, examining the influence of the classical tradition on the British poets of World War I.

Dr. Vandiver is married to Franklin J. Hildy, Ph.D., Professor and Chair, Department of Theatre, at the University of Maryland.

This course is dedicated to the memory
of Gareth Morgan,
teacher of Greek, lover of Homer.

Table of Contents
The *Iliad* of Homer

The *Iliad* of Homer

Scope:

This set of twelve lectures introduces the student to the first of the two great epics of ancient Greece, the *Iliad* and the *Odyssey*. During the course, the student should read the *Iliad* in its entirety to gain the maximum benefit and enjoyment from the lectures, which provide careful, detailed examinations of the most important episodes, address various critical and interpretative issues, and give background information on the cultural assumptions contained in the *Iliad*.

The first lecture sets the stage for our reading of the *Iliad* (and, subsequently, the *Odyssey*) by providing an introduction to the plan of the course and summarizing the mythological background assumed by the Greek epics. The second lecture addresses the question of the 400- to 500-year gap between the events described in the *Iliad* and the *Odyssey* and the time when they were written down. It describes the epics' relationship to traditional orally transmitted poetry, and considers the implications of that oral tradition for the question of who "Homer" was.

Lectures Three through Twelve address the plot, characters, and interpretations of the *Iliad* itself. Each of these lectures focuses on a particular scene, character, or theme as we read through the *Iliad*. Lecture Three introduces the cultural concepts of *kleos* (glory) and *timê* (honor) and explains their significance for understanding the wrath of Achilles. Lecture Four moves inside the walls of Troy to discuss Homer's presentation of the Trojans as sympathetic characters, not as stereotypical enemies. In Lecture Five, we look in detail at Book IX of the *Iliad*, where three of Achilles' comrades try to persuade him to return to battle; we discuss how the concepts of *kleos* and *timê* factor into his refusal to do so. The concept of *kleos* is given a fuller discussion in Lecture Six, which demonstrates that it is one of the key elements in the *Iliad*'s examination of the human condition. In Lecture Seven, we turn to examining the gods in Homer, discussing what types of beings they are and what their presence in the narrative adds to the *Iliad*. Lectures Eight and Nine give a detailed reading of the most important events of the day of Hektor's glory and Patroklos' death, the *Iliad*'s longest day, which lasts from Book XI through Book XVIII; Lecture Eight focuses on

Hektor and Lecture Nine, on Patroklos. Achilles' return to battle is covered in Lecture Ten, which discusses the implications of his actions, his divinely made armor, and his refusal to bury the dead Patroklos. Lecture Eleven examines Hektor and Achilles together, highlighting the contrasting elements in their characters and the inevitability of their final encounter in battle. Finally, in Lecture Twelve, we discuss the resolution of the *Iliad*, which is brought about by Achilles' encounter with his dead enemy, Hektor's aged father, King Priam. Throughout these lectures, we will visit again and again the overriding theme of what it means to be human and what the *Iliad* has to say about the human condition.

Lecture One
Introduction to Homeric Epic

Scope:

This first lecture introduces students to the overall plan of the course. The lecture falls into three main sections. The first of these discusses why the Homeric epics are still worth reading, nearly 3,000 years after their creation. In this section, we consider definitions of the term "epic," the *Iliad* and *Odyssey*'s place in literary history, and possible reasons why they have remained popular for so long. The second section outlines and explains the course's format and approach; lectures will include some plot synopsis, discussion of the epics' cultural background, and examination of larger issues raised by the epics. The third section gives a brief overview of the story of the Trojan War, which is the crucial narrative background of the Homeric epics.

Outline

I. This introductory lecture has three main objects.

- **A.** The lecture begins by discussing what the *Iliad* and *Odyssey* are, and why they still worth reading, nearly 3,000 years after their creation.
- **B.** The second section of the lecture outlines the approach and overall shape of the course.
- **C.** The lecture concludes with a brief summary of the story of the Trojan War, the narrative background for the epics.

II. What are the *Iliad* and the *Odyssey*, and why should modern readers spend time on them?

- **A.** These two poems are the earliest literary works in the European tradition, although they represent the culmination of a centuries-long tradition of orally transmitted poetry.
- **B.** They are the first fully developed epics in Western culture.
  1. By "epic," the Greeks simply meant any long poem in one particular meter, dactylic hexameter.
  2. Because of Greece's influence on later Western culture, the *Iliad* and the *Odyssey* served as models for later epic. The term "epic" thus came to mean narrative poems

dealing with gods and heroes, and often associated with either war or adventure.

C. The Homeric epics were primary cultural texts for classical Greek civilization.

1. They served as educational tools, as moral frameworks, provided examples of proper and improper behavior. They codify information about the value system of ancient Greek culture.

2. They provide the fullest accounts we have of several episodes from the Trojan War myth, one of the most important and pervasive myths of Greek, Roman, and later Western civilization.

D. Why should modern readers spend time on these ancient works? There are two obvious answers. First, these epics have survived because they have continued to speak to readers throughout the ages. In addition, they have exercised an enormous influence on later literature.

1. The epics are much more than merely narratives about war (the *Iliad*) or adventure and homecoming (the *Odyssey*). They both look deep into the heart of what it means to be human.

2. The very fact the Homeric epics continue to seem compelling to us is in itself evidence of their influence. We find them compelling in part because so much of our later literary tradition derives ultimately from them.

3. Their influence on later literature is incalculable; apart from these epics, only the Bible has exercised so profound an influence on later Western culture. Unlike the Bible, however, the Greek epics were not sacred texts.

E. At the same time that they remain compelling and familiar, the society described in the epics is also alien to us in many ways: it is patriarchal, slave-holding, monarchical, polytheistic. They are thus both familiar and strange, both close and remote.

III. These lectures will concentrate on careful, detailed examinations of the two epics. We cannot discuss every episode of both epics, but we will attempt to touch on the highlights of each, especially on those scenes that bring out wider thematic issues. Accordingly, the lectures approach the epics from three angles.

A. Most lectures will include some synopsis of the relevant section's plot.
   1. Lectures Two, Thirteen, and Twenty-Four are exceptions since they discuss material outside the actual epics.
   2. Each lecture's "Essential Reading" will be taken from the epics themselves. Thus, by the end of the course the student will have read the entire *Iliad* and *Odyssey*.

B. When necessary, the lectures will also discuss the cultural background and assumptions of the specific scenes under discussion.

C. Finally, the lectures will address the larger issues being dealt with by the epics: the deeper content for which plot and cultural assumptions are the vehicle.

IV. Before beginning our reading of the epics themselves, we need to cover two types of background information. In this lecture, we will examine the mythic background of the two epics. The next lecture will discuss the poetic background of the epics and the question of when and how they were composed.

A. The mythic background of the poems is the story of the Trojan War, the most famous legend in ancient literature.
   1. This story of a great war between a Greek expeditionary force and the people of Troy provided narrative material not only for the *Iliad* and *Odyssey*, but for many Greek tragedies, for Virgil's *Aeneid*, and for countless later works.
   2. The *Iliad* and the *Odyssey* do not tell the entire story of the war. The *Iliad* focuses on events that happened during a short period in the last year of the war, and the *Odyssey* deals with the hero Odysseus' further adventures after the war.
   3. These two epics were not the only ones to deal with the Trojan War, although they were recognized in antiquity as the greatest epics. There were other epic poems, now lost, that told the rest of the story of the Trojan War.

B. The *Iliad* and the *Odyssey* clearly allude to various episodes of the Trojan War that are not part of their own narrative framework. In other words, these two epics assume that their audience is familiar with the following basic elements of the whole story:

1. The most beautiful woman in the world, Helen, daughter of the great god Zeus and wife of the Greek Menelaos, was abducted by the Trojan prince Paris.
2. Under the command of Menelaos' elder brother Agamemnon, the Greeks mustered an army to go to Troy and fight for Helen's return.
3. The war against Troy lasted for 10 years. The fighting was fairly evenly balanced, with each side having its foremost warrior (Achilles for the Greeks, Hektor for the Trojans).
4. Achilles was the son of a goddess mother, Thetis, and a human father, Peleus. Their wedding was arranged by Zeus, and Thetis was not entirely willing.
5. The greatest Trojan warrior, Hektor, was killed by the greatest Greek warrior, Achilles, who was himself killed by Paris.
6. Finally, the Greeks resorted to trickery. Using the famous ruse of the Trojan Horse, invented by Odysseus, they infiltrated the walled city of Troy and sacked it by night.
7. The Greeks committed many outrages against the Trojans during the Sack of Troy. Foremost among these were the killing of King Priam at his household altar, the murder of Hektor's baby son Astyanax by throwing him from the city walls, and the rape of Priam's daughter Kassandra in the temple of the virgin goddess Athena.
8. These outrages angered the gods, leading to many hardships for the surviving Greeks on their way home. Most importantly, Agamemnon was killed by his wife and her lover when he arrived home, and Odysseus spent 10 years wandering on his way from Troy.

C. There are some famous details of the legend that are not clearly alluded to by Homer, and even some that are clearly excluded.

1. Most scholars think that the *Iliad* alludes to the famous "Judgment of Paris," but this remains uncertain.
2. The story that Achilles was invulnerable except for his heel is definitely not assumed in the *Iliad*.

D. In the next lecture, we will consider how these poems came to be created.

Supplementary Reading:

Timothy Gantz, *Early Greek Myth,* Volume 2, Chapter 16. A very detailed account, listing all the ancient sources for each detail of the legend.

Susan Woodford, *Trojan War in Art*, Chapters 1–2. A simple, easily readable account of the background events.

Questions to Consider:

1. Myths such as the story of the Trojan War, which "everyone knew," provided a stock of common reference points against which the Greeks could map their everyday experiences, frame moral questions, and so on. Does modern American culture have any similar set of common reference points?
2. The Homeric epics use the stories they tell to meditate on great over-reaching themes, such as the nature of mortality. Can the same be said of all great literature? Put another way, can a story told simply for the sake of the story qualify as "literature"?

Lecture One—Transcript
Introduction to Homeric Epic

Hello, and welcome to this first lecture in the course, The Homeric Epics. My name is Elizabeth Vandiver; I teach classics—that is, Latin and Greek language, literature, and culture—at Northwestern University, and for next several hours I am going to be talking to you about the two great epics of ancient Greece, the *Iliad* and the *Odyssey*. In this introductory lecture there are three main things I want to do. First, I want to talk about what the *Iliad* and *Odyssey* are, and why they are still worth reading nearly three thousand years after they were created. Second, I want to outline the approach and overall shape of the course, so that you will have some idea of where I am planning to go with these lectures, how I intend to approach the two great epics; and then finally, this introductory lecture will conclude with a summary of the story of the Trojan War, the mythic background for the narrative of the *Iliad* and the *Odyssey*, the background story that those two epics assume their audiences are completely familiar with.

So, to start out with my first point, what are the *Iliad* and the *Odyssey*, and why should modern readers spend time on them? These two poems are the earliest literary works in the Western European tradition, although they represent a culmination of a centuries-long tradition of oral composition and oral poetry. That is, they began, as we'll discuss in detail in Lecture Two, by being passed on generation after generation, through oral transmission and through memorization, rather than writing. But when writing was introduced into Greece, these were the first two great works of literature to be set down in writing. So they are the beginning of the Western literary tradition.

They're also the first fully developed epics in Western culture. The term "epic" maybe needs a little definition. By epic, the Greeks themselves simply meant any long poem written in one poetic meter, that we call dactylic hexameter. So, no matter what the content was, no matter what the subject matter was, to the Greeks themselves, if a poem was written in dactylic hexameter, it counted as epic. But the influence of the *Iliad* and the *Odyssey* on Greek culture was so great, and the influence of Greek culture on later European culture was so great, that epic came to mean any long narrative poem dealing with the subject matter with which the *Iliad* and the *Odyssey* are concerned—namely gods, heroes, warfare, adventure, sometimes warfare *and* adventure. So, the *Iliad* and the *Odyssey* influenced not only our understanding of epic as a form—that is, a long narrative poem—but also our understanding of what the content of epic is.

Within Greek civilization itself, the Homeric epics were the primary cultural texts for that civilization. What I mean by "cultural texts" is that these epics were much more than just entertainment. They are entertainment, of course; they're very enjoyable just to listen to or to read as stories. But within ancient civilization, they were much important than mere entertainment might seem to indicate. They served as educational tools, they provided moral exempla for people, and they provided paradigms of how one ought to behave or ought not to behave in certain situations; examples of how people should deal with just about every situation that might arise in human life.

This aspect of the *Iliad* and the *Odyssey* was particularly important in their pre-written stage. As I already mentioned, they developed first off as oral poems, as poetry that was transmitted orally through several generations, before they were ever written down. In a preliterate culture, in a culture that does not have writing, story-telling of some kind or another assumes an enormous importance, much more than it has in a literate culture, because—if you think about it this makes sense—in a culture without writing, how does the culture transmit its values from one generation to another? How does a culture that does not have writing explain how humans should interact with the gods, what the gods are, what the nature of reality is, how people should live together, how marriages should be conducted, how parents should deal with children, what an enemy owes to another enemy on the battlefield, all of that sort of thing that we, in a highly developed literate culture, would codify in law books, in history books, in theological texts, in religious treatises? In a culture that has no writing—I tend to use the term "preliterate" rather than illiterate, by the way, to get away from the stigma of "illiterate"—in a preliterate culture, there is really only one way to transmit all of those cultural values, and that is through the traditional stories of the culture. That is true not just for ancient Greek culture, but for any preliterate culture.

So, along with being entertaining, the *Iliad* and the *Odyssey* codify—or "contain under the surface" might be a better way of putting it—

all sorts of information about the values, the moral framework, the belief system of ancient Greek culture.

This function that they served did not disappear once they were written down, however; quite the contrary, once writing was introduced into Greece—probably in the eighth century B.C., and that is another point we'll take up in Lecture Two—once writing was introduced into Greece, the *Iliad* and the *Odyssey* became the foremost primary texts for educational purposes. When a little boy—and it almost always was a little *boy*—in, say, fifth-century B.C. Athens, was going to be taught to read and write, he was taught to read and write off Homer's epics, off the *Iliad* and the *Odyssey*. These were the works that any educated literate person knew; the hallmark of being an educated literate person was familiarity with the *Iliad* and the *Odyssey*. And in that role, once Greece had become literate, they provided a kind of touchstone for settling arguments, for citing precedents in legal cases, for referring to as a fine rhetorical flourish in a speech. In most of the great writers that we have from the Golden Age of Greece—which is fifth-century Athens and on into the fourth century—most of the great writers we have make constant reference, either directly or indirectly, to the Homeric epics.

So, within their own culture they provided this kind of rich storehouse of quotations or reference points for the entire culture to use in its everyday existence, somewhat the way the Bible does—or at least used to provide a reference point for our culture. I tend to shy away from what is very often said, that the *Iliad* and the *Odyssey* were "the Bible of the Greeks," because I think that brings with it some misleading assumptions that do not really apply here. They were not sacred texts in the way that the Bible is a sacred text for Jews and Christians or that the Koran is a sacred text for Muslims; they were not dogma. There is nothing in the *Iliad* or in the *Odyssey* that you had to believe in order to be a good "Zeusist," if I can coin a term. They're not sacred texts in that sense, but they were a storehouse, as I have already said, of exempla, of precedents, so they resemble the Bible in our culture in that respect. They resemble Shakespeare in our culture in that respect; perhaps that is, in a way, a better analogy.

As well as their importance in their own culture they also, as it happens, preserve for us the fullest accounts of several important episodes from the Trojan War myth—events such as Achilles dragging the dead body of his enemy, Hektor, behind his chariot, a very vivid image from the Trojan War story, something that most people who know about the Trojan War have heard of. That particular episode occurs in the *Iliad*; the *Iliad* is our main source for that particular event in the Trojan War. So, many of the important details of the Trojan War story—and the Trojan War itself is one of the most important myths of Western culture—many of its important details are preserved in the *Iliad* and *Odyssey*.

Well, all right, so they were important in their culture; so they preserve a great deal of information about the Trojan War; but still, why should readers today bother to read them, nearly three thousand years after they were created? We know the story of the Trojan War; why go back to the source and see what Homer said about it? We have other cultural touchstones to refer to; we don't use the *Iliad* and *Odyssey* that way any more; why are they still important?

I think there are two obvious answers to that question. First off, these epics have survived in the first place because they have continued to speak to readers throughout the ages and throughout changing cultures. They are far more than merely narratives about war, or about adventures in homecoming. They look beyond those surface storylines deep into the heart of what it means to be human, into the human condition. They examine questions of life, of death, of the meaning of mortality, of how human beings must and can come to terms with the fact of death. Tthey examine age; the effect of time on human beings; the interactions of people with other people—husbands with wives, fathers with sons, and so forth. They resonant with us because they are so much more than merely stories about one particular war or one particular hero's homecoming; they have a much wider significance than that. If they had not continued to speak to readers, if they had not continued to resonate on a deeper level than their surface narrative might indicate, they never would have survived from antiquity to today in the first place.

That perhaps deserves a little explanation. We tend to think that a book, once published, remains accessible even if it goes out of print; you can find a copy in a library somewhere, or something. In the time before the invention of the printing press, of course, the survival of any book, of any written text, was a much more tenuous and dangerous proposition. In order to survive, any book had to be copied over by hand. Whenever one manuscript wore out another had to be made by hand. This was an extraordinarily laborious process. And it is the fact that most of the works of ancient literature, most of the writings of the great authors of ancient Greece and ancient Rome, have not survived. And I am not talking here only about obscure works by authors no one has heard of. To take one very famous example, the Greek playwright Sophocles, the author of *Oedipus the King* and *Antigone* wrote probably about 120 tragedies. Of those, seven—only seven—have survived into the modern world. The rest are gone, lost forever. There are some fragments—quotations in other authors, and literal fragments that have been found, mainly in Egypt. But Sophocles' repertoire now, the entire content of Sophocles' work now, is seven plays out of the 120 that he originally wrote.

Other authors are in even worse shape, of Sappho, the great poet Sappho, we have only a handful of fragments. We have only one complete poem by her, out of three books of poetry that we are told she wrote. So, if the *Iliad* and the *Odyssey* had not been considered extraordinarily compelling and worth preserving, they would not have been preserved. To be compelling was not in and of itself enough to ensure preservation—again, as Sophocles shows—but it was certainly a *sine qua non;* without that, they would have died long before now. So, they survived in part because they continued to be compelling to readers. They still are compelling to readers.

Another reason that they are worth reading today, that they are worth becoming familiar with, is their extraordinary influence on later Western literature. Part of the reason they continue to seem familiar, compelling, reasonable, understandable, to us is simply because they have had so much influence on almost all of later Western culture—not just literature, but art, music, almost anything you can imagine in Western culture as well. But purely in terms of literature, they have had such an enormous influence that we find them familiar, in a sense, because they are the foundation of just about every other literary work in our culture. Apart from these epics, I think it is fair to say the only work that has had more influence on later Western culture is again, the Bible. The Bible on the one hand, the Homeric epics on the other, are really the two mainsprings from which Western culture developed.

And yet, at the same time that these epics remain compelling and familiar is so many ways, the society that they describe is alien and remote to us in the extreme. Some modern readers find it shockingly alien and remote. It's patriarchal, it's slave-holding, it's monarchical, it's polytheistic. Each one of those terms I could probably spend an entire lecture on; but just very briefly, to look at what is so strange about each of those four aspects of Homeric society, when I say that this society is patriarchal I am not referring to some vague sense in which men have a little bit more power than women or a little bit more authority than women. I mean it much strongly than that. The society portrayed in the Homeric epics is a society in which men have all the *public* power, at least, all the public authority. With almost no exceptions, men control the family, the kingdoms, the society. Women's power, if it's there at all, is relegated entirely to the domestic sphere. Very different from our society.

Slave-holding, I don't think really needs any discussion, except to say that in the Homeric epics no-one ever questions the validity of slavery as a system; it never has crossed anyone's mind, in these epics, that there could be another way to construct a society other than to hold slaves. Nobody wants to be a slave himself or herself, and slaves who are slaves very much want to get out of that side of the picture and become masters instead. But the idea that there could be a society that did not focus on slaves, that did not operate through slavery, simply has not occurred to anyone in these epics. Similarly with the fact that the society of the Homeric epics is monarchical. You'll see, when we start talking about the *Iliad*, that we are not talking about one unified Greece under one Greek king; we are talking about a loose confederation of small kingdoms, of small communities, but each one of those small communities is ruled by a king. And again, it does not seem to ever cross anyone's mind, in either the *Iliad* or the *Odyssey*, that there could be any other way to govern a society except to have a king. Once again, you may not like the king you have, you may want to throw him out, kill him and become king yourself, but the idea that there could be another way to rule, another way to run a society, simply isn't there; kingship is what society is in the Homeric epics.

Finally, and in a way this is perhaps the most significant difference for the purposes of this course, the society portrayed in the Homeric epics is polytheistic, believes in a multitude of gods, hundreds if not thousands of gods, if you counted up all the very, very minor ones of rivers, springs, woods and so forth. But even talking only about the main gods, there are a great many of them. This is a great difference between the Homeric society, and ancient Greek culture in general, and our society. In our culture we tend to be monotheistic, whether we believe ourselves or not; atheists in modern-day America tend to disbelieve in one god, agnostics are not sure whether there is or is not one god, believers in modern day America tend to believe in one god. We are almost unquestioningly monotheistic. It doesn't occur to most modern Americans that there could be any other system. The Homeric epics, as we'll see, assume without question that of course there are a multitude of gods. That is important enough that I will in fact spend a later lecture talking about the gods in epic. But just to recap for right now, the society shown in the Homeric epics differs from ours in being patriarchal, slave-holding, monarchical and polytheistic.

So, this society is, these epics are, to us at one and the same time both familiar and strange, both close and remote. I think it is the interplay between the specificity of the culture they describe, which is so different from ours, and the universality of the deeper themes that come out through that strange culture—that interplay between specificity and universality is part of what makes these poems remain so fresh, so interesting, and so repaying of frequent rereading. I honestly don't know how many times I have read the *Iliad* and the *Odyssey*, either in English or in Greek; I lost count a long time ago. But each time I reread either of these epics I notice something in it I have never noticed before; I find something new in it; I say to myself, "I never saw that quite that way before." They repay endless rereading. I am sure when I am rereading them when I am 95 years old, I will still be finding new things in them.

So, I hope I have made a good case for the importance of the *Iliad* and the *Odyssey*, for why you should be interested in them in the end of the twentieth century A.D., when they written somewhere near a thousand years B.C. Next I want to talk briefly about the approach I am going to take in this course, what I'm going to be doing in the subsequent lectures dealing with these epics. I want to do, inasmuch as I can, careful, detailed examinations of various points in both epics; and yet clearly there is no way I can talk about even most of what I would like to talk about, let alone all of it. I've found, in teaching these two epics to undergraduates, that I can take as much time as I am given on them. If I have only three days to talk about the *Iliad*, I manage to talk about it in three days, in three class periods. If I have six weeks, at the end of the six weeks there is still much more I want to say. I think if I had an entire year of classes to talk about either one of these epics, I would still get to the end and be frustrated because there were so many points I did not have time to cover. So clearly, in six hours for the *Iliad* and six hours for the *Odyssey*, there is no way I can hit even all the main points that I would like to in each epic. But I will attempt to touch on highlights of each, and especially on scenes that bring out the wider thematic issues that I have already referred to.

The lectures will approach the epics from three main angles. First off, most lectures will include a little synopsis of the relevant section's plot, and each lecture's essential reading will be drawn from the epics themselves. So by the end of the course, if students do the essential reading, they will have read the entire *Iliad* and the *Odyssey*. Now, I know that some of you are probably listening to these tapes in your car or on the way to work. I know that it is not always convenient to do the readings before you listen to the lectures, or even right after you listen to the lectures. That is why I am going to do enough plot summary, I hope, in each lecture that you can follow the points I am making, even if you haven't had a chance to actually read the relevant section of the epic in question. When necessary, I will also discuss cultural background, terms, and concepts, ideas that are crucial for understanding what is going on at that point in the lecture [sic epic], but that a modern audience would not necessarily know. For instance, in Lecture Three, when we start talking about the *Iliad* I will spend a good deal of time developing the two Greek concepts of *kleos,* which is often translated as glory, and *timê,* which is often translated as honor, and explain how those concepts impact the anger of Achilles, the subject matter of the *Iliad*. The third angle from which these lectures will approach the epics will be to address the larger issues dealt with by the *Iliad* and the *Odyssey* both, the deeper content for which plot and cultural assumptions are the vehicle.

So, the final thing I want to do in this introductory lecture is to cover some essential background material. Before we start actually talking about the *Iliad* and the *Odyssey* themselves, there are two types of background that need to be covered. First, the mythic background, the Trojan War story, which is what I will do for the last few minutes of this lecture. The second lecture, Lecture Two will discuss the poetic background of the epics, and the question of how they came to be composed when they were written down, all of that. But, for now, let's think about the mythic background, the Trojan War story.

These two poems, the *Iliad* and the *Odyssey*, recount episodes out of the Trojan War, which is the most famous and important legend or myth, whichever you want to call it, both of Greek literature, of Roman literature, and arguably of later Western culture itself. The story of the great war between a Greek expeditionary force and the people of Troy, located in the northwestern corner of modern day Turkey, provide narrative material not just for the *Iliad* and the *Odyssey*, but for Virgil's Aeneid, for many Greek tragedies, and for countless later works. Now, one thing that often surprises people who haven't actually read the *Iliad* and the *Odyssey* is to discover how very little of the actual Trojan War narrative is contained in those two epics. Achilles does not die in the *Iliad*; the Trojan Horse does not appear in the *Iliad*; Troy is not sacked in the *Iliad*. The *Iliad* recounts events that take place in one brief period during the last year of the Trojan War; the *Odyssey* recounts the adventures of Odysseus on his way home after the war; many of the most famous episodes of that war do not appear in the Homeric poems at all.

These two epics were not the only ones in ancient Greece to deal with the story of the Trojan War. There were a whole number of other epics that filled in the rest of the story, the events of the time before the *Iliad*, the events that happen after the *Iliad*, during the sack of Troy, and so forth. Those epics unfortunately no longer exist; they are lost. We know what they said, because we have brief prose summaries of them, which I sometimes like to refer to as the Cliff Notes of antiquity. So we do know what was contained in the lost epics, but they no longer exist. Now I should say, even in ancient Greece itself, there was no question in anyone's mind that the *Iliad* and the *Odyssey* were out and away the finest of the epics that dealt with the Trojan War. The others were much shorter, much poorer quality. We're not mourning the loss of seven or eight equally fine epics to the *Iliad* and the *Odyssey*; that is not the situation at all. Still, it would be nice to have the other epics that told the rest of the story; unfortunately, we don't. However, the *Iliad* and the *Odyssey* do assume that you know the rest of the story. They clearly allude to various episodes of the Trojan War story that are not part of their own narrative. They assume that their audience knows, at a bare minimum, the following basic elements of the Trojan War story.

Helen, the most beautiful woman in the world, daughter of the great god Zeus and wife of the Greek king Menelaos, was abducted by the Trojan prince, Paris, and taken to Troy. Under the command of

Menelaos' elder brother, Agamemnon, the Greeks mustered a fleet, sailed to Troy, and fought to get Helen back. The war against Troy last for ten years; during that time the fighting was fairly evenly balanced. Each side had its foremost magnificent warrior, Achilles for the Greeks, Hektor for the Trojans, and the other warriors were fairly well equally matched. Achilles, the greatest Greek warrior, was the son of a goddess mother, Thetis, and a human father, Peleus. The wedding of Thetis and Peleus had been arranged by the main god, Zeus, the king of the gods, and Thetis had been not an entirely willing bride. By the time the *Iliad* opens, Thetis and Peleus clearly have not lived together for years. Thetis returned to the sea—she is a sea goddess. She comes when her son Achilles calls her, but she apparently has absolutely nothing to do any longer with her husband, Peleus. Achilles, the greatest Greek warrior, killed Hektor, the greatest Trojan warrior, and not too long thereafter was himself killed by Paris, the same Trojan prince who had abducted Helen. After the deaths of Hektor and Achilles, the Greeks resorted to trickery to win the war against Troy, built the famous wooden Horse, the Trojan Horse, with warriors hidden inside it, and used it as a means to sack Troy by night.

During the sack of Troy, the Greeks committed many outrages, including the murder of King Priam at his household altar, the murder of Hektor's baby son Astyanax by throwing him from the walls of Troy, and the rape of Priam's virgin daughter Kassandra in the temple of the virgin goddess Athena. These outrages, these acts that went beyond what a conquering army could legitimately do to a conquered city, caused the anger of the gods against the Greeks. This anger played itself out in the Greeks' homecoming. Many of them did not make it home at all; Agamemnon, when he made it home, got there only to be murdered by his wife and her lover; Odysseus spent ten years after the war trying to get home.

Those are the basic elements of the Trojan War story that the *Iliad* and the *Odyssey* clearly assume their audience is familiar with. There are some famous details that are missing; for instance, those of you who know the story may be thinking, "Wait a minute, what about the Judgment of Paris?"—the story in which Paris, who abducts Helen, is asked to judge a beauty contest between three goddesses: Hera, the wife of Zeus; Athena, goddess of wisdom and war, daughter of Zeus; Aphrodite, goddess of sexual passion, also the daughter of Zeus. These three goddesses appear to Paris and ask him to judge a contest as to which of them is the most beautiful. Each offers him a bribe if he will pick her. Hera offers him power over many cities; Athena offers him prowess in warfare; Aphrodite offers him the most beautiful woman in the world for his wife. He chooses Aphrodite. The most beautiful woman is Helen; she is already married; hence the abduction of Helen, hence the Trojan War. Many scholars, most scholars probably, think that the *Iliad* does refer to the Judgment of Paris, but if it does so, it does so very elliptically, only once. Other scholars think that Homer did not know this story, that the Judgment of Paris was a later invention, developed to explain why, in the *Iliad*, Hera and Athena hate the Trojans, and Aphrodite favors them. We simply don't know if Homer knew that story or not.

Another very famous element of the Trojan War story, the idea that Achilles was invulnerable except for his heel, his "Achilles heel"—that is clearly unknown to Homer. In fact, if you think of Achilles as invulnerable, that makes nonsense of a great deal of what goes on in the *Iliad*. Achilles has armor; he has full body armor, and his mother Thetis provides it for him. She doesn't come up out of the sea and say, "Here, son, here is a special little plate for the back of your heel, now you are fine." Clearly Homer does not know the tradition that Achilles was invulnerable aside from his heel.

So, in this lecture we have looked at what the *Iliad* and the *Odyssey* are, why they are important and worth reading still, how they function in their own culture, we have talked a bit about the format of the course, I have given you a very quick run-through of the essential mythic background on the Trojan War. In the next lecture we'll turn to the poetic background of the *Iliad* and the *Odyssey*, how they were formed, who created them, and when they came to be written down. Thank you.

Lecture Two
The Homeric Question

Scope:

In this lecture, we consider how the Homeric epics were created and what their function was in their own society. The lecture traces the historical background of the "Homeric Question": Are the *Iliad* and *Odyssey* the works of one creative genius, or are they conglomerations of shorter poems? We then move on to examine the evidence that the epics were grounded in a tradition of oral (as opposed to written) composition, and discuss the implications this has for their creation and for the very existence of "Homer."

Outline

I. Although the events described in the *Iliad* and the *Odyssey* supposedly took place in the 12th century B.C., the alphabet was not introduced into Greece until the 8th century B.C. How, when, and why did these epics come to be created? Who was Homer?

A. The Greeks of the classical period did not doubt the historicity of either the Trojan War or of Homer himself. They assumed that the Sack of Troy occurred in 1184 B.C., and that the epics had been composed by one poet.

B. As early as the 2nd century A.D., scholars had begun to question whether the *Iliad* and the *Odyssey* were written by the same poet, or even by one poet at all. There are some internal inconsistencies in the works that lead to doubts.

C. In 1795, F. A. Wolf published a book suggesting that Homer had been an illiterate bard, who composed in the 10th century B.C., and that his epics were then transmitted orally, by memory, until the 6th century.

D. This question, of whether or not the *Iliad* and the *Odyssey* are unified wholes created by one supreme poetic genius, is often called "The Homeric Question." In the 19th century, it was the topic of heated debate, with two main camps.

1. The "Unitarians" argued that each epic was the result of poetic composition by a single author, although some of them posited two authors, one per epic.

2. The "Analysts" or "Separatists" argued that the poems could be analyzed into original shorter songs, and thus were compilations, not unified works.

II. In 1928, the American scholar Milman Parry published his research demonstrating that the epics bore many signs of being products of an ongoing oral tradition, rather than of one individual's creative genius.

A. Parry's most important contribution to Homeric scholarship was his definition and discussion of *formulas*.

1. Parry defined a formula as "a group of words which is regularly employed under the same metrical conditions to express a given essential idea."
2. The meter of the Homeric epics is dactylic hexameter. This meter is cumbersome in English, but very flexible in Greek.
3. A formula often consists of a name plus an epithet, but it can also be a phrase or even a whole line of verse.
4. Parry demonstrated that Homer's formulas exhibit "thrift"; that is, different ways to refer to a particular character or concept will not occupy the same metrical position.
5. The implication of this is that a bard, in performance, will have one and only one way of expressing a given idea in any given metrical position.

B. Parry's theory of oral composition also helps to explain two other notable features of the Homeric epics, the "type scenes" and the oddities of the dialect used in the poems.

1. Type scenes are descriptions of feasting, arming, etc., that are repeated in different sections of the epic with only minor variations.
2. Homeric dialect included variations from standard Greek forms and many archaisms.

C. Parry and his pupil Albert Lord studied the poetic practice of illiterate South Slavic bards, or *guzlars,* working in an oral tradition.

1. Formulas, type scenes, and so on served as building blocks with which the Slavic bard could organize his material in performance. He thus recreated his poem in a different version each time he performed it, rather than memorizing it word for word.

2. Parry and Lord argued that the Homeric epics had been composed in a similar fashion.
3. The Serbian bards' poems were much shorter than the *Iliad* and the *Odyssey*, but Parry and Lord remained certain that the Homeric epics were products of oral composition.

D. Thus, these first works of Western literature were not originally "literature" at all. They were performance pieces, recreated each time a bard sang them.

E. The circumstances of the epics' performance cannot be known with certainty. However, it seems quite plausible that they were designed to be performed over three- or four-day periods at religious festivals.

III. Parry's demonstration that the Homeric epics are grounded in traditional oral composition is almost universally accepted by modern scholars. However, scholars disagree on the implications of that fact for our understanding of the epics' genesis.

A. Some scholars think that there was never any one poet who can meaningfully be called Homer. The epics as we have them simply represent one version, from one performance of traditional material, which became canonized through writing but was never the creation of one poet.

B. Others think that the epics show a sophistication and complexity of design that must indicate careful structuring by a single poet, albeit a poet working within the oral tradition.

C. Thus, Parry's work did not put an end to the old quarrel between Unitarians and Analysts; it simply recast it in somewhat different terms.

IV. There is little consensus of opinion about how, when, and why the epics came to be written down.

A. There is no absolute agreement about the date at which the alphabet was introduced into Greece.
1. The majority opinion is that the alphabet was introduced into Greece some time in the 8th century B.C.
2. Some scholars suggest that the introduction came much earlier, and some that it was even later.

B. There is no absolute agreement about how long after the alphabet's introduction the epics were written down.

   1. Most scholars think that there must have been a lapse of several decades, at least, between the introduction of the alphabet and the transcription of the Homeric epics.

   2. A few scholars think, on the contrary, that the alphabet was adapted to the Greek language specifically in order to transcribe these epics.

C. There is no absolute agreement about who wrote them down, or how, or why.

   1. Some scholars assume our versions of the epics are "oral dictated texts," but others have difficulty imagining a workable process of dictation.

   2. Some scholars think that a bard working in thc oral tradition learned to write specifically to transcribe these epics, but comparative study of modern oral bards makes this seem highly unlikely.

   3. Others posit a compromise position, in which a completely illiterate Homer composed the *Iliad* and the *Odyssey*, and his creations were then transmitted orally, being memorized word for word by his successors, until writing had become well established.

   4. The exact process of transcription will probably remain unknown.

D. There is an ancient tradition that the Athenian tyrant Peisistratos commissioned a fixed text of the epics in Athens in the 6th century B.C.

E. The texts were further regularized from the 5th to 2nd centuries B.C.

   1. The great Alexandrian scholars of the 3rd and 2nd centuries began the tradition of Homeric scholarship and textual criticism.

   2. It is at this time, probably, that the standard divisions of each epic into 24 "books" developed.

V. For simplicity's sake, throughout this course I will refer to "Homer" or "the bard" as though there were such a poet, the author of the epics.

A. My overall approach will be far closer to the Unitarian than to the Analytical.

B. I assume that the epics show rich characterization, detailed correspondence backward and forward in plot line, and intricate structure, all elements of design which point to a "designer."

C. However, students should remember that many Homer scholars disagree vehemently with these assumptions.

Supplementary Reading:

Norman Austin, *Archery at the Dark of the Moon*, Chapter 1, clearly lays out Parry's concept of the formula, and then argues strongly against assuming that the presence of formulas precludes belief in an individual genius-poet. This chapter contains a good bit of untranslated Greek, but the argumentation is clear without knowledge of Greek.

Geoffrey Kirk, *The Songs of Homer*, Chapters 13–15.

Albert B. Lord, *The Singer of Tales*, esp. Chapters 3, 4, 5, and 7. Lord examines modern Serbian *guzlars* and discusses possible parallels in Homeric usage.

Gregory Nagy, *Greek Mythology and Poetics*, Chapter 2.

Milman Parry, *The Making of Homeric Verse*.

Barry Powell, *Homer and the Origin of the Greek Alphabet*.

Oliver Taplin, *Homeric Soundings*, Chapter 1. This chapter discusses the possibility that the *Iliad* was composed in a tripartite structure, for performance over three days (or nights).

F. A. Wolf, *Prolegomena to Homer*.

Questions to Consider:

1. Many modern "Unitarians" find something very disturbing in the idea that there was no "Homer," no actual author of the *Iliad* and the *Odyssey*. Do you think it makes a difference in our appreciation of these epics if they were the culmination of a tradition rather than the work of an individual genius?
2. Some modern scholars reject the "compromise" position outlined in IV.C.3 above, because they think it is impossible that anyone could remember, word for word, a text as long as the *Iliad*. Can you think of any modern analogues for such a feat of memory? Conversely, can you think of any modern types of performance that resemble the "oral composition" model suggested by Parry and Lord?

Lecture Two—Transcript
The Homeric Question

Hello, and welcome back to the second lecture in the course "Homeric Epic"; this lecture is called the Homeric Question. In this second lecture I want to talk about how the *Iliad* and the *Odyssey* were created, who, if anyone, was Homer and discuss the whole so-called Homeric Question, its history, its background, why scholars ever came to question the idea that one author was responsible for the *Iliad* and the *Odyssey* in the first place. Then I want to look at the evidence that the *Iliad* and the *Odyssey* in fact did grow out of an oral tradition of composition, rather than being works by one individual genius. I want to discuss the implication of their oral nature, and finally talk a little bit about our evidence for when the two epics were actually written down.

So, let's start with background and rationale for the so-called Homeric Question. The events described in the *Iliad* and the *Odyssey*, the events of the Trojan War and its aftermath, supposedly took place in the twelfth century, B.C. The traditional date for the sack of Troy that later Greek historians gave was 1184 B.C., so near the beginning of the twelfth century B.C. is when the events described in the epics supposedly took place. However, the alphabet probably did not come into to Greece until the eighth century B.C. Therefore, there is a gap of some four hundred years between the events covered by the epics and the earliest time when these epics could have been written down. So the obvious question that presents itself is, how, when, why did these epics come to be written down? Why did Homer, if there ever was such a person, choose to write about events four hundred years before his own time, and how did he know about them to write about them?

The Greeks of the classical period themselves did not doubt the historicity of either the Trojan War or of Homer. They assumed that there had been a sack of Troy; as I already said, the most frequently assumed date for it was 1184 B.C. And similarly, the Greeks of the classical period assumed that the *Iliad* and the *Odyssey* had been written by one individual poet, whom they called Homer. However, as early as the second century A.D., some scholars had begun to question whether there had ever been a Homer, or whether the *Iliad* and the *Odyssey* were in fact conglomerations of shorter original poems, collections of shorter descriptions, of different episodes from the *Iliad* and the *Odyssey* that had somehow been put together after being transmitted by memory for several generations after the Trojan War.

There are enough oddities about the two epics to make scholars start questioning the historicity of Homer. There are some episodes in each epic that seem to disagree with other episodes in the same epic. To give perhaps the most obvious example, in the *Odyssey* in Book Eleven, we're given one very detailed description of the state of souls after death, when Odysseus visits the underworld and talks to spirits of the dead. But in Book Twenty-Four of the *Odyssey*, we are given a very different description of what life after death is like. There seems to be a contradiction there; there seems to be disagreement within the text of the *Odyssey* itself about what might be considered a rather important point. So, as early as the second century A.D. the question had arisen, were these poems actually written by one in individual author, or are they conglomerations of originally shorter separate works?

In 1795, the late eighteenth century, a German scholar named Friedrich Wolf published a book suggesting that Homer had been an illiterate bard, a poet who composed rather than wrote; who composed orally in the tenth century B.C., and whose works were then transmitted by memory, through his disciples and or descendents, until finally they were written down, Wolf thought, in the sixth century B.C. This work by Wolf, which he called *Prolegomena to Homer*, suggesting that Homer had been an oral bard of the tenth century B.C., paved the way for what was called the Homeric Question, which was a raging debate among Homer scholars that continued through most of the nineteenth century. The Homeric Question, in brief, is the question of: Are the *Iliad* and the *Odyssey* unified works created by one poetic genius, who thought them through from beginning to end, put them in the order they are now in, developed the characters in them, etc.,—does what an author actually does—or are the *Iliad* and the *Odyssey* conglomerations of shorter works, with no actual author who ever put them into the shape in which we now have them?

Discussion on the Homeric Question in the nineteenth century divided into two main camps, the Unitarians and the Analysts, or Separatists. The Unitarians—it has nothing to do with religion whatsoever—the Unitarians believed that there was in fact an author discernable behind each of these epics. They saw the epics as so beautifully organized, so richly detailed, with such convincing characterization and so on, that they thought each of these works simply had to be the product of one guiding intellect, of one creative mind, whom they thought we might as well continue to call Homer for lack of a better name for him. Some Unitarians thought that there was one author for the *Iliad* and another author for the *Odyssey*, thus two Homers rather than one Homer, but that is a minor detail. The main point is that they thought each epic was the creation of an individual author, whether that was the same individual for both epics or not. The Analysts or Separatists, as their name indicates, argued that the poems could be analyzed or separated into individual original, much shorter, works, and that they were compilations put together—often not very skillfully—at some later date, after the original songs had been composed.

As I said, this debate raged throughout the nineteenth century—well, raged among Homer scholars' circles, at any rate—throughout the nineteenth century, and there seemed to be no real way to decide it. The Unitarians found it absolutely self-evidentially obvious that epics of this grandeur, beauty, scope, complexity, and richness must have been created by a genius; they did not simply happen as conglomerations of randomly collected shorter songs. The Analysts found it equally self-evident that these badly-connected, inconsistent, poorly-put-together conglomerations of various different tales could not possibly be the work of one individual genius. In other words, you paid your money and you took your choice, whether you were a Unitarian or a Separatist in the nineteenth century. There seemed to be no way of deciding the question; it was largely a matter of an individual scholar's temperament and attitude towards the poems.

In the 1920s, the situation changed because a young American Homerist named Milman Parry, in 1928, published his research, which seemed to demonstrate pretty conclusively that the *Iliad* and the *Odyssey* were grounded in an oral tradition, were the culmination of an ongoing oral tradition, rather than the creation of one poetic genius. Parry's argument, Parry's evidence, seemed to demonstrate that many poets over many generations had worked in an oral tradition, using the same forms of poetic diction, the same stock scenes, the same story-line, most importantly, the same fixed expression—which Parry called "formulas." I will get back to discussing formulas in just a second, but one point to clarify here. It may, at first hearing, sound like Parry was saying very much the same thing that Friedriech Wolf said. After all, Wolf said, in 1795, the poems were composed orally, were transmitted orally for many generations—for about four hundred years, in fact—and were then written down. What is different about what Parry said?

Well, Wolf still posited a single author, a single creative genius, Homer. Wolf's argument was that Homer, himself, had been illiterate; had composed the poems more or less as we have them, as unified wholes; they had then been memorized and passed down, and perhaps some corruption had happened in that process, perhaps some bits that got added, perhaps some bits that got left out. But, basically, there had been a Homer, who thought up these poems himself, but thought them up without the benefit of writing. Parry's argument was something quite different.

Parry said, in effect, that there had never been one "Homer" who created these poems; rather, these poems had been created over a process of oral tradition, generation after generation, in which these various different poets would use, as I already said, the same poetic building blocks to talk about the same episodes of the Trojan War, to talk about other episodes as well—that what we have, in effect, in the *Iliad* and the *Odyssey* is one recorded performance out of a whole epic tradition, that could have been very different had we caught another bard doing it, could have been very different if the same bard had performed the text on another day; that what we have is simply a snapshot, if you like, of the oral tradition in motion, rather than the full-fledged creative production of one individual genius. Parry's most important contribution to Homeric scholarship, and the strongest evidence for his argument, was his discussion of what he called formulas in Homer. To try to make the definition of formula as brief and concise as possible, what Parry meant by a formula, the way he defined a formula, was "a group of words which is regularly employed under the same metrical conditions to express a given essential idea."

Let me talk for just a second about the meter of epic, here, because that is important at this point. As I already mentioned in the first lecture, the meter of the Homeric epics is dactylic hexameter. That is a meter that, in Greek, is remarkably flexible and usable. It consists of an alternation of long and short syllables; the basic unit, the dactyl, is one long syllable followed by two shorts. But the two shorts can be substituted for by one long, so you can have a unit of verse that is two long syllables, long, long, rather than long, short,

short. This meter does not work very well in English. It is cumbersome, clumsy, and tends to sound a little bit too much like "oom–pa-pa" in English.

There are poets who have tried to use dactylic hexameter in English, and I am going to quote you a few lines of perhaps the most successful attempt at it, Longfellow's "Evangeline," just to give you, as best we can in English, some sense of what dactylic hexameter sounds like. One problem, of course, is that English poetry works on an alternation of stressed and unstressed syllables, rather than actual long and short syllables, so the effect is not all that great. But I will start by really exaggerating so you can kind of hear the meter. "This is the forest primeval, the murmuring pines and the hemlocks"—the last foot of a dactylic hexameter's line is always two long beats—"Bearded in moss and in garments green, indistinct in the twilight, / Stand like druids of eld with voices sad and prophetic." Now a little less exaggeration, "Stand like harpers hoar with beards that rest on their bosoms. / Loud from its rocky caverns, the deep-voiced neighboring ocean / Speaks and in accents disconsolate answers the wail of the forest."

It is all right, but it is a little bit "oom-pa-pa, oom-pa-pa" in English. In Greek, dactylic hexameter is an extremely beautiful, fluid, flexible, usable meter. There you just have to take my word for it, if you don't know Greek; but again, just to give you a slight sense of how it sounds, the opening lines of the *Iliad* would be: [Professor Vandiver demonstrates sound with a Greek translation of the *Iliad*.]

Now if you don't know Greek, you kind of have to take my word for it. But the main point is that Greek works much better with an alternation of long and short syllables, that fits into the dactylic hexameter line, than English does. What Parry discovered, with his theory of formulas, to put it the simplest, was that in many, many different situations in Homeric epic when a hero is mentioned by name—Achilles, Hektor, Paris, Menelaos—or when a god is mentioned by name, there will be an adjective associated with that name, an epithet, as it's often referred to, that is not necessarily important for the given context, but that is very important for the given meter. For instance, if the poet wants to refer to Hektor at the end of a line—and that is a great name to end the line of dactylic hexameter, Hektor—if he wants to refer to Hektor at the end of a line and he needs only three beats before Hektor, he calls him *phaidimos Hektor*, "glorious Hektor." But if he happens to need five beats before the name Hektor at the end of the line, he calls him *koruthaiolos Hektor*, "Hektor of the glancing helmet," Hektor's most famous epithet.

But, and this was Parry's essential point, Hektor is not called "Hektor of the glancing helmet" only at moments when it is important that he has a glancing helmet. He is called "Hektor of the glancing helmet" at moments when the poet needs five beats to fill out that part of the line. Similarly, "swift-footed Achilles," *podas ôkus Achilleus*, is called "swift-footed" sometimes even when he is sitting down; at times when he is by no means swift-footed but at times when the meter requires him to be swift-footed. Furthermore, the cases I have just mentioned are the names of these heroes—Hektor, Achilles—in the nominative case; that is, working as the subject of their sentence. Greek, like many other languages, has a case system, in which the form of a noun is a little bit different if the noun is the direct object of verb rather than the subject of the verb, if the noun is in the possessive case, and so forth. In each one of those different cases, these heroes have a different epithet. When Hektor is in the genitive case, the possessive case, suddenly he is "horse-taming Hektor," instead of "Hektor of the glancing helmet," because that is what fits metrically in that position in the line.

So, Parry's basic argument was that Homer's formulas exhibit what he called "thrift;" that is, different ways to refer to a particular character or concept will not occupy the same metrical position. Or, putting it the other way around, for each metrical pattern there is only one way to refer to—usually, only one way to refer to a particular character. The implication of this—and this is the keystone of Parry's argument—is that in performance, a bard is not thinking creatively, "What would be the best adjective to describe Achilles in this particular situation?" Rather, he is using traditional set formulas; when you want to mention Achilles at the end of a line and he is in the nominative case, you call him "swift-footed." This seems to go against what most of us think of as creative or poetic inspiration; and it works very well for a kind of poetry that is done in performance, in which the bard is not so much thinking about shaping wonderful poetic language as he is about producing a song, given the building blocks that he has learned in his tradition to work with.

Parry's theory of oral composition, if you take it beyond purely the formula, helps to explain two other notable features of the Homeric epics, the "type scenes," so-called, and the oddities of Homeric dialect. Type scenes are rather like formulas spread out over several lines; they are exactly as they sound, scenes that are repeated over and over again in an epic, that are done in an exactly the same way, exactly the same wording. Anyone who has ever read the *Iliad* or the *Odyssey* will have noticed these. In the *Odyssey*, for instance, when people are going to have a meal, we don't get a different description of the meal every single time. They sit down and a grave housekeeper comes and sponges off the table; then she puts baskets of bread in front of them, and they put their hands out to the bread; and then when they have taken their fill of eating and drinking, you go on with the story. There is a whole little section, of a good many lines, that the bard can just more or less rattle off when he wants to say, in effect, "then they ate."

Parry's theory of oral composition also accounts for oddities of the Homeric dialect. The dialect of the Homeric poems differs from standard Greek in having several odd forms and many archaisms. The form of Greek spoken by the *Iliad* and the *Odyssey* is not a form of Greek ever spoken, as far as we know, by any actual living Greek person. Rather, it is an amalgamation of very, very old-fashioned words—"forsooth," "quotha," that kind of thing, would be the English equivalent—with odd formations, words that have been stretched a little bit so that they take more syllables than they normally would be, or words that have been compressed a little bit so that they fit into the line in a way that they normally would not. Which again, in Parry's argument, seems to indicate a traditional poetic language that developed for this kind of poetic performance, rather than an individual poet creating as he goes along.

Now, Parry formed his theory by studying the Homeric epics themselves, but he also did some comparative work to try to solidify and validate his theory. He and his pupil, Albert Lord, studied the poetic practice of illiterate South Slavic bards, or *guzlars*, who were a working in an oral tradition—who still are, in fact, working in an oral tradition; there are still some of them today. Parry and Lord found that the Slavic *guzlars* used formulas, type scenes, just as he had found in the Homeric poems, as building blocks with which to organized their material and performance. A South Slavic bard thus recreated his same poem, his same story, in a slightly different version each time he performed it, rather than memorizing it word for word.

And that perhaps is the most important point in what is often referred to as the Parry-Lord hypothesis about how the Homeric poems were formed. Parry and Lord found that if you went to a particular South Slavic bard and said, "Sing me your tale of *x*; sing me your story about this great hero, that you sang to me last year. Sing it to me exactly as you sang it to me last year," the bard would recreate the same overall story, but he would no means recreate word for word the same poem. If you asked him, "Did you sing it word for word the same?" he would say, "Yes, I did." But if you compared your tape recording of the song as he sang it last year and the song as he sang it this year, there would be many differences. Word for word accuracy, therefore, the kind that Wolf theorized for his illiterate Homer in the tenth century B.C., does not seem to exist in a tradition that works around these large building blocks of type scenes, of formulas, and so forth.

If Parry and Lord's hypothesis is accepted, then these first works of Western literature, the *Iliad* and the *Odyssey*, were originally not literature at all. They were performance pieces, recreated slightly differently each time a bard sang them. Now, many critics of Parry and Lord's work have pointed out that the songs sung by the South Slavic *guzlars* are much shorter—the longest ones that have been recorded are much shorter—than the Homeric epics; they don't show nearly the same kind of complexity, they don't show nearly the same kind of cross-referencing back and forth within themselves, that we find, or think we find, in the *Iliad* and the *Odyssey*. Nevertheless, Parry and Lord and their modern disciples remained certain that the Homeric epics were in fact products of oral composition. We don't know exactly why these epics would have been performed. One hypothesis that seems quite plausible is that they were originally performed over three- or four-day periods at religious festivals; or putting that another way, that the performance of sung poetry about the exploits of gods and heroes developed as part of religious festivals in Greece, and out of that performance tradition grew the *Iliad* and the *Odyssey* as we have them today.

Parry's demonstration that the Homeric epics are grounded in traditional oral composition has some very important implications. It is almost universally accepted by modern scholars. There are still a few die-hards who say Parry and Lord are simply wrong, the Homeric poems are not grounded in oral composition and that is that; but most modern scholars, by far the majority of modern Homerists, accept that Parry and Lord did demonstrate that the *Iliad* and the *Odyssey* somehow grew out of oral composition. But that "somehow" is a very important adverb there. Exactly how oral are the *Iliad* and the *Odyssey*? How did they get from where they were then to where they are now? Some scholars think there never was any one "Homer," that it's inappropriate to refer to a "Homer" at all; there was never any such poet; the epics as we have them simply represent one version from one performance of traditional material, which became canonized through happening to be written down at some unimaginable point, for some reason that we don't know. Other scholars think that the epics show a sophistication and complexity of design that must indicate careful structuring by a guiding poet, a guiding intellect, someone we might as well call an author for lack of a better term, albeit an author working within the oral tradition. Thus, Parry's work did not put an end to the old controversy between Unitarians and Separatists; it simply recast it in slightly different terms. There is still the same controversy over whether there was, at some point, a "Homer," who put this traditional oral material into the form that we now have it, or whether there was never any such person.

The next obvious question, then, is when, how, why did these epics come to be written down? After all, they *are* written; Parry seems to have demonstrated pretty clearly that they are grounded in oral composition, but they are written now. We have them; they are books; how did that happen? How did they come to be written down? Once again, there is no absolute agreement among scholars. In fact, there isn't even any absolute agreement about when the alphabet was introduced into Greece. The majority opinion is that the alphabet appeared in Greece, the Phoenician alphabet was adapted to work for the Greek language, some time in the eighth century B.C. We say that because the earliest inscriptions that we know don't date any earlier than the mid-eighth century B.C. Most scholars think the alphabet was brought in some time in the eighth century B.C.—although some scholars think earlier, some suggest much later.

There is also no absolute agreement about how long after the alphabet appeared in Greece the *Iliad* and the *Odyssey* were written down. Again, most scholars think there must have been a lapse of at least several decades, that a new technology such as writing would not immediately have been applied to writing down orally performed poems. It seems obvious, to us, that that is the first thing you do with it; you have got these great poems, write them down before you forget them. But in a culture in which the poems had been transmitted orally—in whatever sense—ever since they were first created, the new technology of writing would not immediately motivate people to start writing down their poetry. So, most scholars think there must have been a lapse of several decades between the introductions of the alphabet and the writing down of the epics. A few scholars, on the contrary, think that the alphabet was adapted to the Greek language specially for the purpose of writing down the Homeric epics; once again there is no consensus.

There is also—and this is probably the most important point—there is no absolute agreement about who wrote them down, or how, or why. Once again, there are several possibilities. There is the possibility that these are what are referred to as "oral dictated texts"; that just as the South Slavic *guzlars* performed into a tape recorder from Milman Parry and Albert Lord, so, at some point, someone sat down with his role of papyrus and his pen and wrote down what Homer was reciting to him. That is a possibility; but many people; many scholars have difficulty imagining that process. Writing on papyrus is a slow and messy business; the bard would have to recite awfully slowly for that to work, and many scholars have difficulty imagining that process. Others think that a bard working in the oral tradition learned to write, specifically to be able to write down these epics. Most scholars think that is also unlikely. Oral bards tend to be rather scornful of writing—using comparative modern material, again. It seems unlikely that someone who is a past master in the art of oral composition would suddenly be motivated to learn to write. Why would he think that is a good idea? Some scholars posit a compromise position, in which a completely illiterate Homer composed the *Iliad* and the *Odyssey*; his creations were then transmitted orally, memorized word for word by his successors, until writing became well-established—i.e. Wolf's position again, more or less, adapted to fit the Parry-Lord hypothesis.

We will probably never know the exact process by which these poems were transcribed; not unless we find some proto-diary of someone who says, "I learned to write last week so I could write down the *Iliad* and the *Odyssey* this week"—and that doesn't seem terribly likely. We'll probably never know exactly how this happened. There is an ancient tradition that the Athenian tyrant Peisistratos commissioned a fixed text of the epics in Athens in the sixth century B.C. A lot of scholars take that as established fact, that Peisistratos gathered together bards who were still performing in his day, compared the versions they were giving of the *Iliad* and the *Odyssey*, had them written down, and that was the basis of our fixed text. Unfortunately the earliest mention of this so-called "Peisistratian Recension" is in the Latin author, Cicero, who wrote in the first century B.C.; Peisistratos lived in the sixth century B.C. It is as though the only evidence we had for Gutenberg's invention of the printing press in the 1450s was someone in the 1950s saying, "500 years ago, someone invented the printing press." How much weight could we actually give that? Maybe not very much.

We do know that the texts of the *Iliad* and the *Odyssey* were regularized, in a continual process of regularization of these texts, from the fifth to second centuries B.C. in the great library at Alexandria, where some of the greatest scholars of antiquity worked and devoted their attention to the Homeric texts. The Alexandrian scholars began the tradition of Homeric scholarship and textual criticism that has continued until the present day. It was probably there, in Alexandria, that each epic was divided into 24 standardized books, or papyrus rolls, of a more or less standard length.

What is my own take on all this? Well, for simplicity's sake, throughout this course I will refer to "Homer," or "the bard," as though there were such a poet, the author of the epics. I don't want, every time I mention Homer, to have to say, "Of course if there ever was such a person, and maybe there wasn't"; I will just take it for granted that you will remember all of that. To be honest, my overall approach is far closer to the unitarian than to the analytical; I assume that the epics do in fact show rich characterization, detailed correspondence backward and forward in plot line, intricate structure—in short, elements of design which point to a designer. I think there was a designer, who put these poems together in the form in which we now have them. But students should remember that many Homeric scholars—probably most Homeric scholars—disagree vehemently with that position. I am in somewhat of a minority these days, in still thinking that there actually was a Homer.

So, in this lecture we have looked at the background of the poems, their composition and development and some of the implications that has for our understanding of them; and I will refer back to some of these questions raised by the Parry-Lord hypothesis in later lectures, in reference to specific scenes. In the next lecture we will begin to examine the *Iliad* itself.

Lecture Three

Glory, Honor, and the Wrath of Achilles

Scope:

In this lecture, we begin looking at the *Iliad* itself. The lecture discusses the epic's *in medias res* beginning, and how the opening scenes identify the primary subject matter of the poem from the very beginning. On the simplest level, the *Iliad* is about the wrath of Achilles; on a more complex level, this anger is the narrative device by which the bard can discuss wider themes, among them mortality, the human condition, and how the warrior ethos affects what it means to be human. Since Achilles' anger and its implications can only be properly understood in the context of its own cultural background, the lecture examines and defines the key concepts of *timê* (honor) and *kleos* (fame/glory), which will be crucial throughout our reading of the *Iliad*.

Outline

I. The *Iliad* begins *in medias res*: "in the middle of the subject."

- **A.** A bard working with traditional material could assume that his audience knew the story and the characters, and so could pick the narrative up at any point.
- **B.** The *Iliad* is not the story of the whole war; it addresses one episode in the last year of that war.
  1. Achilles' own death is not shown in the *Iliad*.
  2. The Trojan Horse and the Sack of Troy do not occur in the *Iliad*.
  3. However, the bard does frequently allude to these (and other) important events from other parts of the story.
  4. On the most basic level, the *Iliad*'s subject is the wrath (Greek *mênis*) of Achilles, which motivates him to withdraw from the fighting, leaving his fellow Greeks to suffer great losses to the Trojans. The word used for Achilles' wrath is normally used only in reference to the gods.

II. Starting his narrative with this particular episode, the quarrel of Achilles and Agamemnon, allows the bard to focus on crucial themes that bear on the entire warrior ethos.

III. Achilles is angry because Agamemnon took away his concubine Briseis. To understand the nature of Achilles' anger, we must examine the Homeric hero's motivations for fighting in the first place.

A. The Homeric warrior fights for honor (*timê)* and glory or fame (*kleos*).

1. *Timê* is often translated "honor." However, its most basic meaning is the tangible, physical expression of honor in the form of booty, gifts, or a particular prize (*geras*).

2. *Kleos* can be translated as "glory" or "fame." In its most basic sense, *kleos* means "what other people say about you," what is spoken aloud about you.

B. *Timê* and *kleos* are closely related; one's *kleos* depends to a large extent on the *timê* offered by one's peers. But *kleos* also serves as the only true form of immortality available to Homeric heroes: they live on in what people say about them after they are dead.

IV. Agamemnon dishonors Achilles because of an affront to his own *timê.*

A. Agamemnon has himself suffered a loss of *timê* since he had to return his *geras,* the concubine Chryseis, to her father Chryses. Agamemnon thus tries to restore his own lost *timê* by taking Achilles' *geras*, Briseis.

B. Agamemnon's action is not justified, since his "dishonor" differs from Achilles' in key ways:

1. Agamemnon's dishonor is required by the god Apollo, while Achilles' is a direct, unnecessary, human-to-human affront.

2. As Achilles says, though there is nowhere to get a replacement for Chryseis now, if ever the Greeks sack Troy, they will pick a fine replacement *geras* for Agamemnon.

V. Achilles responds to Agamemnon's actions by withdrawing from battle and by actively seeking the Greeks' temporary defeat.

A. Achilles declares that he will no longer fight against the Trojans. In fact, he threatens to take the Myrmidons and return home.

B. Achilles also summons his mother Thetis, and asks her to petition Zeus to let the Trojans gain dominance over the Greeks until the Greeks once again give *timê* to Achilles.
   1. Thetis' appeal to Zeus gives the audience a glimpse of the gods on Olympus, and the power dynamics that operate among them.
   2. Zeus agrees that the Trojans will have temporary ascendance, although he can't alter the fated downfall of Troy.
   3. Zeus' intervention allows for the Greeks' temporary defeat without detracting from their valor.

C. Within the context of Achilles' own culture and assumptions, his reaction is not excessive.
   1. By dishonoring him, Agamemnon has removed Achilles' motivation for fighting.
   2. The society reflected in the Homeric poems is in many ways a "shame" culture, in which a warrior's sense of worth is largely determined by how others perceive him and what others say about him.
   3. Thus, Agamemnon has done more than insult or dishonor Achilles; he has called Achilles' whole worth into question.

VI. Books II–IV stress the results of Achilles' withdrawal from battle and Zeus' promise to Thetis, and introduce several of the most important characters in the story: Odysseus, Nestor, Paris, Menelaos.

Essential Reading:

Iliad, Books I–II.

Supplementary Reading:

Mark W. Edwards, *Poet of the Iliad*, Chapter 21.

James V. Morrison, *Homeric Misdirection*, Chapter 2.

Jonathan Shay, *Achilles in Vietnam*, Chapters 1–2. An interesting analysis of *mênis* as a kind of "indignant rage" by no means uncommon among soldiers who feel that "what is right" has been betrayed by their commanders. (Warning: These chapters contain a good deal of profanity in quotations of veterans' own words.)

Laura M. Slatkin, *The Power of Thetis*.

Oliver Taplin, *Homeric Soundings*, Chapter 2, sections 2.1–22 (pp. 46–66).

Questions to Consider:

1. Some modern readers see Achilles' reaction as that of a "spoiled brat," who doesn't want to play anymore when things aren't going his way. In the context of a "shame culture," does this interpretation make any sense?
2. Why do you think the bard chose to focus on the quarrel between Achilles and Agamemnon, rather than on a more obvious highlight of the Trojan War legend (i.e., the Sack of Troy)?

Lecture Three—Transcript
Glory, Honor, and the Wrath of Achilles

This lecture is called "*Kleos*, *Timê* and the Wrath of Achilles." In the first two lectures we covered background material, mythic and compositional, for the Homeric Epics. Now we are going to move on to beginning our look at the *Iliad* itself, and how it puts these mythic and poetic elements into action. In this lecture I will discuss the beginning of the *Iliad*, its *in medias res* opening—how the primary subject matter of the *Iliad* is delineated by the bard in the very first lines, so that in the very beginning we know exactly what the main topic of the poem will be. That main topic is, of course, on the simplest level, the wrath of Achilles. The lecture will also discuss how the poet can use that topic, the wrath of Achilles, to address wider themes, both cultural and narrative; and finally, the lecture will examine and define the key concepts of *timê*, or honor, and *kleos*, or glory, and why they are crucial throughout our reading of the *Iliad*.

So, the *Iliad* begins *in medias res*—that is a Latin phrase, coined by the Roman poet Horace. It literally means "in the middle of the material," "in the middle of the thing," "in the middle of the subject matter." This is what Horace said a good epic poem should do; it should start just right in the beginning of its storyline. Again, this depends on the assumption that the audience for an epic already knows that storyline. A bard working with traditional material, as Homer undoubtedly was, could take it absolutely for granted that his audience knows the story of the Trojan War, knows the characters, knows the basic outline of what happened, when, where and to whom—which of course is why I gave you that basic background material in the first lecture. You will notice, when you start reading the *Iliad*, Homer doesn't tell you who Achilles is, or who Agamemnon is, or where they are, or what they are doing there; all of that is simply taken for granted. Rather, what he does in his opening lines is to zero in one particular episode of the Trojan War on which he wants to focus this particular performance, this particular work that we call the *Iliad*.

As I mentioned in Lecture One, but it bears repeating, the *Iliad* is not the story of the whole Trojan War. Rather this entire book the *Iliad* focuses on one really rather short time period, one main episode in the last year of that war. Achilles' own death is not in the *Iliad*, though it's referred to and foreshadowed over and over again. The sack of Troy, the Trojan horse, are not in the *Iliad*, although, again, the sack of Troy is foreshadowed in many ways that we will talk about in the following lectures. But the bard does frequently allude to these and other important events of the Trojan War stories. So the *Iliad* looks outside of itself; it looks beyond its own textual parameters and engages other aspects of the Trojan War story that are crucial for your understanding of what is going on in the *Iliad*. Achilles' character in the *Iliad*, for instance, would make very little sense if we did not know that he is going to die, if we did not know that he dies at Troy. His death is almost a subtext of the *Iliad*, from its beginning through to its very end.

On the most basic level, the subject matter of the *Iliad*, as stated by the bard in the opening lines, is the wrath—or anger—of Achilles, which motivates him to withdraw from the fighting, leaving his fellow Greeks to suffer great losses at the hands of the Trojans in his absence. The word that is translated as wrath or anger in Greek is *mênis*. The first word of the *Iliad* is the slightly different form, *mênin*, because it is the direct object of a verb; it is the accusative case, if you know your grammar. The first three words of the *Iliad* are *Mênin aeide, thea*—"wrath, sing, goddess;" "Goddess, sing the wrath"—and then the rest of the first line is "of Peleus' son, Achilles."

Now, *mênis* right away is a very interesting and important word for the bard to use to delineate the wrath of Achilles, because elsewhere in the *Iliad* the word *mênis* is used to refer only to the anger of a god. So by choosing this word—rather than another word for anger; there are many other words for anger in Greek—by choosing this word to describe the anger of Achilles, from the very opening word of the *Iliad* Homer has already established that Achilles is somehow different from other heroes, somehow different from other human beings. That is a point we'll return to over and over again in these lectures on the *Iliad*. Achilles is in some sense set apart from the normal run of humanity, and this is reflected in the very first word that refers to him, when he is given a term that normally would be used of a god rather than a human.

The bard begins his narrative not just by stating that he wants the goddess to sing about the anger of Achilles, but also by mentioning the quarrel between Achilles and Agamemnon that follows immediately upon that anger. Listen to the first few lines of the

Iliad—in English this time—and see how the bard jumps right into the thick of the matter, sets out what he is going to talk about very quickly, and then moves on into his story. This is how the *Iliad* begins:

> Sing, goddess, the anger of Peleus' son Achilleus
> and its devastation, which put pains thousand-fold upon the
> Achaians,
> hurled in their multitudes to the house of Hades strong souls
> of heroes but gave their bodies to be the delicate feasting
> of dogs, of all birds, and the will of Zeus was accomplished.

Very abrupt beginning, right into the thick of the action. The bard then goes on, in the next few lines, to say this happened since the moment at which Achilles and Agamemnon began to quarrel with one another, and the will of Zeus was accomplished. We'll talk much more about the will of Zeus as well. But the crucially important themes are all hit right in the very first lines: the anger of Achilles; which was devastating to the Greeks; all of this happened somehow to accomplish the will of Zeus; the anger of Achilles led to the quarrel with Agamemnon; and so on.

So, why is Achilles angry? He is angry because Agamemnon took away Achilles' concubine, Briseis. Now just to remind you of the relationship between Achilles and Agamemnon, Achilles is the greatest warrior that the Greeks have at Troy, without question, but Agamemnon is the leader of the expedition. Agamemnon is not "king of the Greeks" as is often said; there is no unified Greece and there is no unified king of the Greeks at this point in the culture, as reflected in the *Iliad*. However, Agamemnon is the leader of the expedition to Troy. Achilles is the king over his own kingdom, Agamemnon is a king, Menelaos is a king, Odysseus is a king, but Agamemnon is recognized as, in some sense, the leader—at least of this particular expedition, if not the leader in general. So Agamemnon is to some degree Achilles' superior, in terms of authority, but Achilles is without question the greatest warrior whom the Greeks have. Agamemnon has taken away Achilles' concubine, Briseis, and this is the motivation for Achilles' anger, which causes him to withdraw from the fighting. But to understand the nature of Achilles' anger, to understand why he is so outraged and enraged when Agamemnon takes away his concubine, we need to talk a little bit about the Homeric warriors' motivations for fighting in the first place.

What are the Greeks there fighting for? Yes, they are fighting to get Helen back; but on a broader level, on a wider level, why are they fighting? What does the individual Greek warrior want to get out of battle, out of going to war in the first place? Homeric warriors fight for two main things. They fight for *timê*, which is usually translated as honor, and for glory or fame, which is usually translated as *kleos*. The reason I like to use the Greek terms here, rather than just saying they fight for honor and for glory, is because our terms "honor" and "glory" are not exact equivalents for what these Greek words mean. The Greek concepts are little bit different from any concepts that we actually have, and require a little bit of explanation in consequence.

Timê, as I already said, is usually translated as honor, but it does not mean an internalized sense of honor, a personal sense of honor by which you validate yourself no matter what others think of you. Rather, *timê* refers to the externalized, tangible, physical representations of honor. *Timê* is what you are given by your peers; if you are a god, *timê* is what you are given through sacrifices that humans make to you. It is material, physical, tangible—and therefore removable. In fact, *timê*—the kind of honor conferred by *timê*—is often referred to as a "zero-sum game." If I have more *timê*, you have less. It is not like our concept of honor, where it is more or less infinitely expandable and how much honor you may have has no bearing on how much honor I have. *Timê* is a zero-sum game. If I get more of it, by definition, you get less, and vice-versa.

Now, *timê* is most usually expressed, in the Homeric poems at least, by gifts, booty, prizes—the actual objects that warriors gain when they sack enemy cities; gold, cattle, armor, slaves, particularly slave women. Briseis, therefore, is the tangible, visible expression of Achilles' *timê*. When Agamemnon takes her away from him, this is much more than merely a sexual affront. Achilles is jealous, I think, on the sexual level—Briseis is his concubine; Agamemnon has taken her—but there is much more going on in this quarrel between Achilles and Agamemnon than purely, or merely, sexual jealousy. Agamemnon's affront to Achilles' *timê* is much more important, much more serious, than that might seem to indicate. Briseis is, in fact, Achilles' *geras*; another Greek term which means a particular prize. *Geras* is often translated "prize of honor"; it means a representation of *timê*, the best prize that can be given to a warrior by his peers to indicate how great a warrior he is. That is what Briseis is to Achilles; that is what Agamemnon takes away from him.

I will come back to Agamemnon's motivations in a few minutes. But what about other term that I said Homeric warriors fight for, *kleos*? *Kleos* is usually translated as "glory" or "fame" or, sometimes, "reputation." What it literally means is what people say about you, what is spoken aloud about you. And obviously *timê* and *kleos* are very, very closely connected. The more *timê* you have the more *kleos* you are likely to get—the more visible signs of honor are given to you, the more great things people are likely to say about you—so there is an interlocking system here of *timê* and *kleos*. But *kleos* also, very importantly, serves as the only true form of immortality available to a Homeric warrior. *Kleos* is what people say about you at any time, but particularly, what people say about you after you are dead; how your reputation, your fame, your glory lives on after you die is the main point of *kleos*, the main interest that Homeric warriors have in *kleos*. If Achilles loses his *timê*, if he is dishonored, "dis-*timê*d" in the view of his fellow warriors, if he is no longer given these visible, tangible signs of honor, then what happens to his *kleos* after he is dead? Is he remembered as the greatest warrior or not? Probably not.

So Agamemnon has done much more to Achilles than simply take away his sexual partner; he has in effect dishonored Achilles, both in Achilles' own eyes and in the eyes of this assembled Greek army, and has done so in an extremely grievous way. Why did Agamemnon do this? Why would a commander-in-chief treat his foremost warrior this way? Agamemnon dishonors Achilles, or removes Achilles' *timê*, because of an affront to his own *timê*. Agamemnon has suffered a loss that,at first glance, is very similar to the loss he inflicts on Achilles. Agamemnon has had to return his own *geras*, his own prize of honor, his own representation of *timê*, the concubine, the slave woman Chryseis, daughter of a priest of Apollo named Chryses. Agamemnon has been forced to return this girl to her father. (By the way, I know it is annoying that Briseis and Chryseis sound so much alike and just to make matters even worse, Chryseis' father is named Chryses; but there is nothing we can do about it. That is the names that have come down to us, and we just have to deal with them.) Agamemnon, thus, tries to restore his own lost *timê*, the removal of Chryseis, his concubine, by taking Achilles' *geras*, Briseis.

Now Agamemnon, I said, is forced to return his concubine to her father. In the opening section of the *Iliad* the situation is set up very quickly, very abruptly, by the poet. At first Agamemnon refuses to return Chryseis to her father. Her father, Chryses, comes to the camps of the Greeks, begs for his daughter's return; he is carrying the emblems of his rank as a priest of the god Apollo, and in Apollo's name he begs for the return of his daughter. Agamemnon refuses; Chryses therefore goes away and prays to his god, Apollo—who, by the way, is the god of plague and sickness as well as the god of medicine and healing—Chryses prays to Apollo to smite the Greeks and make them regret that they would not return Chryseis to him. Apollo therefore sends a plague; this is the thousand-fold pains referred to in the opening lines of the *Iliad*. Apollo sends a plague upon the Greeks that causes the death of a great many Greek warriors. Agamemnon asks his prophet what he must do to lift the plague, and is told, "You must return Chryseis."

So far, so good; why would Agamemnon take it out on Achilles? Because Achilles had been one of the foremost Greeks who argued that Agamemnon ought to give Chryseis back. From the beginning, Achilles had said, "You should give her back to her father; you should not affront the priest of Apollo by keeping her." Agamemnon, therefore, sees this as somehow, if not Achilles' fault, at least something that it is reasonable to make Achilles suffer for. Also, Agamemnon is reasserting his own rank. He has visibly lost *timê* in the eyes of his men—Chryseis was taken away from him. He has to reassert his rank as the foremost authority among the Greeks; how better to do that than to prove that he is in control by taking away the prize of honor of the greatest warrior, Achilles?

Although Agamemnon has suffered this affront to his *timê*—and as I already said, externally, on the surface, it looks very similar to what he does to Achilles—I, at least, think that Agamemnon's action is not justified; because although he has suffered dishonor, loss of *timê*, his loss of *timê* differs from Achilles in some key ways. First of all, as I just explained, Agamemnon's loss of *timê* is directly required by a god. It is not a matter of another human being just deciding arbitrarily to take away Agamemnon's concubine; rather, his concubine is taken away from him through the direct command, the direct intervention, of a god who is slaughtering his people. And as the commander-in-chief, as the leader of the forces, Agamemnon ought to be able to put the well-being of his troops in front of his own desires, even for *timê*. Since the situation he is in is, "Either Apollo continues to kill your soldiers or you give back Chyrseis," he ought to be able to give back Chyrseis and to accept that. Secondly, as Achilles says to Agamemnon in the early part of Book One of the

Iliad, at this point, the Greeks have no replacement prize to give Agamemnon. They have distributed all the loot they have taken from the most recent sack of cities around Troy—Troy itself has not been sacked but there are all sorts of allied smaller cities around Troy that the Greeks have sacked; that is where they got Chryseis and Briseis in the first place. Achilles points out to Agamemnon, "We have no unallocated prizes lying around in the camp that we can distribute now, but if we ever do sack Troy, then we will give you the finest *geras*, the finest prize of honor imaginable. We will make it up to you; this is a temporary loss of *timê* not a permanent diminution in your status."

So Agamemnon has not suffered the same kind of affront that he imposes upon Achilles. His loss of *timê* is required by a god and has a wider motivation, if you like, a public motivation—lifting the plague from his people. What he does to Achilles, in contrast, is a direct human-to-human affront, intended purely to degrade Achilles in the eyes of his fellow warriors. Achilles responds to Agamemnon's actions by withdrawing from battle and actively seeking the temporary defeat of the Greeks. Achilles announces that he will no longer fight against the Trojans. If this is what Agamemnon thinks of him, if Agamemnon can this easily remove Achilles *timê* from him, then, Achilles says, he will no longer fight against the Trojans. In fact, he threatens to take his group of warriors, called the Myrmidons, and return home; he threatens to leave Troy entirely.

Achilles further reacts to Agamemnon's actions by summoning his mother, Thetis—the sea goddess who is his mother—and asking her to go and petition Zeus, the king of the gods, to grant the Trojans temporary ascendancy over the Greeks, until the Greeks learn what is like to try to wage the Trojan War without the help of Achilles. So Achilles calls to his mother; she comes up out of the ocean and asks him what is troubling him; he tells her the situation; she agrees to go and talk to Zeus and see if Zeus cannot punish the Greeks for Agamemnon's mistreatment of Achilles. Thetis' appeal to Zeus has several functions in this opening section of the *Iliad*; not only does it carry the narrative along—Achilles asks Thetis to get Zeus to help him avenge himself against the Trojans—but also the scene between Thetis and Zeus allows the audience of glimpse of the gods on Mount Olympus, in their own dwelling place, and gives us a view of the power dynamics that operate among the gods.

Now, of course, just as Homer's audience knew the human characters of the *Iliad*, so they were also perfectly familiar with the gods. These were their gods; these were the gods whom they worshipped, and in whom they believed. Nevertheless, Homer is doing something that will be unusual from the normal, every-day human viewpoint; he is telling us how the gods interact with one another, what they say to each other, the conversations that they have with one another on Mount Olympus. And so when Thetis goes to appeal to Zeus, we're given a little vignette of gods interacting with one another, and we are also given a fairly clear delineation, or clear for this early in the epic, of how much even Zeus can change or manipulate or in any way affect the outcome of events. In fact, the scene between Thetis and Zeus is our first glimpse of one extraordinarily important theme of the *Iliad*: the idea of fate and of human destiny.

Now, I will talked much more about fate in a later lecture, but very briefly, for right now, the basic idea is that each human being has an allotted time of death, a time of fate, a time when he or she—but of course in the *Iliad* we are mainly dealing with he's—will die; and that this fate is set, cannot be altered—or at least *is* not altered—even by the gods, even by Zeus himself. For most humans in the *Iliad*, that is about all that their fate means, and all we need to know—that they are going to die at a certain time. They, of course, don't know when; we, of course, don't know when; but when a warrior actually dies in battle, Homer will sometimes say something like, "His fate took him," or "He met his fate," at that particular point. When Thetis goes and appeals to Zeus, we are given an idea that while the endpoint of fate is fixed—Troy is going to fall to the Greeks; the Greeks are going to sack Troy; that cannot be changed; that is set—while that end point is fixed, apparently getting from here to there allows a certain amount of malleability. Zeus can change what happens in the interim. Zeus can, in fact, give ascendancy to the Trojans for a certain amount of time in order to please Thetis, in order to help Achilles establish his importance for the Greeks. So the endpoint of fate is set, but Zeus is allowed a certain amount of leeway with how the humans involved get to that endpoint of fate. Zeus agrees that he will give the Trojans temporary ascendancy over the Greeks; the Greeks will suffer at the Trojans hands; the Trojans will seem to be winning the war. It is only temporary; Zeus knows that—and we know that because we, like Zeus, know that the eventual outcome of the Trojan War is set and cannot be changed.

Now, Zeus' intervention, in narrative terms, works extremely well, because it allows the poet to build a certain sense of suspense in the audience. The Trojans are going to defeat the Greeks, at least for a certain amount of time; Zeus is going to let the Trojans inflict great harm upon the Greeks. Just as Zeus knows the outcome of fate and cannot change it, Homer's audience knows the outcome of the story; they are not sitting on the edge on the edge of their seats worried that perhaps the Trojans will defeat the Greeks, and will destroy the entire Greek fleet, and Troy will become the ruling power in the Mediterranean. This is not going to happen; the audience knows the end of the story. The suspense is built, again, by wondering about the details of that story; what is this bard going to do with the minutiae of the story, the interim details? How much damage are the Trojans going to inflict upon the Greeks? How long will Zeus let that go on? Also remember, the *Iliad* is a Greek epic, for a Greek audience. There is a certain discomfort with showing the Trojans, the enemy, in ascendancy over the Greeks even temporarily, even briefly when Achilles withdraws from fighting. Are the rest of the Greeks really that bad at fighting, that the loss of Achilles means the Trojans almost clobber them? Well, think of what Homer has done. Zeus has intervened, Zeus has ordained that in Achilles' absence the Trojans will get the upper hand over the Greeks. This is a very clever way of letting a Greek audience see Greek soldiers temporarily defeated, and yet not feel like, "Well, we were worse warriors that the Trojans." We are not; it is all Zeus. Zeus has temporarily allowed this to happen.

Now, within the context of Achilles' own culture and Achilles' own assumptions about the nature of being a warrior, about *kleos*, about *timê*, I think that his reaction to Agamemnon's affront is not excessive. Yes, Achilles withdraws from battle; yes, he asks his mother, who can do so, to see to it that a great many of his fellow Greeks get killed because he has withdrawn from battle; and modern readers—I find this a lot with modern students—often think that Achilles at this point has just gone way, way overboard. Agamemnon takes away his girlfriend; Achilles tries to kill all his fellow warriors. This seems like an overreaction in our terms. I think, within the terms of Achilles' own culture and own ethos, it is not an overreaction; it is not excessive. By dishonoring him, Agamemnon has removed Achilles' motivation for fighting, but he has done more than that. It is not just that Agamemnon has taken away this representation of *timê* so that Achilles says, "Well, why should I continue to fight to get *timê*, when you can take it away from me?" It is much more than that.

The society reflected in the Homeric poems is, in many ways, what anthropologists call, or at least used to call, a "shame culture"; that is, a culture in which an individual's sense of self-worth, sense of identity, is constructed by what others say, think, perceive about that person. The opposite of a shame culture is a guilt culture, in which people's self-image; sense of self-worth, is motivated by their internal sense of who and what they are. In a guilt culture, Achilles would be able to say, "I know that I am the greatest warrior among the Greeks; what does it matter to me if Agamemnon has dishonored me in everyone's eyes, when I know in my own heart, in my own soul, what a great warrior I am?" In a guilt culture that makes sense. In a shame culture, there is a very real sense in which, if other people perceive Achilles as having no honor, then Achilles *has* no honor. It is all very externalized; his honor, his sense of identity, his sense of his importance in his society, all of those things are very definitely externalized. Thus, what Agamemnon has done is, as I have already developed, more than to insult or dishonor Achilles; he has called Achilles' whole worth—almost Achilles' whole identity as Achilles—into question. And Achilles' only possible means of retaliation is to prove his worth, through the Greeks' suffering in his absence.

As we'll see in a later lecture, in fact, Achilles does more than that—Achilles comes to question the whole system of *kleos* and *timê*, the whole warrior ethos that has nurtured him. But in the immediate context of Book One, his only possible retaliation against Agamemnon's affront is to prove to the Greeks his worth, by making them suffer in his absence. So, once Book One has set the scene by establishing the reason for the quarrel between Achilles and Agamemnon, by establishing the devastating effects of Achilles' wrath on the Greek army, by giving us a glimpse of the gods on Mount Olympus and how they interact with one another, then the bard can move on into the body of the story. The next three books, Books Two through Four, introduce the audience to both sides, the Greeks and the Trojans; to some particular characters who are especially important in the *Iliad*; and move us into the descriptions of actual battle. In the next lecture we will move on to look at Homer's treatment of the Trojans, particularly of Priam and Helen, and how he delineates the enemy in the *Iliad*.

Lecture Four

Within the Walls of Troy

Scope:

This lecture examines Homer's portrayal of the Trojans, which is sympathetic, three-dimensional, and nuanced. The Trojans are not portrayed as villains; rather, the war is a terrible tragedy for them, and one that they never sought. They fight not just for *timê* and *kleos* but for their lives and their country's survival. Our view of them is colored throughout by the knowledge that they will be defeated. We examine two crucial scenes, one between Priam and Helen and the other between Hektor and Andromache, and discuss both how the portrayal of these characters adds to our overall picture of the war, and how our knowledge of events outside the *Iliad* heightens the pathos of these scenes.

Outline

I. Our first sustained view of the Trojans comes in Book III, where we meet the noncombatants Priam and Helen.

- **A.** The bard shows us Priam and other Trojan elders watching the battle from the city wall.
  1. We are introduced not only to Priam but to Helen. Her ambiguous nature is summed up by the words of the Trojan elders as they look at her.
  2. Priam's first words, when he calls Helen "dear child," set his "character note."
  3. "The gods are blameworthy": these words of Priam's foreground the limitations of human control.
  4. Certain aspects of this scene raise again the "Homeric Question," post-Perry Melman.
  5. The scene in which Helen names the heroes is an excellent example of the "displacement" of episodes that logically should have happened earlier in the war into the narrative of the *Iliad*.
- **B.** The pathos of the Trojans' position is highlighted by a vignette of Paris and Helen together.
  1. Paris is inside Troy because Aphrodite rescued him from the field of battle, where he was fighting a duel with Menelaos, and put him down in his own bedroom.

2. Aphrodite summons Helen to join Paris. Helen resists, but Aphrodite threatens her and she obeys.
3. The fact that Helen now despises Paris as much as anyone else does adds an element of futility to the whole war.

II. The Trojans fight not just for *timê* and *kleos* but also for their country's survival. We see this most clearly in Hektor, who appears in the early books of the *Iliad* both as the leader of the Trojans in the field, and with his family inside the walls of Troy.

A. Hektor appears as the Trojan leader and spokesman in Book III.

1. In his first words in the *Iliad*, Hektor scolds Paris for the shame and hardship he has brought on the Trojans.
2. Although the duel with Menelaos is Paris' idea, it is Hektor who suggests it to the Greeks.

B. We see Hektor inside Troy with his family in Book VI.

1. Hektor goes into Troy to ask his mother to offer gifts to Athena, and to summon Paris back to battle.
2. Hektor meets his wife Andromache and baby son Astyanax on the walls of Troy. Their conversation gives us a glimpse of what the Trojans warriors are fighting for.
3. Hektor's own statement of why he must fight reiterates the importance of "shame," but also highlights his role as protector of his city.

III. Our view of the Trojans is colored throughout by the knowledge that they will be defeated.

A. Hektor's meeting with Andromache and Astyanax lets us see the cost of the Trojan War in human terms.

B. Hektor will be killed by Achilles.

C. Astyanax will be thrown from the walls of Troy.

D. Andromache will be led away into slavery.

IV. Our view of the Trojans is also colored by the obvious disparity between what they are risking (the total destruction of their culture) and what they are risking it for (Paris' and Helen's adulterous affair).

A. This disparity was noticed in antiquity; from the 6th century B.C. on, authors wondered why Priam did not just send Helen back.

B. The *Iliad* itself takes account of this disparity in the encounter of the Trojan Glaukos and the Greek Diomedes.
   1. The two discover that they are hereditary "guest-friends," and decide not to fight.
   2. As a token of their friendship, they exchange armor.
   3. The poet comments that Zeus took away Glaukos' wits, so that he exchanged golden armor worth 100 oxen for bronze worth only 9.
   4. This can be read as a comment on Troy's exchange of all the blessings of peace for Helen.

Essential Reading:

Iliad, Books III–VI.

Supplementary Reading:

Norman Austin, *Helen of Troy*, Chapter 1.

Mark W. Edwards, *Poet of the Iliad*, Chapters 22–23.

James V. Morrison, *Homeric Misdirection*, Chapter 5.

Oliver Taplin, *Homeric Soundings*, Chapter 4.

Questions to Consider:

1. Consider the "dual motivation" of Helen going to bed with Paris, despite saying that she no longer likes him. On one level, Helen can simply say "Aphrodite made me do it"; can her action be understood in modern psychological terms as well?
2. The *Iliad* is a Greek epic, for a Greek audience, and the Trojans' downfall is inevitable. Explain how the impact of the story would differ if Priam, Hektor, and Andromache were portrayed as unsympathetic characters.

Lecture Four—Transcript
Within the Walls of Troy

Hello, and welcome back to Lecture Four, "Within the Walls of Troy." Our previous lecture examined the opening of the *Iliad*, and the ways in which the bard set the scene for the epic by stating the primary theme of the *Iliad*—the wrath of Achilles—and developing the argument between Achilles and Agamemnon. In this lecture I want to turn to discussing Homer's portrayal of the Trojans, the Greeks' enemy. We will see how Homer depicts the Trojans in a very sympathetic fashion; how he points out that they are, unlike the aggressive Greeks, fighting a defensive war, fighting to protect their homes and country. We'll also talk about how our foreknowledge, as the audience, of the Trojan defeat plays into our reading of their characters; and finally, how events outside the *Iliad*—how our knowledge of events outside the *Iliad*—colors our perception of the Trojans as Homer depicts them.

So, to begin with, Homer's treatment of the Trojans; who, despite the fact that they are the enemies of the Greeks in the *Iliad*, are portrayed in an extremely sympathetic, nuanced, and three-dimensional way. These are far from being cut-out-cardboard-villain type enemies. In fact, many readers find the Trojans, and Hektor in particular, far more sympathetic than some of the Greek characters in the *Iliad*.

Our first sustained view of the Trojans comes in Book Three of the *Iliad* and, interestingly enough, focuses mainly on non-combatants. In Book Three, Homer takes us inside Troy and shows us the aged king, Priam, and various other Trojan elders observing the battle from the walls of Troy. We also see Priam interact with Helen, and finally in Book Three we see Helen and Paris interact with one another. I want to look at each of these scenes in some detail, and talk about the implications for our understanding of the Trojans and the implications for our overall reading of the *Iliad* as well.

In Book Three, we see Priam and other Trojan elders watching the progress of the battle from the city wall of Troy. In this scene Helen approaches the spot where the Trojan elders and Priam are sitting and the Trojans look at her, the old men of Troy look at her, and comment on her in a way that sums up her ambiguous nature; she is both the most beautiful women in the world and a cause of great suffering to the Trojans. The Trojan elders, as they watch her walking towards them, say to one another:

> Surely there is no blame on Trojans and strong-greaved Achaians
> if for long time they suffer hardship for a woman like this one.
> Terrible is the likeness of her face to immortal goddesses.
> Still, though she be such, let her go away in the ships, lest he
> be left behind, a grief to us and our children.

Even these old men of Troy, who get no benefit whatsoever from Helen's presence, cannot blame the Trojans and Achaians—that is Homer's most common word for the Greeks—for fighting over Helen. She is so beautiful, she resembles the immortal goddesses; anyone would fight for her. And yet at the same time, the elders want her to leave, they want her to go away again, lest she become a source of even more disaster to them and to their children.

As Helen approaches Priam speaks to her; and the way in which he addresses her sets, I think, his character note, so to speak, for the entire *Iliad*. Remember, Priam is the king of Troy; it is his city that is being devastated by the war over Helen. It is his people who are being destroyed by Helen's presence in Troy; and yet, when he speaks to her, his words could hardly be more gentle or even affectionate. He says to her,

> Come over here where I am, dear child, and sit down beside me,
> to look at your husband of time past, your friends and your people.
> I am not blaming you: to me the gods are blameworthy
> who drove upon me this sorrowful war against the Achaians.

He does not blame her; he calls her "dear child"; and he asks her to sit with him. This is hardly a vicious or a one-dimensional enemy, about whom the Greek listeners of the *Iliad* could feel comfortable in hating him and thinking that he ought to be destroyed.

Clearly, Priam is an extremely sympathetic character; we see this from this very early view of him in Book Three of the *Iliad*. Also, his words in which he says that the gods are blameworthy stress, again, the limitations of human endeavor and of human control, reiterate from the other side that same topic that I talked about a bit in the last lecture, the topic of fate, the idea that the outcome of these events is foreordained and will happen as it happens—whether or not the humans happen to know what that outcome is. Priam does not know, although we do, that Troy will fall; and yet he does know, or he does believe, that all of these events are somehow brought against him by the gods. So, when Priam speaks to Helen we see him as a compassionate, gentle, kind, elderly man, talking to a young woman who has brought devastation against his family and his city, and yet in no way blaming or reproaching her for this devastation.

He asks her to look at the warriors who are fighting on the plain below the walls of Troy; he and the elders and Helen are all sitting on the walls, looking out over the battle, and Priam asks Helen to name to him the warriors whom she sees fighting before the walls of Troy at this point. She does so; she looks out over the battlefield, Priam points out different warriors to her, says, "Who is this one? Who is that one?" Helen names them. She names three in particular, Agamemnon, Odysseus, and Aias the Greater—Agamemnon, of course, the leader of the expedition; Odysseus, the cleverest, most gifted speaker among the Greeks; and Aias the Greater, the best warrior, second only to Achilles himself.

As Helen looks at the warriors fighting before Troy, she says that she recognizes all of them, she can name all of them; but two and only two whom she expected to see are missing. Those are her own brothers, Castor and Polydeuces, or Castor and Pollux, if you know him better by his Roman name. She speculates that perhaps Castor and Polydeuces did not come to Troy, did not come to fight, out of shame over her, her actions, and what she has caused the Greeks. So she speculates that she doesn't see her brothers because they simply did not come to the war. Homer, the bard, comments that this what she thought; but actually, her brothers were lying buried under the "life-giving earth" in their native land, in Sparta.

Now that comment, that little adjective, that these dead heroes are buried under the "life-giving earth," is an example in miniature of the kind of controversies that have been raging in Homeric criticism ever since Milman Parry gave us his oral compositional theory. In the nineteenth century, several critics pointed to this particular line as one of especially poignant poetic beauty in the *Iliad*. Helen doesn't see her brothers; she speculates that they are still at home; the poet says, "Yes, they are, but they are dead, under the life-giving earth"—and the irony of the life-giving earth holding the dead heroes was what particularly appealed to some nineteenth-century critics (and I am thinking particularly of Matthew Arnold, for instance, and other such literary critics). After Milman Parry's work on oral compositional theory, various modern critics said, "Well, that is precisely the kind of reading of Homer that we cannot do any more." Because now, they thought, we know that Homer did not choose adjectives in that way, that if he says *phusizoos aia*, "life- giving earth," he uses that phrase simply because it fits nicely at the end of the line; and there is no way we can any longer think that the poet himself was thinking of the contrast between the life-giving earth and the dead heroes.

But just recently, in what might be called the counter-wave of criticism against the most straightforward reading of the Parry-Lord hypothesis, some critics have started to say, "Well now, wait a minute. Let's look at this a little more closely." That particular, that particular phrase, *phusizoos aia*, "life-giving earth," is very rare in the Homeric poems. It shows up, I believe, only twice in the entire corpus; certainly it shows up very infrequently. Here it is in a context where we are talking about dead heroes; why can't we say that, in this case, Homer chose that adjective intentionally? So, this is the sort of critical problem that we are left with, that the Parry-Lord hypothesis has helped with to some extent, but not with others. Still, as I said, in Lecture Number Two, to some extent it is a matter of individual critics' individual opinions about what sort of poetry this is and how it works, whether you think that this is a wonderful instance of poetic poignancy and irony, when the poet says the dead heroes are held by the life-giving earth, or whether you think that this is just sort of surface effect of the formulaic tradition, and the poet had no such thought in his mind; no more did his audience. Really, that is a matter on which each critic has to make up his or her own mind; we don't, at this point, know which way to go with it.

After Helen looks at the heroes and names them, she is going, very soon thereafter, to be taken by Aphrodite and reunited with Paris in his bedroom. But there is one more point that I wanted to make about this scene in which Helen names the heroes, and that is that it is an excellent example of what is often called "displacement" of narrative episodes within the *Iliad*. Logically speaking, if ever Helen described to Priam who the different Greek warriors were, named them by name, speculated about where her brothers were, and so forth, logically speaking, if ever that happened, it should have happened in the first year of the Trojan War. There is no reason at all why, in year nine and a half of the Trojan War, Priam should suddenly say to

Helen, "Now come and tell me who all these people are, now." Logically, it makes no sense.

This is the sort of episode that Analysts in the last century put their finger on and say, "Aha, look, somebody cobbled this together. Some collector (who did not have very much poetic sense or skill) took a scene that belonged in the first year of the Trojan War—and probably in some bards' recitations *was* in the first year of the Trojan War—and stuck it in here in the *Iliad* where it doesn't fit; and this is evidence that whoever put these shorter poems together was not even trying for narrative consistency or unity." Another—perhaps the most obvious—example of this kind of narrative displacement is the long list in Book Two of the *Iliad* that sometimes is called the "Catalogue of Ships," in which the bard lists all the ships that came from Greece, who commands which ones, how many he commands, what city they came from; again, in narrating the tenth year of the war, there is no point in putting in a muster roll, basically a list of the fleet at that point. It doesn't really belong there.

Well, as I said, this is something that the Analysts often turned to, to say that this indicates a lack of narrative cohesion, a lack of consistency, in the *Iliad*. I am not sure that it does. I think most readers, when they come across the scene in Book Three where Helen and Priam are standing on the walls looking out over the battlefield, I think most readers do not stop and think to themselves, "But wait a minute, this is the tenth year of the war; why are they just getting around to this now?"—any more than when we are watching a play, we wonder why the critical events that are going to start the story happen just the instant after the curtain goes up when we happen to be there to see them. They happen then, because that is what the narrative requires. Yes, this is the tenth year of the war; but this is the third book of the *Iliad*. From the point of view of the audience, we are very early on in the story, and I think it works, poetically, to have this naming of the heroes for Priam by Helen just at this point in the *Iliad*. I don't think that very many audience members, then or now, would stop and think about it, ultra-logically, and say, "But this should have happened in the first year of the war." I don't think that is the way poetry, oral or otherwise, tends to work.

In any case, after this scene, the poet moves on—still inside the walls of Troy—to a vignette that shows us Paris and Helen together and highlights, I think, the pathos of the Trojans' position by showing us the futility of what they are fighting for. Paris is inside the walls of Troy at this point because Aphrodite has put him there. More displacement; Paris was fighting a duel with Menelaos, another event that, if it happened at all, should have happened in the first year of the war. It is a very, very obvious solution; have Paris and Menelaos fight a duel, and the winner gets Helen. But in the *Iliad*, this is only suggested after Achilles has withdrawn from fighting, after the *Iliad* has begun. Then Hektor suggests to Paris that he should fight a duel against Menelaos, and Paris thinks this is a good idea and does so. So in Book Three, Paris and Menelaos have been fighting a duel, and Menelaos is about to win. If there had been no divine intervention, if Menelaos had won the duel, the *Iliad* would be a much shorter book. It would be over right then and there would be very little left to say about the Trojan War.

However, Aphrodite rescues Paris directly. She goes down onto the battlefield, picks Paris up, carries him away from Menelaos, takes him inside Troy, puts him down inside his own bedroom, and then goes to get Helen. So we are shown Aphrodite as the direct embodiment—which she is—of sexual passion, but also as an actor in the story who herself, especially deliberately, puts Helen and Paris together in the bedroom inside Troy. When Aphrodite goes to summon Helen to join Paris, Aphrodite is in disguise as an old woman, but Helen recognizes her and resists the idea of going to join Paris in his bedroom. Helen says, near the end of Book Three of the *Iliad*, that she does not want to join Paris in the bedroom. She is ashamed to leave the walls of Troy so publicly, to go off to bed with Paris; she doesn't want to do this. Aphrodite, in effect, threatens her; says, "I can make you as hated as you are now loved, I can come to hate you as much as I now love you, do what I tell you or you will be sorry"—and Helen does in fact go off to bed with Paris. But as Book Three ends, we see Helen and Paris actually speaking to one another, and one of the first things Helen says to Paris when she joins him in the bedroom is, "I wish Menelaos had killed you." She knows that he was out fighting with Menelaos, and she says she wishes he had died in this duel.

Now, I think the fact that Helen now despises Paris as much as anyone else does, that Helen does not want to be there, that Helen is in no way interested in Paris any longer, I think this adds an element of futility, an element of pathos, underlines the utter frivolity of this war. It is fought over an adulterous relationship to which one of the parties no longer even wants to belong. The Trojans are risking everything—country, city, life, freedom, everything—so that Paris and Helen can continue to live together; and Helen doesn't even want to any more. So the futility of this war is underlined by this scene between Paris and Helen.

So, in his depiction of the non-combatant Trojans inside the walls of Troy—and here I am counting Helen as a Trojan, because for the duration of the war, she *is*, more or less—Homer reminds us that the Trojans, unlike the Greeks, are fighting not for *timê* and *kleos*—or at least not only for *timê* and *kleos*—but for their country's very survival. We see this, however, not just in the non-combatants, not just inside Troy with Priam, Paris, and Helen. We also see this double motivation, the fact that the Trojans are fighting for survival as well as *timê* and *kleos*, in the warrior Hektor, the crown prince of Troy, Paris' older brother.

When Hektor first appears and speaks in the *Iliad*—this is in Book Three—he speaks to his younger brother, Paris, and he scolds Paris for the shame and hardship that Paris has brought upon the Trojans. Hektor calls Paris evil, beautiful, mad about women, a seducer; he really says some very, very harsh things to his younger brother. This is what motivates Paris to agree to fight the duel with Menelaos, the duel that I have just been talking about. Hektor appears as the foremost Trojan warrior, the definite leader of the Trojans; it is Paris' fight with Menelaos, and yet Hektor is the one who walks between the ranks of the amassed Greeks and Trojans and suggests a duel, Hektor is the one who speaks for all the Trojans, Hektor is definitely the leader of the Trojans. We also see Hektor inside Troy. We see him not only on the battlefield, interacting with his younger brother, Paris, and negotiating the terms of the duel with the Greeks; we also see Hektor inside Troy with his family in Book Six of the *Iliad*. Book Six focuses almost entirely on Hektor and his interaction with his wife Andromache and his son Astyanax; to a lesser extent his mother, Hekabe.

Hektor goes inside the walls of Troy, in Book Six, specifically to ask his mother to offer gifts to the goddess Athena, to try to appease her and win her over to the Trojan side. Now, this is a point I have not touched on yet, but it is well worth thinking about for a moment, because it is not immediately what you would expect—namely that the Trojans worshipped the same gods as the Greeks. When Hektor goes inside Troy to ask his mother to offer sacrifices to Athena, he is not saying, "Mother, please offer sacrifices to this strange foreign goddess, who seems to be doing a lot of good for the Greeks; let's see if we can get in touch with her somehow and get her onto our side"; not at all. He asks his mother to go to the temple of Athena; it is taken for granted in the *Iliad* that the Trojans have exactly the same gods as the Greeks, that the Trojans worship the same gods as the Greeks.

It is even, apparently, taken for granted that the Trojans speak Greek, the same language as the Greeks. When we see Greeks and Trojans interacting, talking to one another, taunting one another on the battlefield at times, they speak the same language. Now, Homer recognized that there were people who spoke other languages than Greek, because he mentioned some Trojan allies who speak barbarous languages, who do not speak Greek, who twitter like birds and nobody can understand them. But the Trojans themselves are assumed both to speak Greek and to worship the same gods that the Greeks worship. I think, once again, this is part of the pattern whereby the poet presents the Trojans as fully-developed, likeable people with whom we can sympathize; not as some sort of strange, different, barbarian enemy whom it would be easy to hate, but really as in very few ways different at all from the Greeks. There are some differences—Priam seems to be polygamous; he seems to have more than one wife, which is unlike the Greek practice—there are some differences, but for the most part the Trojans are treated as though they were also Greeks, and they worshipped the same gods; and some of the gods are on their side, some are on the Greeks' side.

So, Hektor goes into Troy, in Book Six, to ask his mother to offer gifts to Athena, and also he goes into Troy to summon Paris back to battle, because Paris is still there in bed with Helen—or is still there, at any rate, whether he is still in bed or not. So Hektor is in Troy to ask his mother to offer gifts to Athena and to summon Paris back to battle. While he is inside the city Hektor meets his wife Andromache and baby son Astyanax, and, in one of the most famous scenes of the *Iliad*, this little family talks to one another, interacts with one another. Andromache asks Hektor please not to go back out to the fighting but to stay inside the walls of the city with her and their baby son. Hektor talks to her about the future, he holds his baby—an extremely vivid picture of Hektor not just as a warrior, not just as a fighter, but as a husband, a father, and a son. We see all of those aspects of him—and an elder brother with a rather problematic younger brother—we see all of those aspects of him in Book Six of the *Iliad*.

His encounter with his wife is particularly important for this full development of Hektor's humanity and of Hektor as a sympathetic character. As I just said, Andromache asks him please not to go back out into the fighting, not to risk his life again, but to stay in the city, at least for a while, with her and with the baby, Astyanax. Hektor's own statement of why he can't do that, of why he must go back out again and fight, gives us a portrait, a picture, of what it is that the Trojans are fighting for; because Hektor refers to honor, to glory, and to shame, to these elements that keep a warrior fighting, but he also refers what the aftermath will be for his family if Troy is destroyed. So after Andromache has asked him not to return to the fighting, in an extremely emotionally appealing speech in which she reminds him that Achilles killed her parents and her brothers and Hektor is literally all she has left—she says you are my father, my mother, my brother, my husband, you are everything that I have—Hektor replies:

> All these
> things are in my mind also, lady; yet I would feel deep shame
> before the Trojans, and the Trojan women . . .
> if like a coward I were to shrink aside from the fighting;
> and the spirit will not let me, since I have learned to be valiant
> and to fight always among the foremost ranks of the Trojans,
> winning for my own self great glory, [*kleos*, of course] and for my father.
> For I know this thing well in my heart, and my mind knows it:
> there will come a day when sacred Ilion shall perish,
> and Priam, and the people of Priam of the great [sic strong] ash spear.

Then he goes on and says that he knows that Troy will fall. We'll see, in just a minute, he doesn't know it; he thinks it might, but he turns right around, just a few lines later, and prays that his son will grow up to be a better man than he, and will delight the heart of his mother. Hektor, in other words, is a normal human being, who is capable of thinking in one instant that his city is doomed, and in the next that he'll live to a ripe old age. He doesn't know the future; he fears that Troy will fall. He goes on to say that if Troy does fall, what bothers him the most, what troubles him the most when he thinks about that, is not the loss of the city, not his loss of his own life, not even the death of his parents, but the thought of Andromache being dragged off into slavery by some Greek, and people taunting her, saying, "There she goes, the wife of great Hektor; now she is a slave."

Now, again, from the audience's point of view, we know that this is exactly what will happen to Andromache. We know that Andromache will be enslaved; we know that Astyanax, the baby, will be killed by the Greeks, by being thrown from the walls of Troy and smashed on the rocks below. And so our impression of this scene is colored throughout by our foreknowledge, which Hektor and Andromache do not share, of what is going to happen to them. The most famous visual detail in this scene, one that people often remember from the *Iliad*, is when Hektor reaches out to hold his baby, and the baby is frightened by the horsehair crest on Hektor's Helmut and starts to cry. Hektor of the glancing helmet takes the helmet off, sets it aside, then holds the baby up and prays that this child may grow up to be greater than he is, and Andromache, we're told, smiles through her tears. An extremely vivid, extremely moving scene, and, as I said, moving in large part because we know that it will not come to pass; that what Hektor prays for will not happen, that Astyanax will be killed by other helmeted warriors, if not by his father.

Our view of the Trojans, I think, is also colored by the obvious disparity between what they are risking—the total destruction of their culture—and what they are risking it for—Paris and Helen's adulterous affair. This disparity was noted in antiquity; as far back as the sixth century B.C., authors wondered why on earth Priam did not simply send Helen back. Why would a king do that? Why would a king let his entire country be destroyed so that his younger son—not even the crown prince, but his younger son—could have an adulterous liaison with someone else's wife? And the obvious answer is, no king would. So various Greek authors came up with explanations, such as Helen had never been there at all; Priam did not have her to give back, and the Greeks simply wouldn't believe him; or other such explanations. In the *Iliad* it is quite clear that she is there. We are not ever told why Priam doesn't just send her back, but I think the *Iliad* itself notices and comments on the disparity between what the Trojans are fighting for, and what they are risking in that fight. I think the *Iliad* comments on this disparity in one particular scene.

Still in *Iliad* Book Six, there is a scene in which the Trojan ally Glaukos and the Greek warrior Diomedes meet on the field of battle.

They discover, by announcing to one another who they are, they discover that they are hereditary "guest-friends"; that is, that a guest-host relationship runs in their family, through their great-grandfathers, grandfathers, fathers, and so on. Now you will notice, as you read the *Iliad*, that these warriors very frequently announce who they are to one another before they fight. This, of course, again has to do with *kleos*; you need to know who it is that you are killing, or about to be killed by, in order to know how glorious a deed you are doing. Glaukos and Diomedes discover that they are hereditary guest-friends and choose not to kill one another. They say, "there are plenty of Greeks for me to kill; plenty of Trojans for you to kill; let's not fight," and as a token of their hereditary so-called guest-friendship, they exchange armor.

Now this is the point I want to bring out. The poet comments that Zeus took away Glaukos' wits—the wits of Glaukos, the Trojan ally—so that he exchanged golden armor worth one hundred oxen for bronze armor worth only nine. It has always seemed to me that that is a comment on the Trojans in general; they have exchanged the blessings of peace, of domestic life, of seeing their children grow up, of their country flourishing—they have exchanged all of those blessings for what? For Helen—and she is not worth it. The reason I think that this can be read as such a comment is because the scene between Glaukos and Diomedes leads directly into Hektor going into Troy. The poet says Zeus took away Glaukos' wits; he exchanged armor worth one hundred oxen for armor worth nine; then Hektor walked into Troy and was immediately surrounded by women asking for news of their brothers, their fathers, their husbands, their sons. It seems to me there is a very clear comment there about what the Trojans in general have exchanged for Helen; the blessings of peace, hope for their country, all of those things, in order to keep Helen.

So, in his portrayal of the Trojans, Homer shows us not an easy-to-hate enemy, but a whole, fully-developed picture of a people—from the old king Priam to the young wife Andromache—caught in a tragic war they never sought, and suffering consequences far out of proportion to any fault that any of them have committed. In the next lecture we'll turn back to looking at Achilles and the Greeks, specifically to the scene in which Agamemnon sends three people to try to persuade Achilles to return to battle.

Lecture Five
The Embassy to Achilles

Scope:

As the battle continues, and continues to go badly for the Greeks, Achilles' absence becomes more and more serious for them. Finally, on Nestor's advice, Agamemnon decides to try to persuade Achilles to return to battle. Agamemnon admits that he was wrong, and sends Odysseus, Phoinix and Aias to speak to Achilles on his behalf and to describe the gifts he will offer Achilles in recompense. Achilles refuses to accept Agamemnon's offered gifts, and does so in terms that call into question the whole *timê*- and *kleos*-based structure of his society. This lecture examines the arguments that the three emissaries make to Achilles, his reasons for rejecting those arguments, and the implications of his rejection for our understanding of his character.

Outline

I. As the battle continues (Books VII and VIII), the Greek leaders realize that they must do something to change their situation.

- **A.** Agamemnon suggests packing up and going home.
- **B.** Diomedes answers that Agamemnon can leave if he likes, but that the other Greeks will stay.
- **C.** Nestor applauds Diomedes' words, and counsels Agamemnon to try to persuade Achilles to return to battle.

II. Agamemnon agrees that he was at fault, proposes a magnificent recompense for Achilles, and selects three men to serve as an embassy to Achilles.

- **A.** The recompense that Agamemnon offers Achilles includes the return of Briseis and many other slave women, the kingship of seven cities and marriage to one of Agamemnon's daughters. These gifts mirror the three types of bribes offered by the goddesses to Paris in the beauty contest that ostensibly started the Trojan War.
- **B.** Agamemnon chooses Odysseus, Phoinix, and Aias as emissaries to approach Achilles. These three men are carefully chosen:

1. Odysseus is the cleverest Greek, and the best persuasive orator. Thus, he can put Agamemnon's case as well as it possibly can be put.
2. Phoinix, an old man, was Achilles' foster-father. He can appeal to emotion, and particularly to Achilles' sense of filial duty toward his father Peleus, whose representative Phoinix is.
3. Aias is the best Greek warrior after Achilles' himself. He can appeal to Achilles' sense of comradeship with other warriors.

III. The embassy goes to Achilles' camp.

A. When the three emissaries arrive at Achilles' camp, they find him sitting by his tent.

1. Achilles is playing the lyre and singing *klea andron* (the "glories of man"). Thus, he is portrayed as memorializing in song the deeds he will no longer perform in reality.
2. *Kleos* is still crucial in the depiction of Achilles, although it is inverted here.

B. Achilles greets his friends cordially and offers them a meal. His quarrel is with Agamemnon, not with them.

IV. After they eat, the three emissaries attempt, in turn, to persuade Achilles to accept Agamemnon's gifts and return to battle. He answers each of them in turn.

A. Odysseus speaks first and repeats Agamemnon's offer, in the exact words that Agamemnon uses earlier in Book IX. This is an excellent example of how the formulaic style can allow for subtle characterizations.

1. Achilles replies to Odysseus in an astonishing speech that seems to undercut the entire basis of his society and the warrior culture.
2. Odysseus appeals to *timê* by listing Agamemnon's gifts. But Achilles responds, in effect, that if *timê* can be taken away irrationally, at a leader's whim, then it has no value.
3. Achilles further remarks that his mother Thetis has informed him he has two possible, alternative fates: to win *kleos* by dying at Troy, or to return home and live a long, but peaceful and inglorious, life. He says that he intends to sail home, and counsels others to do so as well.

B. Phoinix speaks second, and uses two arguments.
   1. First, he appeals to Achilles' sense of affection and obligation.
   2. Second, Phoinix tells a story of a famous hero from an earlier generation, Meleagros, who quarreled with his mother, refused gifts that were offered him to end the quarrel, and only set aside his wrath too late, after he could no longer gain any advantage from yielding.
   3. Phoinix' appeal to the authority of antiquity functions within the epic precisely as the epic functions within its own society: as a paradigm for appropriate behavior.
   4. Achilles rejects Phoinix' plea no less firmly than that of Odysseus.

C. Finally, Aias speaks.
   1. He gives a very short speech accusing Achilles of being pitiless toward his fellow soldiers.
   2. Achilles relents to the extent of saying that he will not sail for home. However, he will not fight until the Trojans' fires reach the Greeks' ships.

V. The emissaries have to be content with this answer, which they report back to Agamemnon. As Book IX closes, the Greeks' situation remains desperate.

VI. Book IX appears at a crucial point in the *Iliad.*

A. If, as some scholars believe, the epic was originally performed over three days, then this book either closes the first day or opens the second day of performance.

B. It is very appropriate to have this sort of restating of the conflict and reiterating of some of the crucial themes at precisely this point of the narrative.

Essential Reading:

Iliad, Books VII–IX.

Supplementary Reading:

Mark W. Edwards, *Poet of the Iliad*, Chapter 24.

James V. Morrison, *Homeric Misdirection*, Appendix.

Seth L. Schein, *Mortal Hero*, Chapter 4.

Oliver Taplin, *Homeric Soundings*, Chapter 2, Section 2.3 (pp. 66–73).

Questions to Consider:

1. Explain the implications of Achilles' stated intention to choose a long, inglorious life over death in battle. Why can this be described as a rejection of his culture's entire system of mores?
2. Why does Aias' appeal to Achilles succeed, at least partially, where Odysseus and Phoinix fail?

Lecture Five—Transcript
The Embassy to Achilles

Hello, and welcome back to Lecture Five, "The Embassy to Achilles." In our previous lecture, we looked at Homer's treatment of the Trojans—specifically Priam; Hektor; his wife Andromache and his son Astyanax—as well as looking at Paris and Helen. In this lecture, we are going to turn back to the Greeks, and specifically to Achilles and his continued refusal to join in the battle and fight the Trojans. This lecture will concentrate on Book Nine of the *Iliad*, in which Agamemnon sends three men as emissaries to Achilles to beseech him to return to battle. We'll examine the arguments that the three emissaries make to Achilles, his reasons for rejecting those arguments, and the implications of his rejection for our understanding of his character.

In Books Seven and Eight of the *Iliad*, which I am not going to talk about in detail at all, the battle continues and the Greeks continue to get the worst of it. This means that by the time Book Nine opens the Greeks are quite dispirited; in fact, to such an extent that the Greek leaders realize they must do something to change their situation. Agamemnon even suggests simply packing up and going home. Now, Agamemnon had suggested this as a ruse in Book Two of the *Iliad*, to try to test his warriors and see if their morale was still high even after the loss of Achilles. In Book Two, Agamemnon was apparently shocked and astounded to discover that most of his warriors thought it would be a very good idea to simply leave and go home, and Odysseus had to talk them out of it. Now, in Book Nine, Agamemnon apparently seriously suggests that they should leave, give up, sail for home. Diomedes, one of the greatest Greek warriors, answers that Agamemnon can leave if he wants, but that the other Greeks are going to stay behind. They have recovered their desire to fight, at least to the extent that they no longer simply want to turn tail and run.

But clearly the situation is desperate, and growing worse, without Achilles; and finally the oldest and wisest of the Greeks, a character named Nestor, applauds Diomedes' words and counsels Agamemnon to do his best to persuade Achilles to return to battle. Nestor had tried in Book One to reconcile Agamemnon and Achilles; he had tried to find some way of getting these two men not to fight with one another in the first place. Now he reiterates some of the arguments that he made to Agamemnon in Book One, reminds him of how valuable

Achilles is, and manages to persuade Agamemnon that in fact he should send an apology and recompense to Achilles. Agamemnon agrees with the aged, venerable, and wise Nestor; admits that he was in the wrong when he took away Achilles' concubine Briseis; admits that the should not have done such an act of dishonor to the greatest Greek warrior; and in fact says he will give Achilles an absolutely magnificent recompense. He will more than restore Achilles' lost *timê*, if only Achilles will return and fight again.

Agamemnon selects three key men to serve as an embassy to Achilles—to go and plead his case, offer the recompense, see if they can get Achilles to return to battle. Now, the recompense that Agamemnon offers Achilles is magnificent in the extreme. He says, if Achilles will return to the fighting right now, he will be awarded seven tripods—those are ceremonial stands used for putting a cauldron, a pot, something like that on; ten talents' weight of gold—a talent was a very large sum of money, that is a lot of money in gold; twenty cauldrons; twelve racehorses; seven picked women from the island of Lesbos, who are extremely good at handicrafts, at weaving; and Briseis, absolutely guaranteed untouched—Agamemnon says he has never slept with her. That is what Achilles will get now; if and when the Greeks sack Troy, Agamemnon says Achilles will be able to load his ship with as much bronze and gold as he likes. He will have his choice of the twenty best Trojan women that he wishes to pick out from the crowd of Trojan women. When they get back to Greece, he will have his pick of one of Agamemnon's three daughters to marry, and Agamemnon will give him kingship over seven well-founded citadels.

So, this is a very large recompense that Agamemnon is offering Achilles. Interestingly enough, also, look at the three main aspects that Achilles is being offered here: recognition of his prowess in war, with things like race horses, gold, bronze, so forth; an advantageous marriage with one of Agamemnon's daughters; and kingship over several cities. Remember the bribes that the three goddesses offered Paris in the Judgment of Paris? Kingship over several cities; prowess in warfare; a wonderful marriage—the same three things are being offered to Achilles here. Now, again, this is one of those impossible knots to untie in Homeric scholarship. If you think that Homer knows about the Judgment of Paris, you can say this is a veiled reference to it, with an offer of the same three possible outcomes. If you think that Homer does not know about the Judgment of Paris, then these are simply the three most obvious things that a warrior would be after—prowess in battle, kingship over cities, and a really great marriage.

In any case, this is what Agamemnon offers Achilles, and he chooses very carefully three people to go and plead his case with Achilles. The three men Agamemnon chooses are Odysseus, Phoinix, and Aias. As I say, they are very carefully chosen. Odysseus, as I mentioned in the last lecture, is the cleverest Greek and the best persuasive orator among the Greeks. He, of course is the hero of the *Odyssey*, and we'll talk about his cleverness and his skill in rhetoric much more in that section of the course. But he is, even in the *Iliad*, depicted as being out and away the best speaker, the most gifted orator, the quickest-witted of the Greeks; not the wisest—that would be Nestor—but the quickest-witted, cleverest, most facile with words of the Greeks is Odysseus. Thus, Odysseus can put Agamemnon's case as well as it possibly can be put; if anyone can persuade Achilles to give over his anger and rejoin the fighting it would be Odysseus.

The second man that Agamemnon chooses to send to plead, with Odysseus, is Phoinix. Phoinix is an old man; he is, in fact, Achilles' foster-father. He lived in the household of Achilles' father Peleus when Achilles was growing up. In his speech to Achilles we'll get to in a little bit; he talks a great deal about the care he took of Achilles when Achilles was a baby. Phoinix is thus, in effect, a stand-in for Achilles' own father, Peleus, who of course is not present. And Phoinix is therefore able to appeal to Achilles in two ways. He can appeal to Achilles' filial emotion, to his sense of duty and obligation to his father, as well his sense of affection to his father. Phoinix can also appeal as an older man speaking to a younger man; he is in every respect a father-figure, and a very good choice for Agamemnon to send to talk to Achilles.

Aias, the third member of this embassy, is the greatest Greek warrior second only to Achilles himself. That is made very clear in the *Iliad*, that with Achilles out of the fighting, Aias is the greatest warrior the Greeks have—he is second only to Achilles. And he, therefore, can appeal to Achilles' sense of comradeship with other warriors. He can, in effect, appeal to Achilles by saying, "Even I am not able to hold the Trojans off without you; we need you because you are the best that we have, and I, as the second best, am in a position to say that in a way that no one else could." So Agamemnon sends an embassy that will appeal to Achilles through the best possible rhetoric; through the strongest emotional appeal that the Homeric culture knows of, the appeal of father or his representative to son; and through the affection of comradeship and shared bond that warriors feel towards one another—a very carefully selected group of emissaries.

So, these three emissaries go to Achilles' camp. When they arrive at his camp Odysseus, Phoinix, and Aias find Achilles sitting by his tent. The Greek camp is on the seashore. Troy, of course, is on a hill or a battlement overlooking a plain; the plain fronts on the sea. The Greeks are encamped along the seacoast; their tents are there, their ships are there, and this is where Achilles has retreated, when he stopped fighting. He has gone back to camp. He is sitting by his tent when the embassy arrives, and he is playing the lyre. Not only is he playing the lyre, but also he is singing, the bard tell us; he is singing *klea andrôn*. *Klea* is the plural of *kleos*, and *andrôn* means "of men." So, Achilles is singing the glories of men, the reputations of men, the fame of men—in other words, Achilles is performing an epic poem at this point. He is no longer taking part in the battle, he is no longer fighting, he is no longer gaining *kleos* for himself; instead, he is now portrayed as memorializing the deeds that he will no longer perform in reality.

And this is exactly what Homer's song, of course, is doing for Achilles, at the same time that Achilles is doing it within the epic. Homer is singing the *kleos* of Achilles, and here he tells us that Achilles is singing the *kleos* of other warriors. So, *kleos* is still crucial in the depiction of Achilles, but is in a sense inverted here; he is no longer gaining it, rather he is memorializing it as something that others have gained in the past. This is one of the *Iliad*'s very few references—really the only sustained reference in the *Iliad*—to bardic performance. There are more references in the *Odyssey* to bards and bardic performances; we see a couple of different bards in the *Odyssey* and observe them singing songs, see how audience members are supposed to interact with bards, and so forth. But in the *Iliad* this is as close as we get to actually seeing a bard in performance, Achilles here in Book Nine.

Achilles greets his three friends cordially and offers them a meal. It is quite clear that he is not angry with them; his quarrel is with Agamemnon. He is willing to refrain from fighting and let his other friends and companions suffer the results of that, but he is no way angry at Odysseus, Phoinix, or Aias. He greets them cordially, he serves them a meal, and then asks them, in effect, why have they come and what they want from him. So, after they eat, the three emissaries attempt, each one in turn, to persuade Achilles to accept Agamemnon's gifts and return to battle, and Achilles answers each of them in turn. Odysseus speaks first, and Odysseus repeats word-for-word Agamemnon's offer of the seven tripods, ten talents, etc, etc, going on through the idea that "once we sack Troy you can take all the gold you want, you can pick the slaves, and you can marry one of Agamemnon's daughters."

This is an excellent example—Odysseus' repeated speech is an excellent example—of how the formulaic style can allow for subtle characterizations. At first glance, all that is happening here is that the poet has worked out a set of lines describing Agamemnon's offer to Achilles. First Agamemnon says the lines; now Odysseus says the lines. And yet Odysseus doesn't just repeat exactly the same lines Agamemnon has said; at the end of them, after he has in effect reported Agamemnon's offer to Achilles, Odysseus goes on and speaks, in his own voice, words that he does not, then, later at the end of the book, report back dutifully to Agamemnon. He says to Achilles, "If you hate him and you hate his gifts, and you won't stop being angry at Agamemnon, at least feel pity for us and return to fighting; and think of the great *kleos* you could win for yourself by killing Hektor." So, Odysseus goes beyond his brief from Agamemnon; he repeats Agamemnon's offer but he adds to it, he elaborates on it, and he recognizes what Agamemnon apparently doesn't recognize at this point—that it is quite possible that Achilles will still be angry, that this recompense will not ease Achilles' wrath.

And in fact, it does not ease Achilles' wrath. Achilles replies to Odysseus, in an absolutely astonishing speech that really seems to undercut the entire basis of his society. Odysseus has, after all, appealed to *timê*, with this offer of recompense from Agamemnon; he said, "You lost the *timê* of Briseis, but look at how much more you will be given back—not just will Briseis be restored to you untouched, unharmed, in no way worse than she was when you lost her, but you will get all these other things as well; there will be absolutely no question in anyone's mind that you are the greatest, most honored warrior of all of us." How does Achilles respond to that? Well, he responds, in effect, by saying that he simply does not care any more about any of this; he responds in terms that seem to say, in effect, that *timê* is no longer a concern to him. This is part of Achilles' speech in answer to Odysseus; it is a very long speech, it goes on for several pages, but near the beginning of it, Achilles says:

> Fate is the same for the man who holds back, the same if he fights hard.
> We are all held in a single honour [that, of course, is *timê* in the Greek], the brave with the weaklings.
> A man dies still if he has done nothing, as one who has done much.
> Nothing is one won for me, now that my heart has gone through its afflictions
> in forever setting my life on the hazard of battle.

In other words, Achilles in effect says that he no longer is concerned with *timê*; he no longer cares about *timê*; it no longer has anything to say to him. In effect, he says that if *timê* can be taken away irrationally at a leader's whim, then it has no value; why fight for something so unstable, why fight for something that Agamemnon can remove from him, at a whim, at a moment's notice? The fact that Agamemnon is now giving it back is, at this juncture, pointless for Achilles; the point is that it could be taken away arbitrarily. So the fact that it can be given back arbitrarily doesn't really help any more; he is no longer interested in *timê*.

He further remarks that his mother, Thetis, has told him he has two possible alternative fates, and he describes to his friends who have come to talk to him—after saying, by the way, that he would not marry one of Agamemnon's daughters, if she was as beautiful as Aphrodite and as skilled in weaving as Athena; he basically says "I would not marry his daughter if she were the last girl on earth, but as it is, there are plenty of other girls for me to marry; so forget it, I am not going to marry one of his"—he continues, though, talking about the two fates that his mother, Thetis, has told him he has.This is an extraordinary passage, unparalleled, really, in the rest of the *Iliad* or in other literature, for that matter. Achilles, again—still Achilles speaking—says:

> My mother Thetis, the goddess of the silver feet tells me
> I carry two sorts of destiny towards the day of my death. Either,
> if I stay here and fight beside the city of the Trojans,

> my return home is gone, but my glory shall be everlasting;
> but if I return home to the beloved land of my fathers,
> the excellence of my glory is gone, but there will be a long life
> left for me, and my end in death will not come to me quickly.

So Thetis has given Achilles two alternative fates, or has described two alternative fates to Achilles—early death in battle and everlasting glory, everlasting *kleos*, or a long and obscure life and no fame, no *kleos*, no glory.

Now, there are a couple of truly extraordinary things about this passage. First of all, it is extraordinary for a mortal to be told his fate at all. As I talked about before, the idea is that we all have a fate, we all have an appointed time of death, a day when we are going to die; but most of us do not know it, most of us cannot know it. There are a few stories in Greek mythology, in Greek literature, of people who do find out what their fate is; the most obvious one is Oedipus, in Sophocles' *Oedipus the King*, who finds out his dreadful fate, that he is fated to kill his father and marry his mother, and then of course the whole unfolding of the story is what happens as Oedipus tries to avoid that terrible fate. But most of us are never told what our fate will be. It is something that can be seen in retrospect. After someone is killed in battle, you can assume that they were fated to be killed in battle on that day; but you don't know it ahead of time. So it is very unusual for human being to be told what his fate is to begin with.

Secondly, it is all but unparalleled for a human to have two separate, alternative fates, as Achilles does here. For Achilles to be able to say, "My mother has told me I carry two kinds of destiny with me," is so unusual as to be almost unique, if not absolutely unique. That Achilles is able to say "I can choose one or I can choose the other," that is not how fate normally works. He says—after telling his friends this remarkable thing, Achilles says—that he intends to choose the long, peaceful, inglorious life; he intends to sail home, renounce being a warrior, give up all hope of *kleos*, and he counsels his friends to do so as well.

Now, this leaves Phoinix and Aias in a very difficult situation. Odysseus has tried the standard appeal to *timê* and to *kleos*, and Achilles has basically said, "But I don't care about *timê* and *kleos* any more. *Timê* is worthless to me because it can be taken away and as for *kleos*, well, I don't care about that; I would just as soon live a long life and die at home in bed, and never mind *kleos*." In effect, in short, Achilles has said, "I reject the entire basis of our society; I reject the entire warrior ethos in which we have been brought up; I reject everything that the rest of you think is important—so now, persuade me." This is a very hard task for Phoinix to be faced with and yet Phoinix tries; Phoinix makes a very good try, in fact. He speaks—after this long speech by Achilles in response to Odysseus, Phoinix speaks next, and he uses two main arguments. First, he appeals to Achilles' sense of affection and obligation; and second, he cites the precedents of antiquity, the precedents of ancient heroes—both of which ought to be extremely powerful arguments.

As I already said, Phoinix is Achilles' foster-father. He reminds Achilles of how he came to be his foster-father; this is a very nice, subtle touch. Phoinix reminds Achilles that the reason, he, Phoinix was living in Peleus' house in the first place was because he had quarreled with his own father over a concubine. His father had a concubine; Phoinix's mother, out of jealousy, tried to persuade her son to seduce this concubine, who would prefer him to the older father and not sleep with the father any more. Phoinix's father became extremely angry of this, the two had a falling out, and Phoinix had to leave his household. A quarrel with an older man in authority over a concubine, devastating effects because of that quarrel—the parallel is fairly clear there. But Phoinix mentions this to remind Achilles of why it is that he; Phoinix, lived in Peleus' household in the first place. Then he reminds Achilles of the great care he took of him, of Achilles, as a baby. He talks about holding him on his knees, cutting up little bits of meat to feed to him, he even mentions how Achilles often soaked his shirt by spitting up wine on him, and all the trouble and care he took with Achilles as a baby. He is very much pushing the substitute father, the "you owe me affection, respect, and devotion because of the care I took of you as a child," and he also tugs at the heartstrings just a little bit more by reminding Achilles that he himself is childless, that Achilles is the closest thing to a son Phoinix will ever have. He also points out that Peleus, Achilles' father, entrusted Achilles to Phoinix for the journey to Troy, that Phoinix is some sense standing in for Peleus right now—but Peleus had said, "Take care of my son at Troy; see to it that he acts as he should act."

So Phoinix hits the substitute father theme from every angle he possibly can. Then he turns to the second prong of his plea to Achilles, which is to appeal to the story of a famous hero from an earlier generation. Phoinix says directly, "In earlier times, heroes would allow themselves to be persuaded and put aside their anger when it was best for them to do so; here is a story to prove to you that this is how things worked in earlier days"—and he cites the story of a hero named Meleagros. Meleagros had quarreled with his mother, and after the quarrel had refused gifts that were offered him to end the hard feelings and to put matters back as they should be. He only set aside his wrath too late, after he could no longer gain any advantage from yielding, after the gifts were no later on offer. And so Phoinix here, quite explicitly, says to Achilles "Learn from Meleagros' story. You are going to have to set aside your anger eventually; do it now, when Agamemnon is offering you all this wonderful loot, because if you wait till later, you may not get the gifts—it may be too late to get these gifts." Achilles answers very much as he had answered Odysseus; he says—in so many words, he says, "Phoinix, I no longer need that kind of honor"; he says, "I do not need this *timê.* He doesn't want the gifts that Agamemnon can offer him any longer.

But one more point about Phoinix's appeal to the authority of antiquity—it's interesting to contemplate how that functions, within the epic, precisely the way the epic itself functions in its own society, as I talked about in the first lecture. Phoinix needs to persuade Achilles to do something. What does he call upon to persuade him, outside of individual emotion? He says, "Look at how heroes behaved in the old days; let me tell you a story; let me cite Meleagros to you; let me tell you how heroes are supposed to behave; this is what happened to Meleagros." This is precisely what Homeric epic does for its own civilization; this is precisely what the *Iliad* did for people who studied the *Iliad* in ancient Greek civilization. How should we behave in a certain situation? Let's look to Homer and see how Achilles behaved, see how Agamemnon behaved, see how Odysseus behaved. So, just as we had Achilles performing epic inside the epic, here we have Phoinix citing epic, or citing the authority of antiquity, inside the epic—which itself is the authority of antiquity. A nice kind of double vision of how epic works.

But Achilles doesn't go for it. He rejects Phoinix's plea no less firmly than he rejected Odysseus' plea. Finally, Aias speaks. Aias, as befits a man of action not words, a bluff, brawny soldier, gives a very short speech, which he begins by saying to Odysseus and Phoinix, "We might as well go home; we are wasting our time here"; and then he accuses Achilles of being pitiless, hard-hearted, forgetting all the honor his friends have always done him, forgetting the comradeship that is so important among soldiers. For some reason, Aias' speech gets through to Achilles—to a certain extent—in a way that neither Odysseus nor Phoinix was able to. Achilles relents to the extent of saying that he will not sail for home. Up until now, he has been saying he was going to pack up and sail for home. Now he says, "All right, I will stay here; I won't fight, but I will stay here in camp until the Trojans reach the Greeks' ships and set them on fire." At that point, Achilles says, he will return to battle. In other words, he says that he will fight a defensive battle, he'll fight to defend his ships, his camp, himself—but he won't fight an offensive battle any more, he won't attack the Trojans. This is where the emissaries have to leave it, this what they have to be content with. They report this answer back to Agamemnon, and of course it is not what Agamemnon wanted to hear; and as Book Nine ends, the Greeks' situation remains desperate.

Now, Book Nine appears at a crucial pont in the *Iliad*. I mentioned very briefly in the second lecture, when I was talking about the composition of Homeric verse, that some scholars think these epics developed out of performances at religious festivals, performances that lasted for perhaps three or four days. If the *Iliad* developed out of a performance at a festival that extended over three days, Book Nine is right about at the time when the first day's performance would probably be coming to an end—perhaps right at the time when the second day's performance would be beginning; probably right at the end of the first day's performance. There are, of course, 24 books in the *Iliad*, so one-third of them, if you count them by books, is eight, and yet the books are of uneven length. In terms of performance time, the *Iliad* takes probably about 23 to 24 hours to recite in Greek, straight through. We don't know exactly; we don't know how fast these poems were recited, we don't know how much musical accompaniment there was—there was some musical accompaniment to them; we don't know how much. But at any rate, it is pretty clear that Book Nine is about one-third of the way through the *Iliad*, and therefore it is fair to guess, to estimate, that if the *Iliad* was performed over three days, this is about the first day's performance would end.

And it is actually a very appropriate point to have this sort of restating of the major themes of the narrative, if this book closes either the first day or the second day of performance. We have a reiteration of the conflict between Achilles and Agamemnon; we have a reminder of exactly what it was that they fell out over, the concubine, Briseis; we have Agamemnon now, instead of taking the concubine away, trying to give her back, Achilles refusing to accept her. We have Achilles directly addressing those issues of *kleos* and *timê* that I said were so important in the first book, and directly rejecting them; and we have a very powerful reiteration of exactly how desperate the situation of the Greeks is, without Achilles' presence. So this is a powerful way to hit, once again, at the primary themes of the *Iliad*, just at the point in performance when those themes need to be reiterated again. As I have said about several other things already, this can neither prove or disprove the theory that the *Iliad* was performed over a stretch of three days, but it is at least interesting to notice that, if you break it up into three more or less even segments, you have these narrative high points—we'll see this again in Book Eighteen—about where you would expect them to be if the *Iliad* was performed over three days.

So, in this lecture we have looked at the attempt of Agamemnon to make recompense to Achilles and to bring Achilles back to the fighting, and how that attempt failed; and how, in rejecting Agamemnon's recompense, Achilles in effect rejects the entire system of his society, his entire cultural framework. In the next lecture, we'll look a little more closely at *kleos* itself, and how it is one of the primary motivating forces of the *Iliad*.

Lecture Six

The Paradox of Glory

Scope:

In this lecture, we look in detail at the concept of *kleos* and its crucial thematic importance for the *Iliad*. *Kleos* is the only kind of immortality available to a Homeric warrior, and is of the utmost importance; every major warrior strives for it, often in a type scene of battle-prowess called an *aristeia*. But *kleos* can be gained only by dying or by killing. Thus, a kind of paradox lies at the heart of the *Iliad*'s depiction of the warrior's quest for *kleos*. Through an examination of the essential duality of Achilles' character, we see how he is the best representative of this paradox of *kleos*. Finally, wc consider how the gods' immortality makes them unable to gain *kleos* in this sense.

Outline

I. One of the central themes of the *Iliad* is "the human condition," and what mortality means.

- **A.** The *Iliad* is often called a "poem of death," and not just because so many people die in it.
- **B.** As we will see later, the resolution of the whole epic turns on Achilles' final acceptance of the human condition, including death.

II. Central to the *Iliad*'*s* conception of the human condition is the paradox of *kleos* (which is related linguistically to the English verb "to call").

- **A.** In his description of his two possible fates, Achilles links *kleos* with the adjective *aphthiton*, meaning "imperishable. "
  1. *Kleos aphthiton*, imperishable glory, is what the Homeric warrior ultimately fights for and what is bestowed by epic poetry itself.
  2. There is a nearly exact parallel phrase in Sanskrit, one of three ancient Indo-European languages with a substantial extant body of literature.
- **B.** Imperishable glory is the only kind of meaningful immortality available to a Homeric warrior, but it can only be gained through losing life or causing someone else to lose it.

1. At death the *psyche* leaves the body and goes to the Underworld.
2. The existence of the *psyche* in the Underworld is vague and unsubstantial. This is not a view of the afterlife calculated to provide consolation for bodily death.
3. Thus, only *kleos* provides any kind of significant immortality.

C. The *Iliad* foregrounds several warriors in turn, in their pursuit of *kleos aphthiton*, by giving each one his own *aristeia,* or extended type scene of special valor, with several recognizable parts. Not all of these elements are always present, but this is the basic form of an *aristeia*:

1. First, the warrior arms himself in gleaming armor.
2. He bursts into the ranks of the enemy, wreaks great slaughter among them, and turns the tide of battle.
3. He is wounded himself, which causes a setback for his side until he prays to a god and is healed and strengthened.
4. He returns to battle and kills an important enemy.
5. A fierce battle ensues over this enemy's body, which is finally taken from the warrior, often through divine intervention.

D. Achilles' *aristeia* is the culmination of the poem; others, of varying length, belong to Diomedes, Agamemnon, Hektor, and Patroklos.

III. The paradoxical nature of *kleos* (immortal fame gained only through acts of death) is confronted over and over again in the epic. One of its clearest articulations comes in Sarpedon's words to Glaukos in Book XII. (Note: see Biographical Notes for information on these and other characters in the *Iliad.*)

IV. Achilles himself is the best representative of the contradictions inherent in *kleos*.

A. His relationship with his mother marks him out as different from other heroes, since Thetis is the only divine parent in the *Iliad* who has long, intimate conversations with her human child.

B. This special relationship with Thetis gives Achilles a kind of view from the outside on mortality, almost a "gods'-eye view," especially regarding his two possible fates.

1. Superficially, Achilles' choice of fates is the same faced by all warriors.
2. But where other warriors *suspect* they *might* die at Troy if they stay, Achilles *knows* that he *will* die there.

C. Achilles' rejection of the mores of his society in Book IX is thus more far reaching than might appear at first. In effect, by rejecting *kleos* he is questioning his world's whole paradigm of what it means to be human.

V. *Kleos* as it appears in the *Iliad* is a human phenomenon; since gods cannot die, they cannot achieve *kleos* in the same sense that a human can.

A. Human mortality is the crucial distinction between human beings and these very anthropomorphic gods.
1. The gods are the *athanatoi*, or deathless ones. They cannot die.
2. Humans are the *thnêtoi*, or dying ones. They must die.
3. Throughout the *Iliad*, Homer stresses the actuality of warrior's deaths. Wounds in the *Iliad* are either fairly minor or result in almost immediate death. This adds to the focus on death as the inevitable outcome of battle.

B. Homer uses the distinction between mortals and immortals to highlight the human condition through contrasting it with the gods' state of "easy living."

Essential Reading:

Iliad, Books X–XII.

Supplementary Reading:

Mark W. Edwards, *Poet of the Iliad*, Chapters 8 and 19.

Jasper Griffin, *Homer on Life and Death*, Chapters III–IV.

Seth L. Schein, *Mortal Hero*, Chapter 3, Section 4.

Jonathan Shay, *Achilles in Vietnam*, Chapter 7. This chapter ("What Homer Left Out") includes graphic descriptions of wounds and lingering deaths, and of civilian suffering, that some students may prefer to skip.

Questions to Consider:

1. Is the choice of fates offered to Achilles a genuine choice? Could he really decide simply to quit fighting and return home to his father Peleus?
2. Do you agree that mortality, i.e., impermanence, is the essential defining hallmark of human life, or do you think that our culture's view of this is essentially different from the view portrayed in the *Iliad*?

Lecture Six—Transcript

The Paradox of Glory

Hello, and welcome back to Lecture Six, "The Paradox of *Kleos*." In our last lecture, we talked about the embassy to Achilles, in which Phoinix, Odysseus, and Aias tried to persuade Achilles to return to battle and to accept Agamemnon's offered recompense for the loss of Briseis. We talked about how Achilles' refusal in effect represented a rejection of the mores of his society, as represented by *timê* and *kleos*. In this lecture I want to look in some detail at the concept of *kleos*, and how and why it is a crucial thematic concept for our understanding of the *Iliad*. We'll discuss how *kleos* is, in effect, the only kind of immortality available to a Homeric warrior, and yet this immortality can only be gained through dying or killing. This is at the heart of what I call the paradox of *kleos*. The lecture will also examine the essential duality of Achilles' character, and how he functions as a best representative of this paradoxical concept of *kleos*. Finally, we'll consider how the gods' immortality separates them from *kleos* in the human sense, and what implication that has for our understanding of the role of the gods in the epic.

So, one of the central themes of the *Iliad* is the human condition, what it means to be human, what the implications are of our humanity and, specifically, of our human mortality; or putting it another way, one of the main themes of the *Iliad* is death and the implications of the reality of death for human nature and human existence. The *Iliad* has been called a poem of death, and that isn't just because so many people die in it; it is because death and our ability or lack of ability to come to terms with it are one of the major themes of the *Iliad*. As we'll see later on, the entire resolution of the *Iliad* centers around Achilles' initial refusal to accept the death of his beloved friend Patroklos, and, later, his coming to terms with, his acceptance, his recognition of the human condition and the implication that everyone, even the most beloved individuals, must in fact die, and that their deaths must be accepted. So, the rejection or acceptance of death is one of the primary themes of the *Iliad*, and lies at the heart of the *Iliad*'s depiction of the human condition. Central to the *Iliad*'s conception of what it means to be human, of this presentation of mortality and the implications of mortality, is the paradox of *kleos*.

As you remember from the lecture on the opening book of the *Iliad*, *kleos*, often translated glory or fame, literally means what people say about you, what is spoken about you. It is, in fact, related to the English word "call"—you can hear the "k" and "l" sounds in both words. *Kleos*—the Greek verb *kaleomai* means to speak aloud, to say aloud, even sometimes to name, and our English word "call" is related, linguistically speaking, to the Greek words *kleos* and *kaleomai*—*kleos* is what is said aloud about you, and it is especially what is said aloud about you after your death. And again, of course, in a preliterate society what is said aloud about you is the only kind of memorialization available. There can no written records, not even any tombstones; the only way to remember someone after death is to speak about that person.

In his description of his two possible fates in Book Nine, which I read aloud in the last lecture, Achilles links *kleos* with the adjective alphthiton, meaning imperishable. He says if he chooses to stay at Troy and die fighting there, his *kleos* will be *aphthiton*, his *kleos* will be imperishable, undestroyable, undying. This concept—*kleos aphthiton*, imperishable glory, undying fame—this is what the Homeric warrior ultimately fights for and, no less importantly, what is bestowed by epic poetry itself. It is a fascinating little linguistic fact that the Greek phrase, *kleos aphthiton*, is paralleled exactly by two Sanskrit words—Sanskrit, of course, being the ancient language of India, one of the three oldest surviving Indo-European languages with major literature still intact; Latin, Greek, and Sanskrit are the major ancient Indo-European languages in which we have substantive literatures. In Sanskrit there is a phrase, *sravas aksitam*, which exactly parallels *kleos aphthiton*. In fact, those who know about Indo-European linguistics tell us that *kleos* and *sravas* are the Greek and Sanskrit derivatives of the same original Indo-European word; so the adjectives *aphthiton* in Greek, *aksitam* in Sanskrit, are the Greek and Sanskrit derivatives of the same original Indo-European word.

That means, back in the mists of dim antiquity, long before writing had ever been thought of, before the original speakers of proto Indo-European had fanned out all over Europe and India taking their languages with them, already they had a phrase for imperishable glory: something that shows up in Greek as *kleos aphthiton*, in Sanskrit as *sravas aksitam*, in proto-Indo-European as—who knows what, but words that meant imperishable glory; and it is possible—

although some scholars disagree about this—it is even possible that there was an ancient Indo-European poetics, and ancient Indo-European praise poetry, in which this imperishable glory was conferred on the memory of heroes by poetry after the heroes' death. That would explain why it is cited as important in the *Iliad*, and why it shows up as important in the Sanskrit poetry as well, in exactly the same words—imperishable fame, imperishable glory, what is conferred by poetry on the memory of the dead.

Imperishable glory in the Homeric epics, *kleos aphthiton*, is the only kind of meaningful or significant immortality available to a Homeric hero. Now, Homer does recognize a kind of afterlife; when the Homeric warrior dies he is not simply wiped out entirely, he doesn't disappear entirely. There is an underworld, there is an afterlife, there is a substance, an entity, that departs the body and goes to the underworld and continues to survive there in a kind of afterlife. This entity is called the *psyche*—that is spelled exactly like the English word psyche, but I give it the Greek pronunciation simply to stress that I am not talking about what psychologists study. I am not talking about the psyche in our sense; I am talking about the Greek *psyche*. The *psyche* was originally the breath; it is almost an onomatopoeic-type word, a sighing kind of sound that originally referred to what it is that visibly, tangibly, leaves the body when a person dies, the breath of life that exits the body at the moment of death. It comes to mean more than just that; it is sort of the soul, sort of the spirit, sort of the essence of the person. It does survive after death; it does pass into the underworld; it is capable of sometimes being recognized there, under certain circumstances, but the existence of the *psyche* in the underworld is, at least as Homer portrays it in the *Odyssey* in particular, vague, unsubstantial, unpleasant, fairly meaningless.

In Book Eleven of the *Odyssey* we are told that the souls of the dead in the underworld, their *psyches*, flit about like bats gibbering meaninglessly; they don't recognize one another, they don't know who they are, until they are given a drink of sacrificial blood from an animal at which point they get their wits back for a while. This is not the kind of afterlife calculated to provide comfort before bodily death or hope for glorious reunions in the afterlife. It is an extremely pallid substitute for life in this world. Thus, only *kleos*, only what people say about you after you have died, can provide any kind of significant immorality, any kind of living on that has any meaning or offers any sense of comfort or validity to a Homeric hero. So this is even beyond *timê*—as I have talked about before, *timê* is significant largely for the amount of *kleos* it confers—even beyond *timê*, *kleos aphthiton* is what Homeric warriors ultimately fight for. And we see—throughout the *Iliad*, we see several warriors, in turn, in their pursuit of *kleos aphthiton*, of imperishable glory, foregrounded each one in a scene of special valor that Homeric scholars usually refer to as an *aristeia*. Various different Homeric heroes have an *aristeia*. That is a scene—it can be as short as a few lines; it can in the case of Achilles' *aristeia*, extend for several books of the *Iliad*—which foregrounds, focuses on, does (in cinematographic terms) a close-up of a particular hero fighting his best in his best moment of valor; focuses on him, and shows us his *kleos*, his glory, in extended detail.

An *aristeia* includes several standard recognizable parts. It will begin with a warrior arming himself in gleaming armor; and the armor will be stressed, will be described. We're told that it is gleaming, that it is bright, that it is flashing, that it is particularly beautiful armor. The warrior arms himself in gleaming armor; he then bursts into the ranks of the enemy, wreaks great slaughter among them, and turns the tide of battle. This can happen on both sides. We see Hektor having an *aristeia*, we see Greek warriors having *aristeias*. Eventually, in the midst of his *aristeia*, the warrior is wounded himself, which causes a set-back for his side until he prays to some god or other and is healed and strengthened and sent back into battle. At this point, he returns to battle and kills an important enemy. A fierce battle ensues over the body of this important enemy, which is finally taken from the warrior—often through divine intervention, sometimes not; sometimes just through the fighting of his enemies—and at that point an individual hero's *aristeia* ends.

Now, not all of those elements are present in each and every *aristeia*, but that is the overall picture of this specific kind of scene of especial valor. This memorialization in epic poetry, this idea of a bard focusing in on your particular battle valor and saying, "This is how Agamemnon, or this is how Menelaos, or this is how Achilles, or this is how Patroklos fought on the day he fought best in his life"—that is the essence of *kleos aphthiton*, and that is what these heroes are after. Achilles' *aristeia* is a culmination of the whole *Iliad*, but various other heroes are granted them as well—Diomedes, Agamemnon, Hektor, Patroklos, and others.

And yet, if this is how a hero gets *kleos aphthiton*, by fighting as magnificently as he can and slaughtering as many enemies as he possibly can, then you can see what I mean when I say that there is a paradox in the heart of this kind of immortality. *Kleos* is the only immortality available to Homeric warrior, but how does he get it? He gets it through killing, or through dying, or often through both. So, the only kind of life after death, the only kind of survival of death, available to a Homeric hero can itself only be gained through acts of death; and this paradox—this contradiction, you might say, or this tragedy, if you like—that is enshrined in *kleos* itself is concentrated on, foregrounded, focused on, confronted over and over again in the *Iliad*, in various different ways.

One of its clearest articulations comes in Book Twelve, when the Trojan ally Sarpedon, who is himself the son of the god Zeus and a very fine warrior, is speaking to his friend, Glaukos. Now, Glaukos is the same Glaukos that we already met in Book Six, the same Glaukos who exchanged armor with the Greek Diomedes, whose wits were taken away from him by Zeus because he exchanged armor worth a hundred oxen for armor worth only nine. This same Glaukos is a close friend of the Trojan ally, Sarpedon, and in Book Twelve, Sarpedon speaks lines to him that sum up the essence of *kleos* and what it is that these warriors are fighting for. Sarpedon says to Glaukos:

> Man, supposing you and I, escaping this battle,
> would be able to live on forever, ageless, immortal,
> so neither would I myself go on fighting in the foremost
> nor would I urge you into the fighting where men win glory
> [and of course "glory" there translates *kleos*].
> But now, seeing that the spirits of death stand close about us
> in their thousands, no man can turn aside nor escape them,
> let us go on and win glory for ourselves, or yield it to others.

As clean an articulation as you could ask for of how *kleos* functions in this society. "If we were immortal, if we did not have to die, then I would not fight, there would be no point in fighting; but since we must die, and it is inescapable that all people must die, let us rush into battle and win glory for ourselves or give it to others." Though is goes against the grain for some modern American students—they would imagine that Sarpedon would say something like, "Since we can't escape death, let's go home, and live there carefully, and try to get away from dying for as long as we possibly can, and live to be as old as we possibly can"—in effect, what Achilles says in Book Nine that he is going to do, rather than Sarpedon's statement, "since we must die anyway, let us die by winning glory." But Sarpedon's statement is very much the attitude that most warriors in the *Iliad* take, aside from Achilles in his very strange renunciation, strange from the point of view of his own culture that we talked about in Book Nine.

So, *kleos* has this contradiction built into it. It's the only kind of immortality available, and yet it can only be gained through imposing death, either on others or upon oneself. Achilles is, in some ways, the clearest embodiment of these contradictions in the *Iliad*. In some ways he contains these contradictions of *kleos* in himself, in his own life. He is in many ways a very, very unusual human being, and some of those ways, some of his unusual aspects, directly affect his portrayal of *kleos* to his friends, and our understanding of *kleos* as it relates to him. First of all, Achilles has a relationship with his goddess mother that marks him out as different from other heroes in the *Iliad*. Most obviously, he is different from other warriors in the *Iliad* whose parents are both humans; it is very unusual to have a god or goddess as a parent at all, and yet Achilles is far from the only character in the *Iliad* who has one divine parent. Sarpedon, as I just mentioned, is the son of Zeus. There are other sons of divine parents fighting on both sides in the Trojan War. Aeneas, the Trojan hero—who is a relatively minor character in the *Iliad* but of course becomes the hero of Virgil's *Aeneid* in Latin literature—Aeneas is the son of the goddess Aphrodite, a goddess mother; so in that respect he is like Achilles. But Achilles is the only offspring of a god or goddess in the *Iliad* whose divine parent has long, intimate, detailed, involved conversations with him. We do see divine parents occasionally intervening for other children; Aphrodite comes to rescue Aeneas when he is about to be killed at one point in the *Iliad*. She picks him up off the battlefield, as she did with Paris in Book Three, but Diomedes, the Greek warrior, scratches her hand with his sword and Aphrodite immediately drops Aeneas and flies away. So, while she begins to react she is hardly the kind of dedicated, devoted mother that Thetis is to Achilles; and no other divine parent in the *Iliad* carries on long involved conversations with their human offspring as Thetis does with Achilles.

It is also noteworthy the kinds of conversations, the subjects of the conversations that Thetis and Achilles have. When Thetis comes to talk to Achilles, over and over again she starts out by lamenting the brevity of his life, by lamenting her own misfortune in being the mother of so short-lived a son. So, clearly, the content of their conversations often revolves around mortality, death, the fact that Achilles is going to die, his status as a human being; and this special relationship with Thetis gives Achilles, in effect, a view on mortality from the outside, what you could almost call a god's eye view of mortality, especially regarding his two possible fates. It is not just unusual that he has two possible fates and that Thetis tells him about; it is unusual that he is in a position to have someone who *could* tell him about it. Most humans do not have that kind of relationship with any god or goddess, that even if they had this oddity of two particular fates they would ever find out about it.

Now, on one level, superficially, the choice between fates that Achilles faces is a choice faced by all warriors. Any warrior, in any culture, in any war, knows that if he stays and fights he is quite likely to die. If he manages to turn tail and go home—leaving aside for the moment the possibility of that for most soldiers in most wars—if he manages to turn tail and go home, he will quite likely live a long and uneventful life. But those "quite likelies" and "probablies" make all the difference in the world. The other warriors in the *Iliad* know that if they stay and fight they *might* die, and if they go home they *might* live a long and uneventful life. Achilles knows that if he stays and fights he *will* die; if he goes home he *will* live a long and uneventful life. Compare him with Hektor, as I talked about Hektor in Book Six of the *Iliad*, when Hektor says, almost in the same breath, to Andromache, "I know that Troy is going to fall, and we're all going to die, and you are going to be taken off into slavery," and then, in almost the same breath, "May our son live to be a greater warrior I am and delight his mother when he comes home from the battle," and so forth. Hektor is in the common position of most human beings, being able to imagine these two alternative fates but not knowing which one is his.

Achilles knows his choice—he knows that if he stays, he dies; if he goes home he lives. So he is given this kind of outside view, this kind of view of mortality from the outside, almost as mortality must look to the gods who know what human fates are before the humans do. Achilles is able to see mortality from the outside, in a way, because of his relationship with his mother, the goddess, Thetis. And when he rejects the mores of his society in Book Nine, when he says that he no longer is interested in *timê*, he no longer needs *kleos*, what he is doing is much more far-reaching than might appear at first. He is not simply rejecting the whole warrior ethos of his society; he is not simply rejecting the whole basis on which he and other warriors have built their entire lives; in effect, he is questioning his world's whole paradigm of what it means to be human—because humans by definition, in the *Iliad*, are the ones who die.

We will talk in our next lecture about what the gods are doing in the *Iliad*, how the gods operate in the *Iliad*, why they are so important in the *Iliad*. But one aspect of the importance of the gods is that they are there to provide a contrast, a foil, to human beings precisely in this question of mortality and immortality. The gods in the *Iliad* are defined as—are often referred to by the term—the *athanatoi*, the deathless ones, the undying ones, the ones who cannot die. Of course that's what our word "immortal" means, but we don't normally think of the resonance of "mortal" and "immortal" in quite the same way any more, in English, as we would if we were Latin speakers and heard the word "death" in them. In Greek *athanatoi* means the deathless ones, the undying ones, and it is a very common term for the gods. Mortals, humans, in contrast, are called the *thnêtoi*, the dying ones, but really it almost means the "dead ones"—as though our lives are so short, and so unimportant against the backdrop of eternity, that we are dead as soon as we come into existence. The gods are "the deathless ones"; the humans are the—almost "the already dead ones."

And this means that for the gods in the *Iliad*, or for the *Iliad* in general, *kleos* is a human phenomenon. Since gods cannot die, gods cannot achieve *kleos* in the same sense that humans can. They do not need *kleos* in the same sense that humans need it; they are already immortal, and they don't need to be remembered in undying song. They don't need to have imperishable fame proclaimed about them openly because they are still there, they are still alive; they have no need of *kleos*. This contrast between the *athanatoi* gods and the *thnêtoi* humans makes for the crucial defining distinction between gods and humans, the crucial defining aspect of what it means to be human in the *Iliad*. The gods of Homer, the gods in both the *Iliad* and the *Odyssey*, are extremely anthropomorphic in many ways. They are conceived of as being human-like in shape, in appearance, in emotions, in activities, in just about every imaginable way. This is not the only ways to conceive of gods; there have been cultures whose gods have not been anthropomorphic, have not been human formed, human-like in character, in appearance, in any other way. But the gods of Homer are extraordinarily anthropomorphic. They eat nectar and ambrosia, not wine and grain like humans eat; but still they drink nectar and eat ambrosia. They sleep, they fight, they have sex, they grow angry, they feel love, they feel hatred—they are in many ways very much like human begins projected on a larger scale. And yet, they are human-like creatures that cannot grow old and cannot die, whereas humans by definition must grow old, and must die. And this is distinction is harped on over and over and over again in the *Iliad*, far more than it is, for instance, in the *Odyssey*.

As I said, the *Iliad* has been called a poem of death and this is part of why. Homer stresses the actuality of warriors' deaths—the inevitability of warriors' deaths, but also what death in battle actually means. There are various sections in the *Iliad*, the battle scenes, in which just about every possible kind of death in battle is described. Warriors are killed by having their heads split in two with axes, by being stabbed in the lower belly, by being stabbed in the base of the throat, by being hit with arrows, just about every possible way that sword or ax or mace can inflict death on a human body is described in fairly gory detail by Homer in the *Iliad*. And yet, as scholars have noticed, wounds in the *Iliad* are always either fairly minor—either someone receives a minor wound, is a walking wounded, is able to be treated by a physician or a comrade, healed fairly quickly and go back to the battle—or he dies almost immediately. Homer never shows us some one lingering for three or four days from a very painful wound and dying slowly and gradually; he also never shows us someone mutilated or crippled by a disabling but not a fatal wound.

I don't think that this is any kind of reticence on Homer's part through wanting not to offend, or through any kind of reluctance to show the realities of battle in all their gory details—because he does show the realities of battle in very gory details. I think, rather, what he is doing by excluding the middle term, the possibility of grievous injury that does not kill or does not kill immediately—I think once again he is focusing on death, the fact that we must die, as the crucial defining characteristic of human existence. So that even in his battles, even in his warfare, humans either are wounded so mildly that they can go back into battle fairly quickly or they are killed; there is no intermediate, there is nothing else that is possible to happen to them in battle. So this focus on death as the defining characteristic of human existence, and this distinction between mortals and immortals, between humans and gods, between the deathless ones and the dying or already dead ones, highlights the human condition constantly throughout the *Iliad* by contrasting human existence with the gods' state of easy living. The gods are often referred to as the *rheia zôontes*, the "ones who live easily," the ones who have no cares, no troubles, no problems, no difficulties—as compared to us humans, who have all the problems, difficulties, troubles in the world, and have to die on top of it.

So *kleos*, to sum up this lecture, *kleos* provides the only possible form of immortality that a Homeric hero can really wish for; and yet that kind of immortality is gained only through inflicting death on another or through suffering death yourself. Above, beyond, behind that very grim picture of immortality gained only through death, stand the gods apart from, exempt from, not only death but age and really from all troubles and worries as well. In our next lecture, we'll look in more detail at the gods and how exactly they interact with humans in the *Iliad*, what they are doing in the *Iliad* in general.

Lecture Seven

The Role of the Gods

Scope:

In this lecture we examine the gods. We begin by considering what effect the gods' appearance as active participants has on the narrative. The lecture then moves on to examine the gods' essential nature and what kind of beings they are, and sketches how, in Homer's treatment of the gods, the essential contrast of immortality and mortality operates to enhance the *Iliad*'s portrait of the human condition and its implications. Finally, the lecture considers the topic of fate (*moira*) and its workings with respect to the gods.

Outline

I. The gods are essential characters in both Homeric epics, but particularly in the *Iliad*. Their actions both contribute to the action of the narrative and reiterate key themes.

  A. The gods take direct, concrete part in the action. Some critics have tried to explain their involvement away as merely a metaphorical way of describing human emotions, but there are many times when such explanations simply will not work (e.g., the Book III scene where Aphrodite physically removes Paris from the battlefield).

  B. The involvement of the gods in the narrative enhances the audience's sense of inevitability.

   1. Often the action of a scene could make sense on the purely human level (cf. the Book XI scene of Aias dropping back from the fighting).

   2. By showing us the divine level as well, Homer makes clear that the events must happen in just this way. This is often referred to as "over-determination."

  C. In their interactions with one another, the gods reiterate some of the most important underlying narrative themes of the *Iliad*.

   1. The power struggle between Zeus and Poseidon in Book XV recalls the power struggle between Achilles and Agamemnon.

2. The seduction of Zeus by Hera (Book XIV), in which a male is distracted by sex from the business at hand, recalls Paris and Helen in Book III, the sexual distraction at the root of the Agamemnon/Achilles struggle, and even the underlying cause of the Trojan War itself (i.e., the over-valuation of sex by Paris).

D. Most importantly, the gods reiterate, by counter-example, the all-important examination of the human condition. To understand this point, we need to look at what kind of beings these gods are.

II. The term "god" is regularly used to translate the Greek *theos*, but for modern readers this translation brings all sorts of misconceptions with it.

A. Let us start with a list of what the Homeric gods are not.

1. They are not consistently good, or merciful, or even (apparently) just.
2. Though they know a great deal, they are not omniscient.
3. Though very powerful, they are not omnipotent.
4. They are not transcendent. In other words, they did not create the universe, but are part of it.
5. They may not even have created human beings.
6. With rare exceptions, the relationship between these gods and humans is not based on mutual love.

B. Next, let us look at what these gods *are*.

1. On the most basic level, they originally represented personified forces of nature. They are much more than that, but their roles as natural forces are still obvious. Aphrodite *is* sexual passion; Ares *is* war.
2. Again, this is not merely metaphor; these gods really do control the forces of nature with which they are associated.
3. The gods are conceived of as anthropomorphic. They share human form, human passions, and human emotions.

III. From the point of view of the *human* characters in the *Iliad*, the gods are awe-inspiring, dangerous, powerful beings whom it is wise not to offend.

IV. When viewed on their own terms, however, the gods of the *Iliad* seem shallow, petty, trivial; they almost seem, at times, like comic relief.

A. They complain loudly about minor injuries.

B. They are easily distracted from the troubles even of their human favorites.

C. They brawl with one another, calling each other names and boxing each others' ears.

D. The scene of Zeus' seduction by Hera gives a very undignified portrait of the "father of gods and men."

V. Why does the *Iliad* present this double view of the gods? What does the epic gain from the apparent pettiness of its divinities?

A. It was by no means necessary for epic to portray the gods this way; the gods are not so petty or shallow in the *Odyssey*.

B. The key point for understanding the gods in the *Iliad* is that their lack of human vulnerability also means a lack of any capacity for nobility. A being that cannot die or even be seriously wounded cannot seriously be at risk, and thus cannot exhibit courage or self-sacrifice.

C. This contrast, between humans faced with the utterly serious issues of life and death and gods who can risk nothing, once again serves to focus attention on the essence of what it means to be human.

VI. Finally, we cannot leave a discussion of the role of the gods in the *Iliad* without looking at the concept of *moira*—fate, as it is usually translated.

A. *Moira*'s most basic meaning is "share" or "portion."

B. When applied to humans, it comes to mean "share of life," thus "time of death."

1. Each person's *moira* is inevitable, but generally not known ahead of time.

2. Thus, *moira* has been defined as "what, in retrospect, was bound to happen."

C. The gods seem generally to know each human's *moira*.

1. Thus, Thetis can tell Achilles about his choice of two *moirai*.

2. Zeus knows that Achilles will kill Hektor.

D. The question of whether or not the gods can change a human's *moira* is left ambiguous by the *Iliad*.
   1. Usually, the answer seems to be no. For example, Thetis clearly cannot change Achilles' fate.
   2. When Zeus considers intervening to save the life of his son Sarpedon, the implication seems to be that he could change Sarpedon's *moira* if he so chose, but that he decides not to.

E. The whole picture of *moira* reiterates that the gods are not transcendent deities outside the universe, but part of the universe. While not bound by *moira* in the same way humans are, they are nevertheless part of the system in which it operates and must respect it.

Essential Reading:

Iliad, Books XIII–XV.

Supplementary Reading:

Jenny Strauss Clay, *Wrath of Athena*, Chapter 3, pp. 133–148, 170–183. Although this book focuses on the *Odyssey*, Clay's discussion of the nature of the Homeric gods is applicable to the *Iliad* as well.

Mark W. Edwards, *Poet of the Iliad*, Chapter 17.

Jasper Griffin, *Homer on Life and Death*, Chapters V–VI. Very good on the gods' sublimity, although (in my opinion) he underplays the significance of the more frivolous elements in their characterization.

Seth L. Schein, *Mortal Hero*, Chapter 2. See especially this chapter's Appendix "On Fate."

Oliver Taplin, *Homeric Soundings*, Chapter V.

Questions to Consider:

1. What are the implications for a culture of believing in gods who are neither transcendent nor omnipotent?
2. Many people have tried to extrapolate a consistent, complete view of the workings of *moira* from the *Iliad*. Is it reasonable to expect such a concept to work consistently?

Lecture Seven—Transcript
The Role of the Gods

Hello, and welcome back to Lecture Seven in "Homeric Epic." In the previous lecture, we looked at *kleos* as the only form of immortality available to a Homeric hero, and discussed mortality and immortality as the crucial distinction between humans and gods. In this lecture, we will examine the role of the gods in more detail. We will look at the effect the gods' actions and active participation have on the narrative, examine their essential nature, and consider how Homer's treatment of the gods enhances the *Iliad*'s portrait of the human condition. Finally, the lecture will conclude with considering the topic of fate and its workings with respect to the gods.

The gods, as we have already seen, are essential characters in both Homeric epics, in the *Iliad* and the *Odyssey* both, but particularly in the *Iliad*. Their actions both contribute to the narrative and reiterate key themes in the *Iliad*. The gods take direct, concrete part in the action of the *Iliad*. Now, some critics have occasionally tried to explain the gods' involvement away as merely metaphorical descriptions of the human characters' own psychological impulses, and therefore say that Homer is not intending to create characters in the gods, but merely to describe, in metaphorical terms, the impulses of these human characters. There are many times when this kind of this kind of psychologicalizing explanation of the gods works quite well. The example that is most frequently cited, for instance, is in Book One of the *Iliad*, when Achilles is considering drawing his sword from its sheath and killing Agamemnon, during the opening of their quarrel. Athena suddenly appears to no-one but Achilles—no-one but Achilles can see her. She grabs him by his long hair and basically says to him, "Stop; you really don't want to do that." Many critics have said this is merely a metaphorical way of saying that Achilles thought better of his action and changed his mind.

However, there are at least as many, I think probably more, instances in the *Iliad* in which an action of the gods cannot be explained away as merely a psychological motivation of the character to whom the gods appear. For instance, to take another very obvious example, as I have already mentioned in passing when we were discussing Book Three of the *Iliad*, there is a scene in which Aphrodite bodily picks Paris up off the battlefield, carries him back inside the city of Troy, and puts him down in his bedroom. It is very hard to see that as merely a description of Paris' own psychological state, particularly since these actions of Aphrodite are narrated to us not by Paris—it is not Paris describing what seemed to him to happen. Rather, it is the narrator, Homer himself, the narrative voice of the epic, saying Aphrodite went, picked Paris up, and carried him off the battlefield. I think we have to assume that these gods are, within the context of the epic, given an actual reality; that they are actual characters who interact with one another and with the humans, and not merely metaphorical ways of describing the humans' own psychological conditions.

The involvement of the gods in the narrative not only motivates and moves along the action of the *Iliad*; there are many times when it also reiterates key themes and key points that have been made elsewhere in the narrative. So, for instance, often the actions of the gods enhance the audience's sense of inevitability, their sense that the storyline must go in precisely this way, at precisely this moment; that things have to happen as we see them happening, and can happen in no other way. There are many time in the *Iliad* when a scene would make perfect sense, when it is sufficiently motivated, merely by human actions and human motivations—when the gods are not necessary to explain what is happening in a scene—and yet Homer gives us both motivations, the human and the divine.

Let me give an example of what I mean there. In Book Eleven, for instance, Aias the Greater, the hero who is second only to Achilles as a warrior—and by the way, I probably should have mentioned in an earlier lecture, Aias is often referred to as Ajax, his name is sometimes transliterated into English as Ajax, rather than as Aias; same character. So if you know of the great Greek hero, Ajax, Aias is the same person. There is a scene in Book Eleven in which Aias the Greater, in exhaustion, drops back from fighting and pauses for a moment, and the Trojans get a momentary bit of ascendancy over the Greeks. This is perfectly understandable; a warrior who has been holding off the ranks of the enemy almost singlehandedly drops back from fighting temporarily—no more motivation for that is needed. And yet Homer tells us that Zeus put fear into Aias' mind, and he drops back from the fighting momentarily. This is the kind of instance I mean, in which there is a double kind of motivation going on. The actions are perfectly understandable purely on the human level, but by adding a divine motivation as well, by saying that the gods are in some sense controlling the humans' perceptions and the humans' actions, Homer adds to our sense of inevitability for how the story is going at this particular point.

This kind of double motivation—showing actions motivated both by the humans' desires, actions, and impulses and showing the same actions motivated at the same time by the gods—this kind of double motivation is often referred to as "over-determination" by literary critics. An action is over-determined, in a work of literature, when it is explained by more than one cause, any one of which would be sufficient to explain why the action or the event happens as it does. There is a lot of over-determination in the *Iliad*. In their interactions with one another in particular—not just in their interactions with humans, but in their interactions with one another—the gods reiterate some of the most important underlying narrative themes of the *Iliad*. Another way of putting that is that we see some of the same themes, some of the same problems, some of the same difficulties occurring between the gods, being worked out on the divine level, as on the human level.

For instance, in Book Fifteen there is an ongoing power-struggle between Zeus and his brother, Poseidon. Zeus, at this point in the *Iliad*, wants the Trojans to have ascendancy. As you remember, he had promised Thetis that he would let the Trojans have ascendancy over the Greeks for a certain time, until Achilles is missed enough by the Greeks that they honor him again. Poseidon, on the other hand, is very much on the side of the Greeks at this point, and he wants them to have ascendancy over the Trojans. In Book Fifteen, Homer refers to these two sons of Chronos—Chronos is the father and Zeus and Poseidon both; he says their hearts are set against one another, and this causes bitter agonies for the fighting men in the *Iliad*. This kind of struggle between two extremely powerful males, who because of their opposition to one another impose difficulties—agonies, even—on the fighting men, obviously recalls the quarrel between Achilles and Agamemnon in the opening of the *Iliad*. So you have a kind of repetition, or reiteration, on the divine level of how a quarrel between two powerful males, a kind of one-upmanship almost between Zeus and Poseidon, has its effect on the fighting men who die as part of Zeus and Poseidon's quarrel, in which they try to work out which of them is more powerful.

Another kind of reiteration of important themes occurs in Book Fourteen, in a scene in which Hera seduces Zeus to distract him from watching the battle, to distract him from presiding over the fighting. Hera seduces Zeus, knowing that he will sleep after they have sex. There, obviously, is a theme that is very important in the *Iliad* in various ways. A male is distracted by sex, distracted by desire, from the business at hand. This, again, reiterates the events of Book One in which—although as I said in Lecture Three, the quarrel between Achilles and Agamemnon is not *only* about sexual jealousy, it is certainly at least in part about sexual jealousy—Achilles and Agamemnon are both to some extent blindsided by their sexual feelings for their concubines, and distracted from the important business of the war. Similarly, of course, this whole war has been caused by a man, a male, Paris, overvaluing sexual attraction, in the person of Helen, and undervaluing everything else: Troy, his society, his duty to his people, all of those things. So when the goddess Hera seduces the god Zeus, we have a reiteration of this same scene. Zeus is distracted from what he intends to be paying attention to at that point—seeing to it that Hektor continues to win glory, that the Trojans continue to have the ascendancy—and he is distracted specifically by Hera seducing him.

Perhaps the most important narrative role or function that the gods play, however, is that they reiterate by counter-example the over-arching theme of what it means to be human, of the human condition in the *Iliad*. Let me explain what I mean by saying they reiterate by counter-example. To understand that, we need to talk a little bit about what kind of beings these gods are. The term "god"—small "g"—is normally used to translate the Greek word *theos*, and it is the best translation we have for *theos*. And yet, to modern American readers and I would assume modern European readers as well, this translation brings all sorts of misconceptions with it. I have often toyed with the idea of teaching a course on the *Iliad* and the *Odyssey*, or a course on Greek mythology and literature in general, in which I never use the words "god" or "gods" or "goddess"—in which I keep the Greek word *theos* untranslated and only use it, and let the students figure out what it means through the course of reading the works, without it being translated into the word "god." The obvious problem with that is I wouldn't be able to use any translations of Greek literature that have ever been published; I would have to translate everything I wanted my students to read myself, and keep *theos* as *theos*. So it is not very practical and this may be a bit extreme, but the reason I thought of doing that is precisely to avoid the misconceptions that we bring with us, without even thinking about them, automatically, when we hear the word "god."

To examine these misconceptions, let's start with a list of what the Homeric gods are not—a rather surprising list of what they are not. They are not consistently good, merciful, or even, apparently, just; these gods are quite capable of committing actions that in any reasonable moral evaluation are evil, are wicked, are unmerciful, and are unjust. These gods are not necessarily good, merciful or just. Though they know a very great deal, they are not omniscient. When a god's back is turned—literally or figuratively—he or she does not necessarily know what is going on behind his back. The best example of that comes in the *Odyssey*, when, at the opening of the *Odyssey*, Athena seizes the opportunity to help Odysseus, to help him back home to Ithaca. Odysseus is being persecuted by Poseidon, who hates him, but at the opening of the *Odyssey* Poseidon is off in Ethiopia, getting sacrifices from the Ethiopians. This is when Athena can move in and help Odysseus, because Poseidon is, so to speak, out of town; he won't know what Athena is doing in his absence. Obviously, Poseidon is not omniscient; when his attention is directed elsewhere, when he is away, he doesn't know what is happening behind his back. Equally obviously, in the *Iliad*, again the scene of seduction of Zeus by Hera—the whole point of that is, while Zeus is concentrating on Hera, he is not going to notice or know what is happening on the battlefield.

So, Greek gods know a great deal, but are by no means omniscient. Similarly, though they are extremely powerful, they are not omnipotent; they cannot do anything and everything that they want to do. The limitation on their power is perhaps most obvious in what seems almost to be an agreement between the gods themselves, rather than an inherent limitation, that they will not trespass—usually—on one another's spheres of influence. Each one of these gods has a particular sphere, or spheres, of influence, a particular realm of power. So, for instance, Poseidon controls the sea; Zeus controls the thunder; that kind of thing, and they tend not to usurp one another's powers, they tend not to take over the roles of other gods. Now, whether they could or not is perhaps questionable, so this may be a voluntary limit on their power rather than an inherent limit on their power; but there also seems to definitely be the sense that they are not in any way absolutely omnipotent. For instance, it seems to be taken as a given that Zeus could not simply annul death, that

Zeus could not simply say, "We are not going to make human beings die any more." Zeus is bound by the way the world works, including the fact that humans die, just as humans are bound by the way the world works.

Perhaps one of the strangest ideas for most modern readers to get hold of is that these gods are not transcendent; they are not outside the universe. In fact, they did not create the universe; rather, they are part of it, they are creatures of the universe, in the universe, bounded by the universe, just as we are. They are no sense transcendent, eternal entities who created the physical universe. That, as I said, is perhaps the way in which they differ the most—that and the fact that they are not necessarily good—is perhaps the way in which they differ the most from our usual conception of what a god is, if there is such a thing at all.

Along with not creating the universe, the gods of Homer may not even have created human beings. This is left ambiguous; Homer doesn't say specifically one way or the other. Other Greek writers, some of them, seem to say that the Zeus or the gods in general did create humans; others say that they did not. But even if they did create humans, that is not one of the most important aspects of these gods. They are not seen as our parents, as our loving protectors, in any way at all. Zeus is often called "the father of gods and men," but really, I think, that refers more to his power and his authority than to any literal paternal relationship between Zeus and men. Certainly Zeus is the father of some gods, but by no means of all of them; and so I think it is pretty clear that that phrase is meant to refer to his power, and not his to his actually paternity.

And, as I just touched on the last main statement of what these gods are not, or do not do, the relationship between Homer's gods and human beings is only very rarely based on any kind of mutual love. These gods, by and large, do not love humans; these humans, by and large, do not love these gods. Now, clearly there are very obvious exceptions to that, most obviously the relationships between gods and their human children. Thetis clearly loves Achilles; Aphrodite probably loves Aeneas in the *Iliad*, although she is not as given to taking care of him as Thetis is of Achilles, as I have mentioned before. Aphrodite, for instance, when she tries to rescue Aeneas in the battlefield in Book Five, drops him shortly after she picks him up on the field of battle. But, by and large, with the exception of human children and god parents, the gods do not seem to love humans; at least, not in the sense that those of us brought up in a Judeo-Christian tradition would expect gods to love humans. So, they are not good necessarily; they can be good when they want to, but they are not necessarily good, or merciful, or omnipotent, or omniscient, or transcendent, or loving. What are they?

On the most basic level, these gods clearly originally represented—or came into being, in some sense, in order to represent—personified forces of nature, and they retain that aspect even in the Homeric epics and in later literature. They are much more than mere personifications of forces of nature; they are much more than mere representations of the natural world or of human culture. But their roles as natural forces, plus additional aspects, are still very obvious in the *Iliad* and in the *Odyssey* both. For instance, Aphrodite is sexual passion. She not only controls sexual passion, she not only inflicts it on humans, gods, and animals; in some sense she is the embodiment of sexual passion. Ares, son of Zeus and Hera, *is* war. Zeus says to Ares, in the *Iliad*, that Ares is more hated than any other god; the reason for that is because Ares is battle, Ares is war. He doesn't just control it or govern it; to some extent, he is the embodiment of war.

Now, again, this is not merely metaphor; these gods really do control the forces of nature with which they are associated. They are not simply metaphorical ways of talking about war; when you say "Aphrodite smote me and made me fall in love with someone," that is not simply a fancy metaphorical way of saying "I fell in love with someone"—at least, not in the *Iliad*. Again, think of Book Three, when Aphrodite makes Helen go to bed with Paris. That is not just a metaphorical way of saying that Helen was attracted to Paris; we are talking about Aphrodite more or less grabbing Helen by the shoulders and marching her into the bedroom. So, Aphrodite is not just a metaphor, but she is deeply associated with the force she embodies—in her case, the force of sexual passion. This works for many of the gods. Zeus perhaps began as a god of the sky, of thunder, lightning, weather; he comes to be much more than that, but he retains some of the aspects of a sky and weather god.

As I mentioned in a previous lecture, these gods are conceived of as anthropomorphic; that is they are conceived of as being human-like in form, in shape, in emotions, in activities. They are greater than humans, physically larger than humans, definitely more beautiful than humans, and always more glorious and powerful than we are, and yet they are anthropomorphic in that they share human form, human passions, and human emotions. Now, the role of the gods in the *Iliad* varies between grandeur and pettiness. There are times when these gods seem awe-inspiring, magnificent, numinous, grand, when they seem, at least in that respect, to be what we would expect gods to be, to be worthy of worship, worthy of awe and reverence, even if they are not necessarily good, kind, or helpful. There are other times, however, when they seem remarkably shallow and petty. And this double nature of the gods, this tension between grandeur and pettiness, has seemed odd to a great many readers of the *Iliad*. There is no question as to why the gods are shown as awe-inspiring and grand; but why are they sometimes shown as petty and trivial?

To understand what is going on there, why Homer treats the gods this way in the *Iliad*, I think we need to realize that there are two distinct viewpoints at play here. When we, the audience, in effect step into the *Iliad* and look at the gods from the point of view of the human characters, when we stand shoulder-to-shoulder with Agamemnon or Hektor or Paris or Achilles and look at the gods, from that point of view they are without question awe-inspiring, magnificent, numinous, glorious, dangerous beings whom it is very wise not to offend. But, when we stand side by side with Homer, the narrator, and look at the gods from the point of view of the narrator of the epic—or, putting it another way, look at the gods on their own terms in the *Iliad*—they sometimes seem shallow, petty, trivial, almost as though they are comic relief.

This is to some extent shocking and surprising—the idea of the gods as shallow, petty, and trivial—and yet it is undeniably there in the *Iliad*. These gods complain loudly about minor injuries. Again, when Aphrodite is wounded by Diomedes—he scratches her hand when she is trying to carry her son, Aeneas, off the battlefield—she drops Aeneas, flies up to Mount Olympus, and cries in her mother's lap because her hand hurts. The gods are easily distracted from the troubles even of their human favorites. They brawl with one another, they call each other names, they box each other's ears, they behave in many undignified ways. Perhaps the most obvious example of the gods as undignified, again, is the scene in which Hera seduces Zeus, in Book Fourteen of the *Iliad*. Hera does this in order to help Poseidon help the Greeks. If she can turn Zeus' attention away from the battlefield, the Trojans can be temporarily overcome by the Greeks; Zeus won't help them. So, Hera decks herself out; she borrows seductiveness from Aphrodite, she makes herself as beautiful as possible, she gets the god, Sleep, to promise to put Zeus to sleep after they have had sex, and then she shows herself to Zeus. And Zeus, looking at her, says that he really wants to go to bed with her right now, and he says to her—apparently thinking that he will gain her approval by so saying—the following lines:

> Never before has love for any goddess or woman
> so melted about the heart inside me, broken into submission,
> as now: not that time when I loved the wife of Ixion
> who bore me Peirithoös, equal of the gods in counsel,
> nor when I loved Akrisios' daughter, sweet-stepping Danaë,
> who bore Perseus to me, pre-eminent among all men,
> nor when I loved the daughter of far -enowned Phoinix,
> Europa,
> who bore Minos to me, and Rhadamanthys the godlike;
> nor when I loved Semele or Alkmene in Thebe. . .

You get the idea; he goes on and on and on. This is not dignified behavior; this is, in particular, not what you would consider appropriate to the father of gods and men, the ruler of the gods, when you consider that Hera is the archetypal jealous wife; she hates the other females that Zeus has been involved with, she particularly hates the sons that they have borne him. For him to think that he will soften her heart, gain her favor, make her feel kindly disposed towards him, by listing this laundry-list of other females that he has had affairs with and the sons they have borne him—it is hard to see this as anything other than comic, as anything other than undignified on Zeus' part and comic on the part of the poet.

So the obvious question is, why does the *Iliad* present this double view of the gods? What does the epic gain from this apparent pettiness of its divinities? It wasn't by any means necessary for epic to portray the gods this way; the gods in the *Odyssey* are much less shallow, much less petty, much less trivial than the gods in the *Iliad*. I think the key point for understanding what is going on here with these gods in the *Iliad* is, once again, to look at them as a means of comparison for humans. The gods lack human vulnerability—they cannot be seriously wounded, they cannot be killed—and along with lacking human vulnerability or the possibility of death, they lack human seriousness and any capacity for nobility.

If you think about that for a minute, I think you will see what I mean. A being that cannot risk anything serious, an entity that cannot be seriously harmed, let alone killed, is incapable, almost by definition, of showing courage, altruism, nobility, self-sacrifice—any of those virtues that we admire most in humans, any of those virtues that perhaps come into fullest detail in a war: courage, self-sacrifice, and so forth. An immortal being that cannot even be seriously wounded cannot exhibit any of those traits. And so, in a very real sense, Homer's gods *are* more trivial than Homer's humans. Homer's humans can display courage, nobility, and self-sacrifice; his gods can't—and I think the treatment of the gods as trivial highlights that difference. This contrast between the humans in the *Iliad*, who are faced with the absolutely serious issues of life and death, and gods, who can risk nothing, once again underlines what it means to be human and how serious a matter that is.

Finally, I can't leave a discussion of the role of the gods in the *Iliad* without looking again at the concept of fate or, in Greek, *moira*. *Moira* is a word that originally meant "lot" or "portion," and continues to mean lot or portion. If you divide a haunch of meat among various different people, you give each of them a *moira*, each of them a portion. But *moira*, perhaps *moira* with a capital "M," comes to mean a human's share of life, portion of life; and therefore, by a very easy transition in meaning, the time of a human's death, the instant at which your share of life is over. As we have already talked about a bit, each person's *moira* is inevitable, but generally not known ahead of time. And *moira* has been defined—I really like this definition—as "what in retrospect was bound to happen." You cannot, ahead of time, see what someone's *moira* is, but you can look at the events afterwards and say it must have always been ordained so; this particular warrior must have been fated to die at this particular time; that was his *moira*. So, *moira* can be defined as what in retrospect was bound to happen.

Now, the gods generally seemed to know each human being's *moira*. Thetis knows that Achilles has this choice that we have already talked about, this very odd choice between two different fates, between two different types of *moira*. She can tell him about it because she knows about it. Zeus knows that Achilles will kill

Hektor; that Hektor will kill Patroklos; Zeus pretty much knows everything that is going to happen in the whole course of the *Iliad*. So, the gods know what humans' *moira* is. The question of whether or not the gods can change it, or can interfere with it, is left ambiguous by the *Iliad*. Usually the answer to that question seems to be no. For example, Thetis can tell Achilles about his choice of *moira*, but she very clearly cannot change it for him. She can tell him the terms of his choice; she can't affect what those terms are.

There is one very famous and very important scene in the *Iliad* where Zeus seems to entertain the idea of changing someone's *moira*. This is when Zeus' son Sarpedon is killed by Patroklos, a scene we'll talk about in more detail in the next lecture, and Zeus considers saving his son, Sarpedon. Hera says to Zeus, in effect, "Go ahead and do that if you like; but if you do, you must realize every god and goddess who has a human child fighting this war will want to change their child's *moira*"—and Zeus, after Hera has said this, allows Sarpedon to be killed. He weeps for his son, he sends the gods of sleep and death to pick Sarpedon's body off the battlefield and carry it off to his own home country; but he does not intervene, he does not change Sarpedon's *moira*. The picture that seems to be given by this is that while theoretically the gods could interfere and could change *moira* they agree—almost by what used to be called a gentlemen's agreement—they agree not to; for if they did, they would be undercutting the entire way the universe works. They would be undercutting the entire right order of things, the way the universe is set out, the way the universe functions.

So, there is an ambiguity. At times it seems that the gods cannot change *moira*; at times it seems that they could, but do not; and so the whole picture of *moira* reiterates that these gods are not transcendent deities outside the universe, but are part of the universe. While they are not bound by *moira* in the same way that humans are, they nevertheless are part of the system in which it operates, and they must and do respect it. In our next lecture, we'll examine in detail the way Homer interweaves divine and human action in one specific section of the *Iliad*, Books Eleven through Fifteen.

Lecture Eight

The Longest Day

Scope:

This lecture continues our comparison of gods and mortals by examining the dual narratives, divine and human, of *Iliad*, Books XI–XV, the books which lead up to and feature Hektor's *aristeia*. We see that in this section of the epic it is possible to extract a coherent narrative which excludes the gods' interventions, and shows the progress of the battle as it would have seemed to the participants. But in the privileged view of the action given to us as Homer's audience, we also see an unusually complex and detailed narrative of the gods' actions intertwined with the human narrative. Once again, this dual level of action stresses the nature and meaning of human mortality.

Outline

I. In Book XI, Zeus sends Iris to tell Hektor to hold back until he sees Agamemnon wounded. Once this has happened, Zeus promises victory to Hektor until the sun sets.

- **A.** This one day lasts from Book XI through Book XVIII, line 240.
- **B.** Hektor's *aristeia* lasts from Book XII through Book XV.

II. The description of battle in these books can be analyzed on two levels, the human and the divine. The characters within the epic normally see only the human level; as the audience, we see the divine level of action as well.

III. On the human level, the action follows the standard give and take of battle, with courage and desperate fighting on both sides.

- **A.** Book XI stresses the Greeks' vulnerability without Achilles.
  1. The fighting begins with Agamemnon's brief *aristeia.*
  2. Once Agamemnon is wounded and withdraws from battle, Hektor rallies his men and rushes into battle, where he kills many.
  3. Diomedes and Odysseus are both wounded. This means that the only outstanding Greek warrior still in the battle is Aias the Greater, who fights valiantly to hold the Trojans from the ships.

B. Book XII stresses the Trojans' prowess during Hektor's promised day.
  1. At Hektor's urging, the Trojans attack the Greeks' trench and wall, which they had built as a defense for their camp. Sarpedon makes the first breach in the wall.
  2. Hektor smashes the gate of the wall. This leaves nothing between the Trojans and the Greeks ships but a mass of demoralized Greeks, lacking their foremost warriors (Agamemnon, Diomedes, Odysseus, Achilles).
  3. The narrator stresses the greater physical prowess of the heroes of Troy as compared to "modern" men (i.e., Homer's contemporaries).

C. In Book XIII, the Greeks rally, and the tide of battle turns temporarily against the Trojans.
  1. The Trojans retreat to take counsel.
  2. Hektor continues to fight, with Paris beside him.
  3. Hektor and Aias the Greater meet face to face.

D. The Greeks continue to gain strength throughout Book XIV.
  1. In a conversation with Nestor, Diomedes, and Odysseus, Agamemnon expresses despair and again suggests that the Greeks should sail away by night. Diomedes suggests instead that they should return to the field of battle, wounded though they are, to encourage the other Greeks.
  2. Aias the Greater wounds Hektor by hitting him with a boulder. Hektor is dazed, and this encourages the Greeks further.

E. In Book XV, Hektor regains his strength and returns to battle. With Hektor leading, the Trojans break through the Greeks' wall and reach the ships.
  1. Hektor calls for fire to burn the ships.
  2. Aias the Greater leaps from deck to deck, urging his fellow Greeks to rally and protect the ships.

IV. The narrative in these books* thus makes perfect sense, and is excitement-packed and suspenseful, without even considering the gods. But the action works on the divine level as well.

A. Zeus has promised victory to Hektor, and so works against the Greeks in this section.

1. In Book XI, Zeus puts fear into Aias' mind, so that he temporarily falls back.
2. In Book XII, Zeus strengthens Sarpedon, who makes the first breach in the Greeks' wall.

B. Poseidon takes the form of Kalchas and rallies the Greeks in Books XIII–XIV.

C. Hera observes Poseidon rallying the Greeks, and decides to aid the Greeks by diverting Zeus' attention from the battle. Accordingly, she seduces him so that he will sleep.

D. It is while Zeus is sleeping that Hektor is wounded by Aias.

E. Zeus awakes in Book XV, and reestablishes the Trojans' dominance.

1. He sees Hektor dazed and vomiting blood, and sends Apollo to heal him. Apollo leads Hektor and the Trojans into battle; he kicks down part of the Greeks' wall and the Trojans pour through.
2. Zeus sends Iris to tell Poseidon to stop helping the Greeks.
3. He scolds Hera for seducing him and diverting his attention.
4. Zeus describes what will happen next in the battle: Hektor will kill Patroklos, Achilles will return to battle, and Hektor will die at Achilles' hands.

V. The narrative in these four books thus includes exceptionally intricate double-level action, which leads to the crucial turning point of the *Iliad*: Patroklos' entry into battle in Achilles' armor.

Supplementary Reading:

Mark W. Edwards, *Poet of the Iliad*, Chapters 25–26.

Oliver Taplin, *Homeric Soundings*, Chapter 6.

Questions to Consider:

1. Explain how the impact of this section of the *Iliad* would suffer if the gods' interventions were removed from the narrative.
2. Hera's seduction of Zeus strikes some readers as out of place in this section of the *Iliad*; its tone seems inappropriate to the surrounding battle narratives. Do you agree or disagree? What do you make of the tone of that scene?

*Note: The numbering of the books was done by scholars in the Great Library of Alexandria in the 3rd or 2nd century B.C. The numbering scheme is based on the number of papyrus scrolls needed to copy out the narrative. The divisions, although artificial, are now accepted as convention.

Lecture Eight—Transcript

The Longest Day

Hello, and welcome back to Lecture Eight. In our previous lecture we discussed the nature of the gods, what kind of beings they are, and how Homer's portrayal of them enhances and highlights his picture of the human condition. In this lecture we are going to turn to examining the dual narratives, divine and human, of *Iliad* Eleven through Fifteen, and see how in this section of the epic we can extract a narrative that is motivated purely in human terms, and another that is motivated purely in divine terms. It is the privileged view of the action given to us as Homer's audience that allows us to interweave these two narratives, divine and human, and to see how the dual level of action stresses the nature and meaning of human mortality.

In the beginning of Book Eleven, Zeus sends Iris, the messenger goddess, to tell Hektor that he should hold back from the fighting until he sees Agamemnon wounded. Once Agamemnon has been wounded and has withdrawn from the fighting, Zeus promises Hektor "power to kill men," as he puts it, until Hektor reaches the ships of the Greeks and the sun sets. So Zeus promises Hektor power in battle, victory in battle, power to kill his enemies, for the space of one day. This one day, which dawns at the opening of Book Eleven, is the longest day in the *Iliad*. It is an extremely long day, in fact; it lasts from this beginning in Book Eleven up to line 240 of Book Eighteen. So it stretches over a full third of the *Iliad*, ending only when the sun sets in Book Eighteen. During this longest day of the *Iliad*, Hektor's *aristeia*—that is his scene of special valor, the scene in which he is able to kill his enemies more thoroughly, more effectively, than he is has before, fights better than he ever has before, is given his spotlight, so to speak, on his special valor—Hektor's *aristeia* covers most of Books Twelve through Fifteen. So this is both the longest day in the *Iliad*, and this is one of the longest focal points on a particular hero's special valor in the *Iliad*.

The description of battle in these books, as I said in the introduction, can be analyzed on two separate levels. We can look at the description of battle on the purely human level, which is what I am going to start by doing, and we can look at the events of these books on the divine level. The characters within the epic itself, of course, normally by and large see only the human level of action. Just as I talked about in the last lecture, the humans, the characters within the

Iliad, see the gods only from the human's-eye view, and therefore perceive the gods as numenous, awe-inspiring, and dangerous. So also, the human characters within the *Iliad* normally see the action only from their own point of view. They are unaware of the upper level of divine motivation, the level above or behind or beyond—whatever spatial metaphor we choose to use—that Homer shows us as his audience. But we, of course, are given the privileged view, which allows us to see both the human motivations and the divine level of action as well.

Let's start by looking at the human action in this section of the *Iliad*, Books Eleven through Fifteen. Analyzed purely on the human level, the action of these books follows the standard give-and-take of battle, in fact is an almost surprisingly realistic description of what a desperate day-long battle would be like. There are acts of courage or despair on both sides. The balance of power in the midst of the fight shifts between Greeks and Trojans rather frequently. Some great heroes are wounded; others fight absolutely magnificently; there is confusion; there is disorder. On the human level, these books provide an extraordinarily realistic description of what it would be like to take part in this sort of battle.

I am going to go through the human narrative of Books Eleven through Fifteen in some detail, within the timeframe that I have to do this in. Book Eleven stresses the Greeks' vulnerability without Achilles. This book—in which we, as the audience, know that Zeus has promised one day's valor to Hektor—from the Greek point of view, this book opens with the Greeks fighting very, very well. In Book Eleven, the fighting begins with Agamemnon's brief *aristeia*. It is a very brief one, but we see Agamemnon go through the regular parts of an *aristeia*; he puts on his armor, he fights very valiantly, he withdraws after he is wounded. Agamemnon is the first major Greek warrior to be wounded in this section of the *Iliad*. He is wounded in the arm; he's stabbed through under the elbow, and, we're told, clean through the flesh of his arm. While the blood flows, Agamemnon continues to fight valiantly. When the blood dries, Homer tells us, Agamemnon is overcome with pains—pains that the narrator likens to the pains of a woman in childbirth—and he has to withdraw from the fighting. After Agamemnon's withdrawal, Hektor rallies his men and rushes into battle, where he kills a great many Greeks. From the Greek point of view, all they see is that Hektor notices Agamemnon has been wounded and comes rushing into the battle. Again, we as the audience know that Hektor had been told by Zeus, "Wait until Agamemnon is wounded and then start fighting." But from the purely human point of view, no extra motivation is needed; Hektor sees that Agamemnon is wounded, seizes his opportunity, runs into battle.

Diomedes and Odysseus, in the meantime, are both fighting very bravely, but both are also wounded in quick succession after Agamemnon. Paris shoots Diomedes in the foot with an arrow, and Diomedes and Paris have a very interesting little conversation in which Paris taunts Diomedes. He shoots an arrow through Diomedes foot, and the arrow goes into the ground on the other side; so Diomedes is momentarily pinned to the spot, literally, by the arrow. Paris taunts him, and Diomedes gives a very interesting comment on Paris' choice of weapon. He says that the bow is a coward's weapon, because with a bow you can stand at a distance and inflict injury on your enemy; you don't have to come into actual face-to-face danger. Diomedes says, "If you have the nerve to fight with me sword-to-sword, face-to-face, we would have a very different outcome here." Diomedes also says, "You have only scratched me; you have inflicted no more damage on me that a woman or even a child could inflict on me." However, Diomedes' wound is painful enough that he too, like Agamemnon, withdraws from the battle.

Odysseus, meanwhile, is stabbed in the ribs by a spear. The point is deflected by his ribs; it does not go through to his vitals, it does not reach any vital organs, but he is fairly badly disabled by this, at least momentarily. He is rescued; Odysseus is rescued by Aias the Greater and Menelaos, who come to his aid. Aias holds off the Trojans while Menelaos helps Odysseus out of battle. So, at the end of Book Eleven Diomedes, Agamemnon, Odysseus are all wounded. This means that the only outstanding Greek warrior, the only truly magnificent Greek warrior still in the battle, is Aias the Greater who fights valiantly to hold the Trojans back from the Greeks' ships. Again, just to remind you of where we are, the battle has almost reached the Greeks' ships. The Trojans are trying to break through to the Greeks' ships; if they can burn the ships, then they have the Greeks basically pinned between the Trojans' ranks and the sea, with no means of escape. So the battle, from the Greek point of view, is quite desperate at this point.

Book Twelve—as we move into Book Twelve with Agamemnon, Diomedes and Odysseus all wounded—Book Twelve stresses the

Trojans' prowess during Hektor's promised day of glory. At Hektor's urging, the Trojans attack the Greeks' defensive trench and wall. I haven't mentioned this defensive wall before, I don't believe. This is a wall that the Greeks built purely to defend themselves against this eventuality, that the Trojans should ever reach their camp; and it is quite a magnificent wall. Book Twelve opens with a description of the Greeks' defensive wall. It is made out of stone, it has timbers reinforcing it, and in front of the wall, between the wall and the plain of Troy, the Greeks have dug a deep ditch, so that it is a double defensive mechanism. If the Trojans are going to try to scale this wall, they are going to have to go down into the ditch first and thus have that much more height to scale over to get to the Greeks' ships. The wall is probably not scalable; what the Trojans are trying to do, and what everyone on the Greek side fears they will do, is break through the wall, and that is what Hektor in Book Twelve urges his men to do—to attack the Greeks' trench and wall. And it is Sarpedon, the son of Zeus, who will later be killed by Patroklos, who makes the first breach in the Greeks wall. He does this immediately after the speech to Glaukos that I mentioned in a previous lecture, in which Sarpedon, speaking to his friend Glaukos, talks about the nature of *kleos*. You remember the speech; he says, "If we were immortal and ageless we would not need to fight; but since we must die let's win as much *kleos* as possible for ourselves or let someone else win it by killing us." It is immediately after Sarpedon says those words to his friend Glaukos that he rages into battle and actually manages to pull away part of the Greeks' wall to form the first breach in the wall.

More importantly, after Sarpedon has made the first breach in the wall, Hektor smashes the gate; Hektor actually smashes an opening through the Greeks' wall. He does this by picking up a boulder, carrying it to the gate, and smashing the door leaves of the gate with the boulder. And in a very interesting little comment given us by the narrator, by the poet, Homer tells us that this stone, this boulder that Hektor has and uses to smash the gate, is a boulder that two men, the best in their community, would be unable to lift from the ground onto the bed of a wagon today, so much more feeble are men today than the heroes of old. But Hektor lifted it easily, carried it to the gate, and smashed it through the doors. This is a theme that is mentioned several times in the *Iliad*, the idea that the heroes of old, the heroes who fought before Troy, were somehow physically larger and stronger—not just more heroic, not just braver, not just closer to the gods in terms of their descent from the gods and their interactions with the gods, but actually larger, stronger—than modern day men. The sense of degeneration, the sense that there has been a falling off of human stock from the ancient days to the days when Homer is singing, is very clear in both the *Iliad* and the *Odyssey*, but especially in the *Iliad*.

So Hektor lifts a boulder that no two men today could lift, smashes the gate with it, and this means—since the wall has now been breached, the gate is gone—this means, really, nothing is left between the Trojans and the Greeks' ships but a mass of demoralized Greeks, lacking their foremost warriors. Agamemnon, Diomedes, Odysseus, and of course Achilles are all out of the action at this point, and the Greeks are greatly demoralized. However, as we move into Book Thirteen, the Greeks begin to rally. Kalchas, the prophet who reads omens for the Greeks, moves among the ranks of the Greeks and encourages the warriors, tells them it is a shameful thing for young, strong men to shrink back from the fighting, that now, if ever, when they see the Trojans bursting through the wall and the Trojans getting close to their ships, now is the moment for them to fight more valiantly than they have ever fought before. And as often happens in a battle, a commander—or, Kalchas is not necessarily a commander, but the speech of a person in some sort of authority does manage to rally the men, and the tide of battle turns temporarily against the Trojans.

The Trojans retreat to take counsel; the Trojan troops back away from the smashed gate and start to counsel with one another about best to proceed at this point. However, Hektor continues to fight, trying to work his way past the gate into the ranks of the Greeks and, interestingly enough, Paris fights beside him. As Book Thirteen comes to an end, Hektor and Aias the Greater meet face to face and taunt one another; they trade insults. They don't actually harm each other at this point, they simply trade insults with one another. They will meet again a little bit later in the narrative.

The Greeks continue to gain strength throughout Book Fourteen; the narrative continues to progress so that the Trojans are doing less well, the Greeks are doing better, in Book Fourteen. However—and again, this is a very realistic touch of how things wound really be in battle—Agamemnon does not know that the Greeks are gaining strength. Agamemnon is wounded, remember; he, Diomedes, and

Odysseus are off apart from the fighting, leaning on their spears, walking, talking to one another. They are not so grievously wounded that they can't return to the battle; remember, as I said in an earlier lecture, Homer tends not to show us wounds that are so grievous that warriors can't continue fighting, unless the wounds are grievous enough to kill them. So, Agamemnon, Diomedes, and Odysseus are not so badly wounded that they even have to sit down; they are walking and talking to one another, but they are apart from the fighting and they assume that things are going badly for the Greeks. In fact, Agamemnon is wondering if everyone is angry at him as Achilles is angry at him, if every one is holding back from the fighting, if all of the Greeks have decide they won't fight for Agamemnon's cause any more.

Nestor comes and talks to Agamemnon, Odysseus, and Diomedes, and mentions that the wall has been breached, that Hektor has smashed the gate; there is now a breach in the wall. At this point, for the third time in the *Iliad*, Agamemnon says "maybe we should just pack up and go home." He suggests that perhaps this very night, as soon as the sun sets, before the Trojans have burned the Greeks' ships, the Greeks should simply give up and sail away. Odysseus and Diomedes are both angered by this suggestion, and Diomedes says, "No, rather than doing that, let the three of us, wounded though we are, go back into battle and see if we can encourage the other Greeks"—and this is in fact what happens; Agamemnon, Diomedes, and Odysseus go back into battle. They arrange for the Greeks who are fighting to do an odd little armor exchange; they say, "Let's give the best armor to the best fighters, the worst armor to the worst fighters"—so that the man who is most likely to succeed in fighting has the best weapons and the best shield. The people who are not so good at fighting, well, they can more or less just fend for themselves. And this strikes me as yet another very realistic detail. At this point in the Greeks' fighting, things seem to be pretty desperate, and therefore it makes good sense to give your best weapons to your best fighters. The main point now is to hold the Trojans away from the ships, and Agamemnon arranges to do whatever it will take to accomplish that.

So, Agamemnon, Diomedes, and Odysseus, even though they are wounded, return to the battle and this encourages other Greeks, and the tide of battle continues to go against the Trojans. In the most important episode of Book Fourteen, Aias the Greater wounds Hektor by throwing a boulder at him, another one of those boulders that two men today would not be able to lift. Aias lifts, throws at Hektor, hits Hektor in the chest, and stuns him. So as Book Fourteen comes to an end Hektor is dazed, the wind is knocked out of him; his chest is hit by a boulder, he is dazed, and this encourages the Greek fighters further. Hektor's companions pull him out of battle and take him to one side. As we move on into Book Fifteen, Hektor regains his strength and returns to battle. With Hektor leading, the Trojans finally actually break through the Greeks' wall. They expand the opening where Hektor had smashed the gate, they break through the wall, they pour through in a swarm and reach the Greeks' ships. So that moment that the Greeks have been dreading, of the Trojans actually reaching the ships, occurs in Book Fifteen with Hektor leading his men against the Greeks' ships, Hektor having recovered from his dazed state after Aias hit him with the boulder. Hektor actually seizes hold of the stern of a ship and calls for fire to set the ships afire. And as Hektor is calling for fire, as the battle is continuing to rage around the ships, Aias the Greater is leaping from deck of ship to deck of ship, calling on his comrades, urging them to fight bravely, urging the Greeks to rally and protect the ships. Aias is, in effect, basically holding the fort almost singlehandedly now. Agamemnon, Diomedes, Odysseus are back in the battle, but they are wounded and not at full strength; Achilles is of course still off in camp doing nothing; Aias is really almost singlehandedly holding the Trojans away from the ships.

So, purely on the human level—I haven't said anything about any gods in this little summary—purely on the human level, the narrative in this section of the *Iliad* makes perfect sense, is excitement-packed, suspenseful, without considering the gods at all. It is also extremely realistic, as I have already mentioned. The give and take of battle; the switching back and forth; the confusion; the leaders not knowing what's happening in another part of the battlefield; the rumors—there is a breach in the wall, maybe there is, maybe there isn't; the warriors being wounded, withdrawing for a while, coming back to battle; the encouragement on one side, the despair on the other side—all of that is extraordinarily realistic as a description of battle, and works perfectly well. You can—if you extract all the references to the gods, you can read this section of the *Iliad*, Books Eleven through Fifteen, as I have just delineated.

Let me reiterate at this point, by the way, that these book divisions I keep referring to are utterly artificial, are a later addition to the *Iliad*.

As I mentioned in the second lecture, when we talked about how the *Iliad* and the *Odyssey* came to be written down, the book divisions were made by scholars in the great library of Alexandria in the third or second century B.C. It takes about twenty-four average length papyrus scrolls to write out the text of the *Iliad* and the *Odyssey*—that is a stunning example of how much more efficient a writing technology the codex is—what we call a book—than scrolls are. It takes twenty-four scrolls to write out this length of text if you keep the scrolls at a usable length. Probably in the first several centuries of the transmission of the *Iliad* and the *Odyssey*, any scribe copying them would just write to the end of a reasonable-length scroll and stop, start the next one in the middle of a sentence or whatever. Somewhere in the third or second century B.C.—we don't really know whose idea this was—it occurred to one of the great scholar-librarians at Alexandria that it would be a good idea to come up with standardized book divisions for the *Iliad* and the *Odyssey*, so that the first roll would stop at the same place, the second roll would stop at the same place, and so on. Part of what this does, of course, is allow for ease of reference. Instead of saying, "you remember that scene about a third of the way through the *Iliad*, when Hektor talks to Andromache on the walls of Troy," I can say, "You remember that scene in Book Six?"—and even give specific line numbers for Book Six. So it aids in reference; it is a great tool for scholars working with the *Iliad* and the *Odyssey*. That is why we still use the book divisions today. But in this kind of discussion, like I am doing now, about the narrative, it is important to remember that the original performer of the *Iliad*, Homer or whatever we want to call him, had no such book divisions in mind. When I say, "At the beginning of Book Fifteen, Hektor regains his strength," that is a completely artificial construct; this narrative that I just delineated would have been a seamless continual narrative of battle.

And as I have said, it works beautifully, just on the human level. But now let's consider what the divine level adds to this narrative of battle in this section of the *Iliad*. As I have already said, Zeus has promised victory to Hektor in this longest day of the *Iliad*, and so Zeus is working against the Greeks through out this section. In Book Eleven, for instance, Zeus puts fear into Aias' mind so that Aias temporarily falls back, as I already mentioned in the previous lecture. In Book Twelve, Zeus strengthens Sarpedon when he makes the breach in the wall. Sarpedon, as I said, is the first Trojan to actually harm the Greeks' wall. What he does is, he reaches up and grabs a piece of it and pulls it away. We're told he does that because Zeus puts extra strength into him. In Books Thirteen and Fourteen, when I said Kalchas moves among the Greeks, rallying them and encouraging them, actually it is not Kalchas. It is the god Poseidon, disguised as Kalchas, rallying the Greeks, encouraging them to fight. Some of the Greeks actually recognize this; the two Aiantes—that is the plural of Aias—Aias the Greater and Aias the Lesser, talking to one another say, "This was not Kalchas; this must have been a god, who put heart back into us to fight again."

In Book Fourteen, Hera observes that Poseidon, disguised as Kalchas, is rallying the Greeks and she decides to aid the Greeks by diverting Zeus' attention from the battle; and this, of course, is the famous seduction scene, when Hera thinks, "How can I get Zeus away from the battle, make Zeus stop paying attention to the battle, so that Poseidon can keep doing what he is doing so well?"—encouraging the Greeks, getting them to fight better, helping them directly and indirectly. And so she seduces Zeus, so that he will fall asleep. And the whole scene of Zeus' seduction, which is described in great detail by Homer, takes place at the same time as the Greeks are gaining ascendance. So again, there is a double level of action. On the battlefield, the Greeks are gaining ascendance over the Trojans; up on Mount Ida, Zeus and Hera are making love, and then Zeus is sleeping.

And it is worth noting, I think—this is a wonderful little detail in Homer's control of these two layers of narrative—that it is while Zeus is asleep that Aias is able to throw the boulder and wound Hektor. Zeus, of course, had promised Hektor power during this one day. Hektor could easily have been killed by that boulder-toss from Aias. He certainly could have been wounded more seriously than he was. It is while Zeus is asleep that Aias is able to do this to Hektor; and Hektor's regaining his strength, Hektor recovering from being dazed, occurs when Zeus awakes in Book Fifteen. In the beginning of Book Fifteen Zeus wakes up; he sees Hektor dazed and vomiting blood, and Zeus immediately springs into action. He sends Apollo to heal and strengthen Hektor. He sends Iris, the goddess who takes messages for Zeus, to tell Poseidon to back off and stop helping the Greeks. Zeus also scolds Hera; he is extremely angry at Hera for tricking him, seducing him, putting him to sleep, and he threatens her with violence if she interferes in such a way again. He reminds her that once, in time long past, when she had interfered with his desires, he had hung her by her ankles from Mount Olympus, tied a chain to her and hung her by her ankles as a punishment, and he threatens her with violence if she interferes again. So, when Zeus wakes up, this is when Hektor is restored to his strength; this is when the Trojans regain dominance in the battle.

As I said, Zeus sends Apollo to heal Hektor. Apollo doesn't only heal Hektor; Apollo leads Hektor and the Trojans back into battle. In the scene in which the Trojans knock down the Greek wall, we're told that Apollo is running in front of them, spreading panic among the Greeks by looking at them; when he stares into the eyes of a particular Greek, that Greek is overwhelmed with dread and terror and panic. And the most vivid detail of all—as I said when I was doing the human narrative here, the Trojans manage, in their massed ranks, to break down the wall around the breach that Hektor has made in the gate; but what is going on there at the divine level, Homer tells us, is that Apollo kicks the wall down, and Homer describes the way Apollo kicks the wall in an extremely vivid little simile. I haven't said any thing yet about the use of similes in the Homeric epics, and yet they are one of the most characteristic elements of Homer's style. One thing is compared to something else. Hektor rushes into battle after Apollo strengthens him, like a horse rushing out of his stall when he has been fed with grain, a stallion rushing toward the mares; that indicates Hektor's eagerness. Here, Apollo kicks down the Greek wall, like a little boy who has built a sand castle on a beach kicks the sand castle down. An extremely vivid image for how easy it is for Apollo to overturn this wall—he kicks it like a child kicks down a sand castle. And the Trojans pour through the breach in the wall.

So, the narrative in these five books, in Books Eleven through Fifteen, includes an exceptionally intricate usage of double-level action, of this divine motivation and human motivation, of the action explained both on the human level and the on the divine level; and of course, just to reiterate, the characters themselves by and large see only the human level motivation. We are privileged to see both. This intricate double motivation works even to the level of minute details. For instance, remember when I said that Odysseus was wounded; he was stabbed in the ribs with a spear, but it did not go through to his vitals, it did not pierce any important organ. What Homer actually says is that Athena did not let the spear-point to go through to Odysseus' vitals. So the separation that I have done here, into human narrative and divine narrative, is actually doing a little bit of violence to Homer's text; the two are intricately interwoven as Homer tells us the story. We see the gods, we see the humans interacting at the same time; and yet when you analyze it, you can see that the humans themselves usually have no idea what is going on, on the divine level.

This double-level action leads to the crucial turning point of the *Iliad*. We are reaching the point in the narrative now where Achilles' beloved friend, Patroklos, will go into battle dressed in Achilles armor, and will fight on behalf of the Greeks in Achilles' place, so to speak. This section that I have been talking about in this lecture leads up inevitably to Patroklos' entry into battle, and the inevitability of Patroklos' entry into battle is stressed by Zeus describing what is going to happen in the rest of the *Iliad*, when Zeus wakes up in Book Fifteen. After he sent Apollo and Iris to help Hektor and to tell Poseidon to stop helping the Greeks, after he scolded Hera, Zeus prophesied what will happen next in the battle. He says that Patroklos will go into battle; Hektor will kill Patroklos and Achilles will return to battle; Hektor will die at Achilles' hands. So the culmination of this double-level narrative is that Zeus describes what will happen from here on out and this, I think, stresses our sense of the inevitability of the action as it moves inexorably on its way. The next thing that must happen is Patroklos must go into battle, and must die at the hands of Hektor; and in the next lecture we'll look at Books Sixteen and Seventeen, in which Patroklos does indeed do just that, go into battle in Achilles' place and die at the hands of Hektor.

Lecture Nine

The Death of Patroklos

Scope:

In this lecture we focus on Books XVI–XVII, the crucial turning point of the *Iliad*. The events of this book lead to Achilles' return to battle, his killing of Hektor, and the eventual resolution in the *Iliad*'s final book. The lecture begins by discussing Patroklos' character and his role as Achilles' substitute in battle. We then examine Patroklos' *aristeia* and death, noting how the death of Zeus' son Sarpedon at Patroklos' hands prefigures Hektor's later death and, outside the narrative framework of the *Iliad*, the death of Achilles himself. We also consider how the scene in which Hektor kills Patroklos highlights both these characters' human ignorance, as opposed to Achilles' foreknowledge of his fate. The lecture concludes with an interpretation of the scene in which Zeus pities the immortal horses of Achilles as they weep for the dead Patroklos.

Outline

I. Books XVI and XVII, which feature Patroklos' *aristeia*, his death, and the fight over his body, are the crucial turning point of the *Iliad*, since the loss of Patroklos will cause Achilles' return to battle.

II. Patroklos is Achilles' dearest friend and, in some sense, his alter-ego. The bard gives us several glimpses of him before Book XVI, in which he becomes crucial to the unfolding of the narrative.

- **A.** In Book I, Patroklos delivers Briseis to Agamemnon's heralds.
- **B.** In Book IX, Patroklos is present with Achilles when the embassy comes to try to persuade him back to battle.
- **C.** In Book XI, Achilles sends Patroklos to find out from Nestor who has been wounded in the fighting. During their conversation, Nestor suggests that Patroklos should go into battle wearing Achilles' armor.
- **D.** At the end of Book XI, as Patroklos is on his way back to Achilles, he stops to tend to a wounded Greek warrior, a fitting example for his epithet "gentle" or "kind Patroklos."

III. Patroklos is thus established as an important companion to Achilles and one worthy to serve as Achilles' surrogate. In Book XVI, he takes on this role by going into battle wearing Achilles' armor.

A. At the beginning of the book, Patroklos tells Achilles that Diomedes, Odysseus, and Agamemnon are all wounded, and asks to wear Achilles' armor into battle himself.

B. Achilles reiterates his intention to keep out of the fighting until it reaches his own ships. He agrees to let Patroklos borrow his armor and chariot, but warns him just to drive the Trojans back from the Greek camp and not to try to go all the way to the walls of Troy.

C. As they are speaking, the Trojans fire the first of the Greek ships. Achilles urges Patroklos to hasten into the fight; he also urges the Myrmidons to fight bravely.

D. Achilles prays to Zeus to let Patroklos fight gloriously and return safely. The bard comments that "the father granted him one prayer, but denied the other."

IV. Patroklos' *aristeia* includes the killing of many Trojans, most importantly Zeus' son Sarpedon. Sarpedon's death prefigures the deaths of Patroklos, Hektor, and even Achilles by setting up three themes that will recur in those later deaths.

A. The dead man's armor is stripped from his body.

B. There is a fierce fight for possession of the corpse.

C. The gods intervene to protect the body from destruction or corruption.

V. Ignoring Achilles' advice, Patroklos rushes on to the wall of Troy, and tries to mount it. Finally, he is slain by Hektor, with the aid of Apollo.

A. With his dying words, Patroklos prophesies that Achilles will avenge him.

B. Hektor does not accept the prophecy, even though in ancient Greek culture, dying prophecies were usually respected as being true.

C. Hektor and Patroklos are both essentially human, able to misinterpret, forget, or overlook predictions about their future fates.

VI. In Book XVII, the Greeks and Trojans fight fiercely over Patroklos' body. Hektor strips the armor from the body and puts it on.

A. Zeus observes that Hektor overlooks the possibility of his own death, but says that he will invest Hektor with great strength, to compensate him for the fact that he will be killed by Achilles.

B. Achilles' immortal horses weep for Patroklos, and Zeus pities them.

1. These horses stress once again the preeminence of death for what it means to be human, since they themselves are immortal.
2. Zeus' words to them are one of the *Iliad*'s starkest statements about the human condition.

C. A messenger is sent to tell Achilles of Patroklos' death. This sets the stage for Achilles' return to battle.

Essential Reading:

Iliad, Books XVI–XVII.

Supplementary Reading:

Mark W. Edwards, *Poet of the Iliad*, Chapter 27.

Oliver Taplin, *Homeric Soundings*, Chapter 7, Sections 7.1–7.2, pp. 179–192.

Questions to Consider:

1. At lines 686–691, the poet comments that if Patroklos had only listened to Achilles and not tried to scale the wall of Troy, he would have escaped death. How does this fit in with the idea that all these events are fated, that Patroklos must die so that Achilles will be moved to fight Hektor?
2. Book XVII shows Zeus pitying Sarpedon, Hektor, and Achilles' horses. What purpose do you think is served by this? Why do we see Zeus feeling more pity here than elsewhere in the *Iliad*?

Lecture Nine—Transcript
The Death of Patroklos

Hello, and welcome back to Lecture Nine. In our previous lecture we analyzed the dual level of narrative, divine and human, in *Iliad* Books Eleven through Fifteen, and saw how, through this dual motivation of the narrative, the poet stresses the inevitability and inexorability of the courses of events. In this lecture we are going to look at the crucial turning point of the *Iliad*, Books Sixteen through Seventeen, in which Patroklos goes into battle wearing the armor of Achilles. We'll examine Patroklos' *aristeia* and death, see how the death of Zeus' son Sarpedon at Patroklos' hands prefigures Hektor's later death in battle; and we'll also consider how the scene in which Hektor kills Patroklos highlights both of these characters' human ignorance as opposed to Achilles' foreknowledge of his fate. This lecture will conclude with an interpretation of the famous scene in which Zeus pities the immortal horses of Achilles as they weep for the dead Patroklos.

Books Sixteen and Seventeen of the *Iliad*, which feature Patroklos' special scene of valor, his *aristeia*, and his death and culminate with the fight over his body, are the crucial turning point of the *Iliad*, since the loss of Patroklos will motivate Achilles' return to battle. It is Patroklos' death, not any recompense from Agamemnon, that finally returns Achilles to his mode of being a fighter, a warrior, and leads to his killing of Hektor and the end of the *Iliad*. Patroklos is Achilles' dearest friend, and in some sense his alter ego. We have been introduced to Patroklos several times earlier in the *Iliad*, though I haven't mentioned him before now. The bard gives us several glimpses of him in the sections of the *Iliad* leading up to this segment, which focuses on Patroklos. In Book One, we see Patroklos deliver Briseis to Agamemnon's heralds, so when Achilles has to hand his concubine, Briseis, over to Agamemnon, Patroklos is the trusted friend whom he chooses to perform this very unwelcome task for him. In Book Nine, when the embassy of Phoinix, Odysseus, and Aias comes to plead with Achilles to return to battle, Patroklos is there. Patroklos serves the three emissaries dinner and is there listening to Achilles as Achilles plays his lyre and sings what is, in effect, an epic song. In Book Eleven, Achilles sends Patroklos to ask Nestor who has been wounded in the fighting.

So, in the segment of the *Iliad* that I discussed in the last lecture, there is a scene in which Achilles speaks to Patroklos and says, "Go ask Nestor who it is that has been wounded, what is going on in the battle. It sounds like the Trojans are getting very close; what is happening?" Patroklos goes out to get news for Achilles in Book Eleven. At the end of Book Eleven, Patroklos is on his way back to camp to tell Achilles who has been wounded, how the battle is going, what the situation is, when he stops to help a wounded Greek warrior. He stops to tend to a wounded friend. Now, that gives us a glimpse into Patroklos' character; he is compassionate, he is kind, he is helpful to others, and in fact, his most common epithet in the *Iliad* is "gentle" or "kind" Patroklos. It is stressed over and over again how gentle Patroklos is. We see this in his reintroduction in Book Sixteen, when he comes in to ask Achilles either to return to battle himself, or to lend his armor to Patroklos so that Patroklos can go into battle in his stead. Patroklos comes in weeping with grief over the wounds that he has seen his friends among the Greek army suffer. In fact, the description of Patroklos in Book Sixteen that Achilles gives contains a rather surprising simile. Achilles asks Patroklos why he is weeping like a little girl who tugs at her mother's gown, and asks to be picked up, and follows her mother around crying until her mother lifts her up and soothes her. Not exactly the kind of description you would expect to find attached to a warrior, and yet one that very vividly stresses this gentle, compassionate, kindly side of Patroklos' nature.

As I said already, Patroklos is sent, all the way back in Book Eleven, to ask Nestor what has happened in the battle. He only reappears and is described as weeping like a little girl in Book Sixteen. Thus, his journey to ask Nestor who has been wounded, to get news for Achilles, to ask what is happening very neatly frames the whole battle section that I talked about in the last lecture. And this is a point that I always like to bring out, because I think it is such an excellent example of the suburb narrative control our bard has over our material. He is able to put Patroklos on hold, so to speak, in Book Eleven, tending to a wounded warrior, then pick him again in Book Sixteen, remembering exactly what Patroklos was doing, where he was, what was going on. This is also a means to remind us, the audience, that though four or five hours of narrative time have passed in this description of the longest day of fighting the day in which Hektor has glory, in terms of real time, lived time, battle time, only a very short space of time has passed. It takes many, many more hours to describe the give and take of the battle then it would take for it actually to happen. So Patroklos, in Book Eleven, is seen tending a wounded warrior; in Book Sixteen he comes back in and says to Achilles, "I have just been tending this wounded warrior, and now I am here to tell you what Nestor said to me." It is a superb example of how completely in control of his material—as complicated as it is—our bard always remains.

So Patroklos has been established—by the time he goes into battle in Book Sixteen, he's been established as an important companion to Achilles, someone who is Achilles' trusted and beloved friend. He's also been established as someone worthy to serve as, in a sense, Achilles' surrogate, and this is what the does in Book Sixteen. When he goes into battle wearing Achilles' armor, he is in some sense standing in for Achilles himself. Patroklos starts by asking Achilles to return to battle himself. He calls Achilles "pitiless," he tells Achilles how badly the Greeks need him, and he asks Achilles to go into battle himself. But, he says, if Achilles will not return to battle, if Achilles will not be motivated by the fact that Diomedes, Odysseus, and Agamemnon are all wounded, that Achilles is needed very badly, then Patroklos says, "At least let me go into battle wearing your armor, in the hope that the Trojans will think I am you, and that will terrify them momentarily and give us some advantage in the battle." Obviously, this implies that a Greek warrior's—or, for that matter, a Trojan warrior's—armor is distinctive. Achilles' armor is recognizable as Achilles' armor. If Patroklos goes into battle wearing Achilles' breastplate, Achilles' helmet, carrying Achilles' shield, it would be very reasonable for the Trojans to think that Achilles had returned to battle.

So Patroklos is hoping for some psychological advantage here, for some space of time, at least, when the Trojans think that Achilles has actually returned. Now, Achilles reiterates his intention to stay out of the fighting until it reaches his own ships, which of course is any moment now. The Trojans are at the gate, literally; the ships are about to be set on fire; however, Achilles says he is not going to go back into the battle until the fires reach his own ships. Interestingly enough, he tells Patroklos at this point that he had not intended to be angry forever. He reiterates very briefly what Agamemnon has done to him, how Agamemnon has dishonored him; he says Agamemnon had treated him as thought he was an honorless vagabond, a vagabond with no *timê*. But, Achilles says, "Let's let all that be; it was not my intention to be angry forever." An odd thing for Achilles to say at this point, particularly since he then reiterates, "But I said I wouldn't go back into fighting until the battle reached my own ships, and I am not going to." It is almost as though, at this point, Achilles' motivation for staying out of the battle is simply not wanting to go back on his sworn word that he would not fight till the battle reached his own ships. He does agree to let Patroklos borrow his armor; however, Achilles warns Patroklos only to drive the Trojans back from the Greek camp and not to try pursue them all the way to Troy. Achilles reminds Patroklos that Apollo is very much on the Trojans side, that Apollo is very definitely fighting for the Trojans, and he says he is concerned that is Patroklos tries to pursue the Trojans, if he turns the Trojans, makes them flee, and then tries to pursue the battle all the way back to the wall of Troy, he, Patroklos, will suffer for it.

As they are speaking, at the exact instant that Achilles and Patroklos are carrying on this conversation, the Trojans drive Aias the Greater—Aias the Greater has to fall back from protecting the ships, and the poet tells us that it is the will of Zeus that forces him back and the Trojans that force him back. So that double motivation that I have talked about so much is encapsulated right there, in the instant when Aias the Greater has to give up his defense of the ships; he is forced back by the will of Zeus and by the Trojans. At this instant, when Aias the Greater falls back, the Trojans set fire to the first of the Greeks' ships. So that instant in which Achilles said he would return to battle is upon him—the ships are being set on fire even as Achilles and Patroklos speak—and yet Achilles does not, at this moment, say, "Wait a minute, Patroklos, stop putting on my armor; give it back to me, I am going into battle myself." Rather, he tells Patroklos, "Hurry up, finish putting on my armor, go into battle in my stead," and he says that he will encourage their own people—the Myrmidons, their own soldiers—to fight.

So Patroklos arms, puts on Achilles' armor, dresses himself as Achilles. He also takes Achilles' chariot, rides the chariot of Achilles into battle. Achilles' chariot is drawn by three horses—two of them immortal, one of them mortal. The two immortal horses were given by Zeus to Achilles' father Peleus, and once again, in some way, mark Achilles out as an unusual, a special, hero, because he has these horses who themselves are deathless. We'll come back to these horses at the end of this lecture. As Achilles sends Patroklos into battle he prays to Zeus to let Patroklos fight gloriously and return safely, and the bard comments that "the Father heard and granted one prayer, but denied the other." Patroklos will indeed fight gloriously and bravely, but he will not return safely. He will be killed by Hektor instead. So, Patroklos goes into battle wearing Achilles' armor, driving Achilles' chariot, and most of Book Sixteen is taken up with Patroklos' *aristeia*, with his special scene of valor. This scene includes the killing of many Trojans; Patroklos fights very gloriously indeed. The most important death that he inflicts is the death of Zeus' son, Sarpedon.

As I mentioned in the last lecture, Zeus, with his foreknowledge of what is going to happen on the battlefield, considers rescuing his son Sarpedon from his fate, but is deterred by Hera from doing so. Zeus weeps tears of blood for Sarpedon but lets him die nevertheless. Sarpedon's death is important, in narrative terms, not only because of the implicit comment it gives us on the workings of fate and whether or not Zeus can control fate; it is also important because it prefigures the death of Patroklos, the death of Hektor, and even, outside the narrative of the *Iliad* itself, the death of Achilles. Sarpedon's death prefigures these three other deaths in three very important ways. In each of these slayings, the death of Sarpedon, the death of Hektor, the death of Patroklos, outside the *Iliad* the death of Achilles, the dead man's armor is stripped from his body immediately after he is killed. There follows a fierce fight between Greeks and Trojans for possession of the dead man's corpse, and the gods intervene in some way to protect the body from destruction or corruption. In the case of Sarpedon, Zeus, as I mentioned in the last lecture, sends the twin gods sleep and death to pick Sarpedon's body up off the battlefield and carry it back to his own homeland of Lykia, where he can be buried at home. So, Sarpedon's armor is stripped from his body, a very fierce battle ensues over his corpse, finally the gods intervene to protect his corpse; we'll see this same pattern, stripping of armor, battle over the body, gods protecting the corpse, in the death of Patroklos and in the death of Hektor.

Ignoring Achilles' advice, Patroklos rushes on to the wall of Troy and tries to climb it. He is not content just to push the Trojans back from the ships; rather, he follows them. Going directly against what Achilles advised, he follows the Trojans to the wall of Troy, and tries three times to scale the wall, is pushed back three times; he can't manage to scale the wall. Finally, Patroklos is slain by Hektor with the aid of Apollo. With his dying words, Patroklos prophesies to Hektor that Achilles will avenge him. Patroklos is dying, and he points out to Hektor that Hektor had not even actually managed to kill him by himself in a fair fight. Patroklos points out to Hektor that he got the assistance, first, of Apollo and, secondly, of another Trojan warrior named Euphorbos. Apollo came into the battle against Patroklos, and stood behind him, and hit Patroklos in the back between the shoulderblades with his hand. This stuns Patroklos, and then Apollo knocks Patroklos' helmet off his head and leaves Patroklos defenseless, helmetless, breaks his corselet, breaks his armor, so that it falls away from Patroklos' body. While Patroklos is thus dazed and helpless, and with his armor literally falling from his body, a Trojan named Euphorbos comes up behind Patroklos and hits him between the shoulderblades with a spear.

So Hektor actually gives Patroklos the *coup de grâce*; he actually kills Patroklos, with a stab of a sword through the lower belly, but when Patroklos speaks to Hektor and points out that Hektor did not kill him alone, he is certainly not exaggerating. This is what Patroklos says to Hektor; he is talking about what will be the aftermath of his death, and he says,

> Deadly destiny, with the son of Leto [that of course is Apollo], has killed me,
> and of men it was Euphorbos; you are only my third slayer.
> And put away in your heart this other thing that I tell you.
> You yourself are not one who shall live long, but now already
> death and powerful destiny are standing beside you,
> to go down under the hands of Aiakos' great son, Achilles.

So, in his moment of death, Patroklos prophesies what will happen to Hektor. Now there is a fairly common idea in Greek literature, that someone who is about to die is gifted with prophecy and is able to speak true prophecies of the future. Socrates plays on this, in Plato's *Apology of Socrates*, near the very end of it, when he says to his judges who have condemned him to death, "I take the privilege of someone who is about to die, to prophesy to you; because since I am about to die, I now have the gift of prophecy," and he says, "You are going to basically regret executing me; this is going to cause a lot of trouble for you." So, here, Patroklos is not just any average warrior saying, "I think this what is going to happen"; he is prophesying to Hektor, and as someone who is at the point of death, his prophecy should be given a certain amount of respect.

And yet Hektor does not accept the prophecy. Hektor responds to Patroklos as follows; he says,

> Patroklos, what is this prophecy of my headlong destruction?
> Who knows if even Achilleus, son of lovely-haired Thetis,
> might before this be struck by my spear, and his own life
>   perish?

So, once again, as we talked about in the discussion of Book Six, when Hektor speaks to Andromache and says in one breath, "I know that Troy is going to fall," and in the next breath says, "I hope that our baby son will grow up to be a greater warrior than I am and to rule over our people," Hektor is completely and essentially human; he does not accept prophecy even when perhaps he ought to. He doesn't understand that Patroklos is speaking the literal truth here; instead, Hektor interprets this as a "maybe yes, maybe no" sort of prophecy. Patroklos hopes that Hektor will die, Hektor thinks, but Patroklos doesn't know that Hektor will die. This all adds to the sense, I believe, of irony and of doom that we see gathering around Hektor. We know—because we have been told by the bard, we have been told by Zeus within the *Iliad*, and we have been told by our own knowledge of the Trojan War story—we, as the audience, know that what Patroklos says is literal truth; Hektor will be killed by Achilles. But Hektor does not share our knowledge.

In Book Seventeen, the Greeks and Trojans fight fiercely over Patroklos' body. Hektor takes the body, takes the armor from the body—that is, the bits of armor that haven't already been knocked off by Apollo Hektor takes from the body—and puts it on himself. This is an act that shows, of course, his superiority over the dead Patroklos; it is a kind of flaunting, a kind of vaunting of what he has just done—"I can take the armor of Achilles himself, and wear it into battle myself." And yet, at the same time, Hektor by putting on Achilles' armor in some sense almost puts on his own death, metaphorically. There seems to be a sense that wearing the armor of Achilles in the *Iliad* equals dying. Patroklos puts on Achilles' armor, goes into battle, and dies. Hektor puts on Achilles' armor, goes into battle, and, we know, dies. This idea that wearing Achilles' armor equates to death is stressed by no one less than Zeus himself. Zeus, in Book Seventeen, looking down over the field of battle, sees Hektor putting on Achilles' armor and Zeus speaks directly to Hektor—though of course Hektor does not hear him. Zeus says the following words:

> Poor wretch!
> There is no thought of death in your mind now, and yet death stands
> close beside you as you put on the immortal armour
> of a surpassing man. There are others who tremble before him.
> Now you have killed this man's dear friend, who was strong and gentle,
> and taken the armor as you should not have done, from his shoulders
> and head. Still for the present I will invest you with great strength
> to make up for it that you will not come home out of the fighting,
> nor Andromache take from your hands the glorious arms of Achilleus.

So, Zeus seems to perceive Hektor's putting on of Achilles' armor as, in a sense, enacting or prefiguring or sealing Hektor's death. "Death stands close beside you; you have put on the arms of a man that you should not have put on"; and Zeus says he will once again instill strength into Hektor, once again give Hektor some *kleos*, some glory, to make up for the fact that Hektor is not going to survive, now that he has put on Achilles' armor and now that Achilles is going to come to avenge Patroklos' death.

There is one other extraordinary scene in Book Seventeen, which in some ways reiterates the same themes that Zeus has just here articulated, when he speaks to Hektor as Hektor puts on the armor he stripped from Patroklos. This second extraordinary scene that I am referring to is the scene in which Achilles' immortal horses weep for the dead Patroklos, and Zeus looking at the horses, pities them, speaks to them, and says words that, at least in their beginning, are rather similar to what he says to Hektor. You remember, as I mentioned a few moments ago, Achilles has these two immortal horses who pull his chariot, and Patroklos drove these immortal horses into battle when he went to fight and, he hoped, gain great glory; he did not know that he was going to be killed by Hektor. The immortal horses are standing and weeping for Patroklos, and they are described in really rather beautiful detail. They are standing the way horses carved on a grave monument would stand—and if you have ever seen pictures of a Greek grave monument you can imagine this; they are standing with their heads down, their manes are drooping down towards the dust, and because these horse are themselves rather anthropomorphized, they are weeping, they are weeping great tears for Patroklos, and their tears are falling into the dust.

Zeus looks at the horses and he pities them, just as a few minutes previously he had pitied Hektor. And he speaks to the horses—this is Zeus talking to the immortal horses of Achilles—the exact same words he used to address Hektor a few moments ago:

> Poor wretches,
> why then did we ever give you to the lord Peleus,
> a mortal man, and you yourselves are immortal and ageless?
> Only so that among unhappy men you also might be grieved?
> Since among all creatures that breathe on earth and crawl on it
> there is not anywhere a thing more dismal than man is.

Now these words of Zeus' are, I think, one of the starkest comments on the human condition, on what it means to be human, on the implications of mortality, that we get in the *Iliad*. And I would like to take a little bit of time to explore what is going on here, how these immortal horses work as a narrative element in the *Iliad*. What does Zeus mean when he says that there is nothing more dismal, nothing more wretched, nothing more grief-stricken than man, than human beings? Why does he say this when he is talking to a pair of animals? Specifically, why does he say this when he is talking to a pair of immortal animals?

Consider, in the Homeric world scheme as we have seen it, that there are three different kind of living sentient entities—there are gods, there are humans, and there are animals—and then consider how death figures into that picture. Gods are immortal and ageless forever, as we know, and as we have talked about a good bit. Gods know about death, certainly; they are cognizant of the reality of death for humans and for animals; but gods themselves are immune to death. They do not die. Animals, who are normally considered as being below humans, die, certainly; and yet I think we can safely assume that Homer assumed that animals do not normally know that they are going to die. So while animals, like humans, are caught by death, have no escape from the reality of death, animals do not have an awareness of that. Humans are the only living creatures who both must die and know that they must die; and so this, I think, is what Zeus is stressing here. There is a sense in which humans are more wretched even then animals, because we not only have to face death, both for ourselves and, perhaps more importantly, for those we love, but we know that we have to face death.

These horses are the perfect entities to bring that point out, because they are such a strange hybrid. They are representative of the ways in which gods and animals differ from humans, by combining the two characteristics; they are themselves animals, they are horses, and yet they are immortal. They are deathless, ageless horses. So by creating them, by talking about them, Homer throws into stark relief what it means to be human—to be more sentient than an animal, to be gifted with speech, understanding, a certain degree of foreknowledge; and yet, at the same time, to have to die. And this, I think, is what Zeus means when he says that these horses are in a sense better than humans. "Why did we give you to the lord Peleus, when you yourselves are immortal and ageless? Why did we give you to a mortal owner, when you are immortal?" From Zeus' point of view, from a god's point of view, the horses are better than humans; from Zeus' point of view, the fact that humans die and know they must die is an emblem of our wretchedness, of our dismalness, of our unhappiness.

But of course, again, from the human point of view, what Zeus does not seem to see, but what we see, is that, again, the very fact that we die and we know we are going to die is what allows us the possibility of nobility, of courage, of self-sacrifice, of all of those human virtues that we prize the highest. So Zeus' description of the human condition is valid from one side; perhaps from the human's own view it is not so valid however. Yes, in one sense we are even more wretched than the animals that crawl upon the earth, because we know we are going to die; but in another sense, it is that very knowledge of death that allows us to be noble and to be courageous, to be self-sacrificing, to be all those things that we like to think are the better part of being human.

So, as Book Seventeen ends—after Zeus' words of pity to the immortal horses of Achilles—as Book Seventeen ends, the fighting continues over Patroklos' body, and finally a messenger is sent to tell Achilles of Patroklos' death, something that I have always thought has got to be one of the most unenviable tasks ever set to anyone in literature. Can you imagine being the person picked out to go and tell Achilles, "Well, by the way, Patroklos was killed while he was fighting in your armor?" Not an enviable task at all.

So in this lecture we have seen how Patroklos' going into battle in Achilles' stead sets into action the events that will lead to Achilles' eventual return into battle. In the next lecture, we will look at Achilles' return to battle, and discuss how the death of Patroklos changes him, so that he is not longer motivated by a desire for regaining his lost *timê*. Rather, from Book Eighteen of the *Iliad* onward, Achilles is motivated by a desire for revenge against the killer of Patroklos; and that is the point at which we will take it up in the next lecture.

Lecture Ten

Achilles Returns to Battle

Scope:

This lecture discusses Achilles' reaction to Patroklos' death, and his re-entry into battle. The lecture begins by noting how Patroklos' death changes Achilles; no longer withdrawn from battle, he is fixated on vengeance. The lecture describes Achilles' informal return to battle in the scene that ends Hektor's day of glory and his later formal return after he receives the armor made for him by Hephaistos; we then turn to examining the dual treatment of Achilles in this section of the *Iliad*. He is described in vocabulary and imagery appropriate to a dead person, and thus is in some way treated as though he were already dead; but at the same time, Achilles is surrounded with fire imagery and with descriptions of battle prowess that are more appropriate to a god than to a human. The lecture concludes by suggesting that this dual portrait of Achilles stresses his refusal to accept Patroklos' death and, in a larger sense, to accept mortality itself.

Outline

I. Patroklos' death is the crucial turning point of the *Iliad*; the events of Books XVI–XVII change the focus of the narrative, and change Achilles.

   A. From now on, Achilles is no longer withdrawn because of rage over his lost *timê*. His anger at Agamemnon is no longer the motivating force of the narrative.

   B. Rather, he is raging in battle over his lost friend. His desire for revenge, his pursuit of Hektor, and its aftermath motivate the rest of the *Iliad*.

II. Achilles' reaction to Patroklos' death is twofold: he is overwhelmed with grief, and utterly determined on vengeance against Hektor.

   A. Thetis comes to mourn with him, and reminds him that he will die soon after Hektor. Achilles accepts this, thus finally choosing which fate to follow.

   B. Thetis leaves to visit Hephaistos, who will make new armor for Achilles. Book XVIII ends with a description of the armor, particularly of the great Shield, on which Hephaistos pictures the entire cosmos, and two cities, one at war and one at peace.

III. Achilles returns to battle, first informally and then after formal reconciliation with Agamemnon.

A. Iris comes with a message from Hera, telling Achilles to show himself to the Trojans, so that his comrades can rescue Patroklos' body.

1. Achilles has no armor, but Athena wraps a cloud around his head and crowns him with flame.

2. He stands by the Greeks' ditch and shouts, and Athena shouts with him.

3. The Trojans panic.

4. The *Iliad*'s longest day ends here, as the sun sets behind Achilles.

B. This scene has had a particular resonance in later literature. One example is Patrick Shaw-Stewart's untitled poem, written during his leave from Gallipoli in 1915.

C. After Thetis returns with the armor made by Hephaistos, Achilles and Agamemnon formally reconcile their differences. Achilles then returns to battle carrying the shield made by Hephaistos.

IV. From Book XVIII through Book XXII, Achilles is portrayed as essentially inhuman, in two respects.

A. Achilles is portrayed as though he were already dead.

1. Patroklos' death symbolically almost seems to equal Achilles' death.

2. The imagery and vocabulary used to describe Achilles as he mourns is typically used to describe dead heroes.

3. Thetis' actions and words are indicative of a woman mourning a dead male, in this case the still-living Achilles.

B. Achilles is portrayed as though he had the powers of a force of nature, or a god.

1. He is described over and over again with fire imagery, to an extent that seems almost to equate him to fire, a force of nature.

2. From the time he returns to battle through Hektor's death, no other mortal kills anyone; Achilles seems to take over the operations of death itself.
3. He kills entirely without pity, even when he ought to show mercy (e.g., when he kills Lykaon, the young son of Priam).
4. The only entity that can stop his excessive killing is a god, the river Skamander (or Xanthos).
5. He goes into battle carrying a representation of the entire world on his shield.

C. Thus throughout this section of the *Iliad*, the two halves of Achilles' nature—his divine side, inherited from his mother, and his mortal side, inherited from his father—are highlighted and the opposition between them is stressed.

V. This sub- and super-human Achilles rejects the human condition.

A. Death itself is put on hold, as Achilles cannot reconcile himself to Patroklos' death. He will not hold a funeral for Patroklos.

B. Life is put on hold as well; Achilles will not eat, sleep, wash, or have sex.

C. In Book XIX, one of Achilles' horses, Xanthos, speaks and prophesies Achilles' death.

1. This horse, an animal who will not die, is in some ways anomalous just as Achilles is, a human who knows too much about death.
2. Their conversation thus stresses Achilles' division from normal humanity.

D. Achilles' reintegration into humanity will depend on his encounter with Hektor.

Essential Reading:

Iliad, Books XVIII–XXI.

Supplementary Reading:

Mark W. Edwards, *Poet of the Iliad*, Chapter 28.

Jonathan Shay, *Achilles in Vietnam*, Chapters 3–5. (Warning: These chapters, especially Chapter 5, contain unexpurgated transcripts of veterans' conversations with Dr. Shay. The language contains a great deal of profanity, and the descriptions of violence are very graphic. Some students may therefore prefer to omit this selection.)

Oliver Taplin, *Homeric Soundings*, Chapter 7, Section 7.3, pp. 193–202.

Questions to Consider:

1. What is the significance of the scenes that appear on Achilles' shield? Are they connected to the wider themes of the *Iliad*?
2. After the stress throughout so much of the *Iliad* on Achilles' anger at Agamemnon and his refusal to accept Agamemnon's gifts, do you find his sudden change of heart in Book XIX believable? Why or why not?

Lecture Ten—Transcript
Achilles Returns to Battle

Hello, and welcome back to Lecture Ten. In our last lecture we talked about Patroklos' *aristeia* and death and how they paved the way for Achilles' return to battle, and thus are the crucial turning point of the *Iliad*. This lecture will consider Achilles' reaction to Patroklos' death, and his re-entry into battle. We'll begin by noticing how Patroklos' death changes Achilles, so that he is no longer withdrawn from battle but now fixated on vengeance. The lecture will then move on to discussing Achilles' informal return to battle before he has armor provided for him by his mother, Thetis. We'll then look at his formal return to battle, after he receives his new armor. Next we return to examining the dual treatment of Achilles in this section of the *Iliad*; we discuss how Achilles is treated as both sub- and super- human. And finally, the lecture will suggest that this dual portrayal of Achilles stresses his refusal to accept Patroklos' death, and in a larger sense his refusal to accept mortality itself.

As I have already said, Patroklos' death is the crucial turning point of the *Iliad*. The events of Books Sixteen and Seventeen change the focus of the narrative, change Achilles, and motivate everything that happens from this point of the *Iliad* on. After Antilochos brings the very unwelcome news to Achilles that Patroklos is dead, Achilles is no longer withdrawn from battle, no longer interested in regaining his lost *timê*, or motivated by rage over the loss of that *timê* in the first place. His anger at Agamemnon is set aside and is no longer in any way the motivating force of the narrative. From this point on, rather, Achilles is raging in battle over his lost friend. His actions for the rest of the *Iliad* are motivated by his desire for revenge for Patroklos' death, his desire to kill Hektor and thereby avenge his friend. This desire, Achilles' pursuit of Hektor, his killing of Hektor, and its aftermath are the motivating forces of the rest of the *Iliad*.

Achilles' reaction to the death of his friend, Patroklos is twofold. First, and understandably, Achilles is overwhelmed with grief; secondly, he is utterly determined, utterly fixated to take vengeance against Hektor. When Achilles first learns of the death of Patroklos, he calls out again to his mother Thetis and she comes to mourn with him. She comes out of the sea accompanied by many other sea goddesses, joins Achilles, and grieves with him; ostensibly over Patroklos, although it seems in many ways is though Thetis is grieving as much for Achilles himself as she is for his dead friend. Thetis reminds Achilles that he will die soon after Patroklos; that it is fated that, if he goes into battle and kills Hektor in vengeance for Patroklos, his own death will follow soon after the death of Hektor. Achilles says that he realizes this, and he accepts it completely. So this is the moment at which Achilles finally really makes his choice between those two possible fates that Thetis had delineated to him so long ago in the *Iliad*. He chooses death, if death is the price of avenging Patroklos.

After the scene in which Thetis and Achilles discuss his forthcoming death and mourn together, Thetis leaves to visit the god Hephaistos, the blacksmith god, who will make new armor for Achilles. Achilles' original armor, of course, is now in the possession of Hektor; this is the armor that Patroklos wore into battle, that Hektor stripped from Patroklos' dead body. Achilles is therefore, at this point, without armor and thus unable to re-enter battle fully, even though he now desires nothing more than to re-enter battle. So Thetis, at the end of Book Eighteen, goes to speak to the blacksmith, god Hephaistos and get a new set of armor made for her son Achilles. We will return to this set of armor that Hephaistos makes for Achilles later in the lecture. For right now, I will just note that the centerpiece of Achilles' armor, and the most significant element of his armor, is a great shield on which Hephaistos pictures, really, the entire cosmos; this shield has constellations on it, the sun, the moon, the river Okeanos—which in the Homeric worldview is an ever-flowing river that flows around the edges of the disk of the world; the world is a flat disk surrounded by an ever-flowing river. All of this is on the shield, as are two depictions of two cities, a city at war and a city at peace, and many other scenes of human culture and human civilization—dancing, sheepfolds, herds of cattle, and so forth. So, Hephaistos depicts on Achilles' shield, really, a representation of the entire known world, and as I said, we will return to that shield near the end of the lecture.

Achilles returns to battle not only after he has been given his new armor, but also he returns informally before his armor is given to him, when he is waiting for Thetis to bring the armor back from Hephaistos. At this point in the narrative, shortly after Achilles has heard of Patroklos' death, Iris comes, the messenger goddess comes, with a message for Achilles from Hera, in which she tells Achilles simply to show himself to the Trojans; just to stand where the

Trojans can see him, so that the Trojans will be terrified and the Greeks can recover Patroklos' body. If you remember, throughout Book Seventeen, the battle has been raging over the body of Patroklos. The Greeks are defending it; Menelaos in particular is defending Patroklos' body very valiantly. The Trojans are trying to drag it away and keep it, and so Hera tells Achilles, through the messenger Iris, to go and show himself to the Trojans and enable his comrades to rescue Patroklos' body. Achilles points out, very reasonably, that he has no armor; he says, "How can I go into the battle, how can I expose myself, how can I show myself to the Trojans when I have no armor?" Iris tells him simply to do so, simply to go and stand by the ditch, by the ditch the Greeks had dug in front of their famous wall, the wall that has been so thoroughly breached by the Trojans.

As Achilles moves out to the ditch, Athena wraps a cloud around his head and crowns him with flame. So Achilles appears to the Trojans, standing by the Greek ditch with flame encircling his head; he shouts aloud and Athena shouts with him and the poet tells us that at this shout, the shout of Athena and Achilles together, the Trojans panic and scatter. The horses panic; the men panic; they run in different directions, and the Greeks are able to recover Patroklos' body at this moment. Also at this moment, the sun sets behind Achilles. So the sun goes down behind the flame-capped Achilles; you can imagine him silhouetted against the sky, with sunset and flame both playing around his head, and this is the end of the *Iliad*'s longest day, the end of Hektor's promised day of glory.

Now this image of the flame-crowned Achilles standing by the ditch and shouting and scattering his enemies has had a particular resonance in later literature; it is one of the most memorable scenes, one of the most visually compelling scenes, in the *Iliad* and many, many later authors have picked up on it. I always like at this point, when I am teaching the *Iliad* to undergraduates, to talk about one particular poet who used this scene in the *Iliad* to remarkable effect, a British poet who wrote during World War I, named Patrick Shaw-Stewart. Shaw-Stewart was, like many hapless British soldiers, stationed at Gallipoli in 1915. Gallipoli, of course, is on the Chersonese peninsula, just across from the historical site of Troy. And the fighting there in World War One was devastating for the British; the Turks practically wiped out the British expeditionary force at Gallipoli. Patrick Shaw-Stewart was on leave for three days from the battle of Gallipoli. He was on an island called Imbros, just a few miles away from Gallipoli, but a completely peaceful island. While he was there he wrote a poem that I am going to recite to you at this point, because it shows so beautifully how the *Iliad* has continued to be a living presence in European literature, up until this century. So this is Patrick Shaw-Stewart's untitled poem:

> I saw a man this morning
> Who did not wish to die;
> I ask, and cannot answer,
> If otherwise wish I.
>
> Fair broke the day this morning
> Upon the Dardanelles:
> The breeze blew soft, the morn's cheeks
> Were cold as cold sea-shells.
>
> But other shells are waiting
> Across the Aegean Sea,
> Shrapnel and high explosives,
> Shells and hells for me.
>
> Oh hell of ships and cities,
> Hell of men like me,
> Fatal second Helen,
> Why must I follow thee?
>
> Achilles came to Troyland
> And I to Chersonese;
> He turned from wrath to battle,
> And I from three days' peace.
>
> Was it so hard, Achilles,
> So very hard to die?
> Thou knowest and I know not;
> So much the happier am I.
>
> I will go back this morning
> From Imbros o'er the sea;
> Stand in the trench, Achilles,
> Flame-capped, and shout for me.

"Stand in the trench, Achilles"—picking up on the imagery of the Greeks' ditch and the actual trenches of World War One, bringing them together. As I said in the first lecture, the *Iliad* has survived because it has continued to speak to modern readers and modern writers, and I think Shaw-Stewart's poem is one of the most beautiful examples of that that I know. By the way, he was, of course, killed; he did not survive World War One.

After Thetis returns at the beginning of Book Nineteen with the armor made by Hephaistos, Achilles is able to return formally to battle; and before he does that he and Agamemnon finally reconcile their differences. But there is a real sense of anti-climax here; this hardly matters any more. Agamemnon says to Achilles, "I will give you the gifts that I offered you in the embassy," and Achilles says, "Agamemnon, keep the gifts; give them to me; I don't care." At this point, Achilles is no longer in any way concerned with his *timê*. He says that gifts do not matter to him now; what his heart is set on now is blood and slaughter. Achilles also says that he will not eat or drink until after he has wreaked great vengeance on the Trojans. Agamemnon tries to persuade him to eat something before he goes into battle; Agamemnon takes a very practical view—you can't fight on an empty stomach—and tries to persuade Achilles to eat. Achilles is so focused on vengeance that not only is he no longer interested in *timê*, he is not even interested in the every-day, human acts of eating and drinking and preparing himself for battle.

He does return to battle, carrying the shield made by Hephaistos, and from this point on, from his learning of Patroklos' death in Book Eighteen on through Achilles' killing of Hektor in Book Twenty-Two, Achilles is portrayed as essentially inhuman, in two very different ways. He is portrayed as sub-human and as super-human; he is portrayed as being in a sense already dead, and as being almost a god. Let me explain each of those, in some more detail. First of all, Achilles is portrayed—particularly in Book Eighteen, but really throughout this section—as though he were in some sense already dead. Another way of putting that is that Patroklos' death seems symbolically almost to equal Achilles' death; Achilles in some sense died with Patroklos. And I am not speaking purely symbolically or metaphorically here; Homer brings this point home very vividly by the language and the imagery he uses to describe Achilles. When Achilles hears that Patroklos has been killed, we are told that Achilles collapses on the ground, he lies stretched in the dust weeping for his friend. Now the Greek verb that is used there when Homer says that Achilles lies stretched in the dust is a verb that elsewhere is used only of the dead bodies of warriors who have fallen in battle, when they lie stretched on the ground. So this is the only time in the *Iliad* when this particular Greek verb is used of a living person.

More than that, as I already mentioned, Thetis and various of her companion sea goddesses come to help Achilles mourn over Patroklos. Thetis stands behind Achilles as he is lying stretched in the dirt, takes his head in her hands, and laments over him. Now, this gesture of a woman standing behind a male who is lying stretched on the ground, of a woman standing behind him and putting her hands on his head—that is a standard iconic gesture of mourning in Greek literature and Greek art. If you see a carving of a woman standing behind a man, the man lying down, the woman with her hands on his head, he is dead and she is mourning for him. It is a standard gesture that indicates mourning; not grieving with someone over someone else's death, but mourning for a dead person. So we are shown Thetis, here, grieving over the dead Achilles—even though Achilles is still alive, and even though supposedly they're both grieving over Patroklos. In fact, Book Eighteen, some scholars think, probably picks up a lot of the language and descriptions of one of the lost epics that I have mentioned in the earlier lectures, in which the funeral of Achilles himself was described—some of the descriptions of Thetis' mourning, some of the things that she cries out in her anguish when she speaks to Achilles. She refers to herself in one long wonderful Greek word, *dusaristotokeia*, which means "unhappy in the best of childbearing." She refers to herself as someone unhappy in the best of childbearing because her son is doomed to die so young. Clearly, Thetis seems to be grieving for Achilles himself and not for Patroklos, and doing so in a way that almost indicates that Achilles is already dead.

Interestingly enough, we see another example of a grieving woman in these books that stress Achilles' re-entry into battle. In Book Nineteen, after Patroklos' body has been recovered, after Achilles has shown himself at the ditch and Patroklos' body has been recovered, there is a scene in which Briseis speaks, for the only time in the *Iliad*, and mourns over Patroklos. She is standing behind him with her hands on his head, just as Thetis stood behind Achilles. Briseis laments for Patroklos' death, says that he was always very kind to her. Now Briseis is Achilles' concubine; you would expect to see her mourning the death of Achilles, not the death of Patroklos. Once again, it is almost as though an element of mourning for

Achilles, an element for the funeral of Achilles, has been displaced into the *Iliad*, onto mourning for Patroklos.

As well as being treated in an imagery and vocabulary that almost indicate he is already dead, Achilles is also portrayed, on the other hand, as super-human, as though he had the powers of a force of nature or of a god. Over and over again, once he returns into battle, over and over again in this great long scene of his *aristeia*, he is described with fire imagery, to an extent that almost seems to equate him to fire or to a force of nature. Most obviously, of course, is the scene I have already talked about, in which Athena crowns him with flame, and he stands by the ditch, and the sun sets behind him; clearly there is a lot of fire in that image. But elsewhere, and throughout the description of his return to battle, we're told that his armor blazes like fire; that he comes down against the Trojans like fire coming down a hillside; that he blazes like fire; that his eyes glitter like fire. Now all of these phrases have been used elsewhere in the *Iliad* to describe other warriors in their *aristeia*, other warriors in the heat of battle, but the sheer weight of repetition in Books Eighteen through Twenty-Two hammers home the idea that here Achilles is somehow almost embodying fire, acting as though he actually were fire.

Furthermore, from the time Achilles returns to battle in Book Nineteen, after arming himself in armor made by Hephaistos the blacksmith god, the god who uses fire—Hephaistos is himself almost a god of fire, and therefore Achilles has been armed by fire—after returning into battle armed by the god of fire, until the point of which he kills Hektor, no-one but Achilles kills anyone; or at least, no other mortal but Achilles kills anyone. In this whole long section of the *Iliad*, Book Nineteen through Book Twenty-Two, Achilles is the only mortal who inflicts death on anyone else. In a way, you can almost say that Achilles seems to take over the operations of death, that Achilles seems to become the force of death in the *Iliad* in this section. He kills entirely without pity; he kills when he should not kill; even when he ought to show mercy he kills inappropriately.

There are a couple of examples of that that I want to mention. First off, Achilles promises Patroklos' dead body—in Book Nineteen, he makes a promise to Patroklos' dead body—that he will sacrifice twelve Trojan youths on Patroklos' funeral pyre. Now, human sacrifice was not a normal activity in the society depicted by the

Homeric epics, and is considered beyond the pale, outside the bounds of reasonable behavior, something that ought not to be done. So when Achilles says to the dead body of Patroklos in Book Nineteen, "I will sacrifice twelve picked Trojan youths for you," he is doing something, he is promising something that is inappropriate, that is beyond the proper bounds of human behavior—and he does follow through on this promise In Book Twenty-Three, in fact, he does sacrifice twelve Trojan youths on Patroklos' funeral pyre.

This is not the only way in which he kills excessively or inappropriately. In Book Twenty-One, Achilles has an encounter with a young son of Priam, a young man named Lykaon, who is represented as being really an adolescent, just a teenager. Now, Lykaon had met Achilles in battle once before and had been taken prisoner by Achilles, who then allowed Priam to buy the boy back for ransom. This was a fairly standard activity; we get the impression from the *Iliad* that you would take a prisoner in battle, and then the prisoner's comrades or, in the case of Lykaon, the prisoner's family would pay ransom to get him back. And this, of course, is a way of getting more booty, more *time*, for yourself, and that is what, normally, a warrior in the *Iliad* is fighting for in the first place. So Lykaon and Achilles have met before, and Lykaon was taken prisoner, and Achilles took ransom to return him to his father.

When they meet again in Book Twenty-One, Lykaon supplicates Achilles; he goes on his knees in front of Achilles, and he asks him to have mercy. Now, the act of supplication, the act of being a suppliant to an enemy on the battlefield, is very important in the *Iliad*; we'll see it come up a couple of times in the *Odyssey* as well. And there is a standardized from of supplication. You take one arm and put it around the knees of the person you are supplicating; with your other hand you reach up and usually grab their chin or their beard. Lykaon grabs Achilles' spear, but it works out to the same thing. You put one arm around their knees; with the other hand you reach up and grab their chin or their beard and you beg them for mercy. Now this accomplishes several things; first off, if I am on my knees—imagine I am supplicating a giant here—if I am on my knees, and I have one arm around my enemy's own knees and one hand holding onto his beard, clearly I have no concealed weapon. My hands are both accounted for; I am not about to stab this man surreptitiously when he isn't expecting it. Secondly, it really focuses his attention—imagine now some one is doing this to me—I can't walk; I can't get away; if I am a man with a beard, so I am told, I also can't even look up without causing myself pain. So it focuses the attention on the suppliant. Finally—now I am supplicating the giant again—look at my throat. It makes me utterly vulnerable; my throat is completely open to my enemy's weapon, so it is almost a kind of stylized submission behavior: "I am completely at your mercy; have mercy on me."

This is what Lykaon does in Book Twenty-One, when he approaches Achilles and begs him for mercy, and reminds Achilles that Priam will pay ransom for him, for Lykaon. Listen to Achilles' answer. Achilles says, first off, that in the old days when Patroklos was alive, yes, he would take ransom. Then, he was interested in such things, but now, he says, there is no way he would take ransom for anyone; he has no interest in that. And he continues:

> So, friend, you die also. Why all this clamour about it?
> Patroklos also is dead, who was better by far than you are.
> Do you not see what a man I am, how huge, how splendid
> and born of a great father, and the mother who bore me immortal?
> Yet even I have also my death and my strong destiny,
> and there shall be a dawn or an afternoon or a noontime
> when some man in the fighting will take the life from me also
> either with a spearcast or an arrow flown from the bowstring.

And with those words he stabs Lykaon in the throat and kills him.

So Achilles in this section of the *Iliad* is impervious to pleas of mercy, is impervious to this extremely powerful form of supplication, which he ought to pay heed to. Furthermore, when he kills Lykaon he throws the young boy's body into the River Skamander, the river of Troy, Skamander or Xanthos—it is called both. He throws the body into the river, and it is not the first body he has thrown into the river. Achilles has killed a lot of people in this section of the *Iliad* and he's thrown most of them into the river. This rouses the anger of the river god against Achilles. Rivers have particular gods, rivers are personified as gods; so are streams, lakes, ponds, so forth. This particular god, the god of the river Skamander, is furious at Achilles because Achilles is choking the river by throwing bodies into it. The river rises up against Achilles, and very significantly, the river Skamander is the only entity in this whole section of the *Iliad* that almost stops Achilles, the only entity that can put an end to his killing spree and can almost overpower him. Think again of what I said about Achilles as an embodiment of fire; it is water, a river in full spate, and a river in flood that comes closest to stopping Achilles. And how is Achilles rescued from the river? Hera sends Hephaistos—again, the god of fire—who uses fire to force the river back, to force the river to let Achilles escape. So this whole segment shows Achilles almost as a force of nature, almost as fire, and that is reiterated by Achilles' encounter with a river god as the only entity that can oppose him. This encounter with the river god also reiterates again Achilles' almost god-like status here. No mortal can oppose him; he cuts his way through mortals like someone reaping grain. It takes a god to cause any hesitation or any fear in Achilles whatsoever.

Finally, in the representation of Achilles as in some sense more than human. Achilles goes into battle carrying a representation of the entire world on his shield. I have already mentioned that representation on this shield. Think of this again, visually; Achilles goes into battle carrying before him, on his shield-arm, a representation of the entire world; and most significantly, within that representation of the entire world the focus is on human culture; human society; what it means to be human; a city at war, a city at peace. Within the city at peace there is a judge giving judgments, there is a picture of a dancing floor, there is agriculture, sheepfolds, cattle herds. Achilles goes into battle carrying before him a representation of humanity—and yet it is precisely humanity and the human condition that, at this point, he is still rejecting throughout this whole section of the *Iliad*.

One way of looking at what is going on is that the two halves of Achilles' nature—his divine side which he draws from his mother and his human side, his mortal side, which he draws from his father—are highlighted, but are highlighted in opposition. In this section of his story, Achilles is in no way a complete or integrated or unified character. He is an already dead mortal, on the one hand; and remember, as I said in an earlier lecture, the term *thnêtoi*, which means mortals, really almost means "dead ones" rather than "dying ones." So on the one hand, Achilles is portrayed as being almost already dead; on the other hand he is portrayed as being super-human. What he is not portrayed as here is being a normal, reasonable, every-day human being, who is able to feel grief for

Patroklos, experience it, and then let it go. And I think the key point here is that this sub- and super-human Achilles, this Achilles who is both less than and more than human, rejects the human condition as strongly as he possibly can.

Death itself is put on hold by Achilles in this section of the *Iliad*, when he refuses to bury Patroklos. He refuses to hold a funeral for Patroklos; he quite literally refuses to accept Patroklos' death. He simply says "no" when confronted with the fact that Patroklos is dead. He will not bury him, and he will not hold a funeral for him. Just as Zeus removed the body of Sarpedon from harm's way by having Sleep and Death take him off to Lykia, so the gods intervene here; Thetis instills ambrosia and nectar, the food and drink of the gods, into Patroklos' nostrils to keep his body from decaying and so, in a very real sense, death is put on hold. Patroklos is in a kind of stasis, a kind of suspended existence, when he is no longer alive but he is not yet been given a funeral and is not yet therefore truly a member of the dead.

Life is put on hold as well. Achilles will not sleep; he will not eat; he will not wash; he will not have sex; and he will not, in any way, act like a normal living human being. His mother Thetis asks him to do all of these things, asks him, in effect, to re-engage with life—to sleep with Briseis now that Agamemnon has given her back to him; to eat; to drink; to do all the things that normal human beings do. Achilles will not. Life is on hold; and at the end of Book Nineteen one of Achilles' horses, the horse Xanthos, is given a human voice by Hera and speaks aloud to his master, Achilles. Achilles has blamed the horses for not protecting Patroklos as they carried him into battle, and Achilles says he hopes they will do a better job of protecting him. Xanthos is given speech, speaks aloud to Achilles, and says:

> We shall still keep you safe for this time, o hard Achilleus.
> And yet the day of your death is near, but it is not we
> who are to blame but a great god and powerful Destiny.

Xanthos goes on to say that they did not fail in protecting Patroklos but it was his fate to be killed; and then Xanthos finishes his speech by saying, "still for you / there is destiny to be killed in force by a god and a mortal."

So we see, once again, this anomalous creature, a horse that is immortal, a horse that is cannot die, here gifted with human speech and speaking to Achilles, who is in some ways as anomalous as this horse. Achilles is a human who, because of the viewpoint given him by his mother, knows too much about death and refuses to accept the reality of death. Xanthos is a horse that will never die. Xanthos speaks to Achilles about Achilles' own death; their conversation, I think, stresses just how far removed Achilles is, at this point, from normal humanity. And the reintegration of Achilles into humanity, his return to some sort of acceptance of the human condition, of what it means to be human, will depend on his encounter with Hektor; and it is to a comparison of Hektor and Achilles that we will turn in the next lecture.

Lecture Eleven

Achilles and Hektor

Scope:

In this lecture, we examine the characters of Achilles and Hektor. The lecture addresses both the bard's characterization of the two men and their interactions with one another. The *Iliad* presents Achilles and Hektor as polar opposites to one another in several key ways; the lecture identifies several of these contrasts, and discusses how they underscore Hektor's place in his community and Achilles' essential isolation. We then analyze the scene in which Achilles kills Hektor, and consider how this conflict of opposites is crucial for the final resolution of the *Iliad*.

Outline

I. Achilles and Hektor, the most important characters in the *Iliad*, are in many ways polar opposites of one another.

- **A.** Hektor is a fully realized human, connected with his family and his community. Many readers find him the most sympathetic and accessible character in the *Iliad*.
- **B.** Achilles is inhumanly isolated, cut off from family, friends, and community.

II. The poem stresses this opposition in their characters through several key contrasts: their family situations, their knowledge of and attitude toward the future, and their motivations for fighting.

- **A.** Their family situations are contrasted.
  1. Hektor's human parents are present, watching the battle. Achilles' human father is far away; his goddess mother appears when he calls her, but is not regularly there.
  2. Hektor's mother is aged and pitiable; Achilles' mother is eternally young and immortal.
  3. We see Hektor interact with his wife and child; Achilles is unmarried, and his son Neoptolemos is not present.
- **B.** There is an opposition in their knowledge of the future, and in their attitude toward death.
  1. Hektor is humanly fallible; he often misunderstands or disregards prophecies. Throughout the *Iliad*, he continues to hope for life.

2. Achilles' special knowledge of his two possible fates marks him out as different from most humans. After Patroklos' death, he knowingly chooses death for himself.

C. There is an opposition in their motivations for fighting.

1. Hektor would prefer not to fight, but recognizes that he must, to defend his city and people. Thus, he subordinates his individual desires to the good of his society.
2. Achilles first refuses to fight, and then desires only revenge for Patroklos. Thus, he overvalues one individual.

III. Hektor accepts the implications of the human condition, however great the cost to himself may be. Achilles rejects the implications of the human condition by refusing to be reconciled to Patroklos' death.

IV. Hektor's humanity and Achilles' inhumanity are highlighted in Book XXII, when they fight and Hektor is killed.

A. Hektor considers retreating; is overwhelmed by fear; runs from Achilles; feels as though he were caught in a nightmare. Achilles is described as looking like the "lord of battles."

B. Achilles' pursuit of Hektor takes them by the springs where Trojan women used to wash clothes, thus giving us a glimpse of Trojan society at peace.

C. When Hektor stops running, he proposes to Achilles that each promise to return the other's body to his people. Achilles refuses.

D. After he is wounded, Hektor begs Achilles not to defile his body. Achilles responds brutally, still showing himself to be in the "sub-human" mode.

E. As Achilles defiles Hektor's body, Priam and Hekabe watch from the walls, and Andromache faints at the sight. This defilement is even more serious because it prevents Hektor's *psyche* from entering the Underworld.

V. The conflict of these two contrasting characters is crucial for the resolution of the *Iliad*, since only through killing and defiling Hektor does Achilles find a way eventually to reintegrate himself into humanity. The importance of their encounter is highlighted by Zeus' weighing their two fates in a scale.

Essential Reading:

Iliad, Book XXII.

Supplementary Reading:

Mark W. Edwards, *Poet of the Iliad*, Chapter 29.

Seth L. Schein, *Mortal Hero*, Chapter 6. Gives an excellent, detailed analysis of the Achilles/Hektor contrast.

Oliver Taplin, *Homeric Soundings*, Chapter. 8.

Questions to Consider:

1. Compare the characters of Thetis and Hekabe. How do their similarities and their differences enhance the contrast between their two sons?
2. Compare Achilles' words to the dying Hektor with Hektor's words to the dying Patroklos in Book XVI. What do these two speeches tell us about the speakers?

Lecture Eleven—Transcript
Achilles and Hektor

Hello, and welcome back to Lecture Eleven. In our last lecture we discussed Achilles' return to battle, his desire for vengeance for the death of Patroklos, and his dual status as simultaneously both less and more than human. In this lecture, we are going to turn to a comparison of the characters of Achilles and Hektor, and discuss how these two characters are contrasted with one another, and how the contrast between them is crucial for the final resolution of the *Iliad* and our final understanding, particularly of Achilles' character.

I think most readers of the *Iliad* will have noticed that the two characters of Achilles and Hektor, as well as being the most important characters in the epic and the most frequently mentioned characters in the epic, are also, in many ways, polar opposites of one another. Hektor is a fully-realized human being; in his community, living with his family. We see him in every form of social human connection that is possible for us to see him in. We see him as a prince leading his people; as a commander in the battlefield leading his warriors; we see him as a son; as a brother, and an older brother of a particularly troublesome younger brother; as a husband; as a father—we see him in just about every possible human relationship. And many readers find Hektor the most sympathetic and accessible character in the *Iliad*, the character who seems most immediately recognizable as in many ways like us. Achilles, in contrast, is inhumanly isolated in the *Iliad*; first through his own choice, when he withdraws from his community of warriors, retreats to his tent, refuses to take part in the fighting. He isolates himself, but he is isolated in a deeper sense as well. He has no contact with his family, in the normal human sense, the way Hektor has contact with family. Achilles' father, of course, is absent; his mother is nearby, but a goddess. He is not part of a normal human family as Hektor is, and this serves to stress Achilles' essential isolation.

Now one point of explanation here; modern Americans have a certain tendency to admire and valorize what we tend to call rugged individualism—the idea of someone who goes his own way, who walks his own path, who isolates himself to some extent from the normal run of humanity. We tend to see a kind of rugged grandeur in that; or at least, one strain of our popular cultural mythology sees a kind of rugged grandeur in that. In the context of Homeric culture, and in ancient Greek civilization, there would be nothing admirable at all about someone isolated the way Achilles is isolated. This would seem strange, bizarre, and in a very real sense inhuman. Human beings are defined in Homeric society by their position in a community—by whose father they are, whose son they are, where they fit in a community, what role they play in a community. A human being without community is, in a very real sense, not a human being at all, in Homeric epic and in Greek civilization in general. So Achilles' isolation is not to be seen as somehow indicating his grand status as a truly great hero. Quite the opposite; it makes him odd, it makes him anomalous, it makes him, once again as we talked about in the last lecture, less than human.

The opposition between Achilles and Hektor is stressed throughout the *Iliad*, through several key contrasts in these two characters—their family situations, their knowledge of and attitude toward the future, and their motivations for fighting. The family situations are probably the most obvious contrasts between the two characters. As I have already touched on, Hektor's parents are present. Hektor's parents are human, to begin with, but they are physically present at Troy, watching the battle; they watch from the walls as Hektor's body is dragged around Troy behind Achilles' chariot after Hektor's death; Hektor's parents are right there.

Achilles' human father, while still alive, is far away and utterly inaccessible to Achilles. His goddess mother appears when he calls her, and yet the very fact that Thetis is a goddess gives a kind of separation between her and her son. She cannot empathize with him the way a human mother can empathize with a human son, because Thetis' experience is, by definition, different from human experience, since she is a goddess. Hektor's mother is aged and pitiable, and appears in the standard role in which you would expect an elderly mother worried over the death of favorite—or at least her most important—son would appear. For instance, when Priam and Hekabe beg Hektor not to go into battle, right before he is killed by Achilles, Hekabe actually bares her aged breasts, shows them to Hektor, and reminds him that she nursed him when he was an infant; reminds him, in effect, that she has grown old carrying for him and his brothers; uses this as an appeal for pity from her son, that he will not go off and be killed and leave her vulnerable to the destruction of the Greeks.

Achilles' mother, of course, is the opposite in many extremely significant ways. Because she is a goddess she is forever young, she is forever ageless, she is forever untouched by the sorrows and the effects of time. She is, of course, shown as grieving over Achilles, and yet the grieving of an immortal, ageless, invulnerable goddess is a very different thing from the grieving of an aged human mother who is about to see her son, her hope for the future, killed. Thetis, to some extent, knows that Achilles' life is going to be only a very short episode out of her life, no matter how long he lives; she will go on forever. Hekabe, as a human mother, has a very different view about her son's and grandson's possible deaths.

We see Hektor interact with his wife and child, as I have talked about before; we see him in Book Six of the *Iliad*, with Andromache and Astyanax. We see him as a loving husband and a loving father. Achilles, in contrast, is unmarried; he has his concubine, Briseis, of course, although she is taken away from him for most of the *Iliad*, but he is unmarried; and although he has a son named Neoptolemos, in the *Iliad* Achilles' son is not present. In other epics of the epic cycle that dealt with the Trojan War. Achilles' son Neoptolemos did take part in the fighting of the Trojan War—and there is a certain chronological problem here, how Achilles could have a son old enough to fight at the Trojan War, but that is beside the point for right now. The point in the *Iliad* is that, although Achilles has a son, that son is not present. So, again, we see Hektor surrounded by family: father, mother, brother, sisters, brothers-in-law and sisters-in-law, wife, child. We see Achilles in complete isolation, except for the occasional visits of his goddess mother, Thetis.

There is also an opposition between these two heroes in their knowledge of the future and their attitude towards death, both their own and others. Hektor, as I have talked about so often by this time, is humanly fallible. Very frequently in the *Iliad* we see Hektor misunderstanding or disregarding prophecies, misreading omens, not understanding, when Patroklos prophesies his death, that Patroklos is in fact speaking a prophecy. Throughout the *Iliad*, really up until the very last moment of his life, Hektor continues to hope for life. So Hektor is very human, both in his fallibility—that is, his ability to misinterpret omens, to misunderstand prophecies, and he is very human in his blindness to fate. He does not know what his fate is, as we have talked about before, and he is very human in his continued hoping that he will somehow survive, and he will somehow live.

Achilles' special knowledge of his two fates, of course, as we have already covered, marks him out as different from most other human beings. Unlike Hektor who is able to misinterpret prophecies, to misunderstand what the prophecies of the future mean, Achilles doesn't even need prophecies of the future. When his speaking horse, Xanthos, for instance, prophesies Achilles' death to him, as I mentioned at the end of the previous lecture, Achilles says, in effect, "But I know that already; why are you telling me about it?" So quite the opposite of Hektor, who misunderstands, does not accept prophecies, and does not know what his fate will bring, Achilles knows only too well. And of course, after Patroklos' death, Achilles knowingly chooses death for himself when he chooses which of his two fates to follow.

There is also an opposition between these two heroes in their basic motivations for fighting in the first place. Hektor—thinking once again back to Book Six of the *Iliad*—Hektor would prefer not to fight if he did not have to. He would prefer not to fight at all; he would prefer—I think it is quite clear that he would prefer to stay at home with his wife and his child, and simply live a life of peace in a flourishing Troy that had never gone to war. But Hektor accepts that if he must fight to defend his city and people, then he must fight; he accepts that. He admits that this is part of his responsibility as crown prince of Troy. So, although I think that Homer makes it quite clear that Hektor would prefer for the Trojan War never to have happened, that he would prefer to be able to continue his life with his wife and child, nevertheless, as a good prince, as a good leader, he is able to subordinate his individual desires to the good of his people and fight even at the risk of his own life, even at his almost certain death, when he comes face to face with Achilles, because that is what is required of him by his position in his community. So Hektor can subordinate what he himself might wish to the good of his community, and the good of his society.

Achilles, once again, is pretty much a polar opposite. First, he refuses to fight at all, when he has lost his *timê* because of Agamemnon's taking away Briseis. Then, when Achilles returns to the fighting, he does so not because of Patroklos' appeal, telling him that the Greeks need him; not even because the fire has reached the Greeks' ships which is the moment at which Achilles said he would return to battle; he returns to battle to get revenge for Patroklos. Thus, Achilles overvalues one individual, overvalues the significance of love for one individual, as compared to the greater good of his community, where Hektor is able to subordinate his individual desires to the greater good of his community. So this opposition between the two characters works on a great many levels: in their attitudes towards their families; in their knowledge of the future; in their foreknowledge, or lack thereof, of their own deaths; in their motivations for fighting—in just about every way, Hektor and Achilles are contrasted to one another, or set against one another, and need to be read in conjunction with one another to understand both of their characters.

Part of what is going on here, I think, is that Hektor accepts the overall implications of the human condition—to use that phrase that I have used so frequently—of what it means to be human, even when the cost to him is very great. He accepts the realities of life as a human being, in this world as we have it. Achilles rejects the implications of the human condition, by refusing to be reconciled to Patroklos' death; by refusing to accept the reality of Patroklos' death; by refusing to accept that death in battle is one of the hazards of sending your friends into battle. Achilles gave Patroklos his armor, sent him into battle—yes, he told him "don't fight on to the wall of Troy; come back after you have driven the Trojans away from the ships"—but surely Achilles must have known that there was some chance that Patroklos would be killed, even in trying to drive the Trojans away from the ships. This is not an extraordinary circumstance; warriors die in battle. And yet Achilles refuses to accept it. Achilles reacts as though this is something that has never happened before. In short, Achilles refuses to accept the limitations, the implications, of being human.

Hektor's humanity and Achilles' inhumanity—or Hektor's acceptance of the human condition and Achilles lack of acceptance of the human condition—are highlighted particularly in Book Twenty-Two, when the two of them fight and Hektor is killed. As Achilles approaches and Hektor realizes a fight within him is inevitable, after the scene in which Priam and Hekabe have begged Hektor not to face Achilles, Hektor does consider retreating. There is a long scene, a soliloquy if you like, in which Hektor talks to himself and considers the possibility of retreating, of not standing and facing Achilles. However, Hektor is stopped by shame. Just as he said to Andromache in Book Six, that he would feel shame in front of the Trojans and the Trojan women if he did not go into the fighting as befits a crown prince of Troy, so when he considers retreating and not facing Achilles, he reminds himself of the shame that that would bring to him, and decides he must stand and face Achilles. However, although Hektor has decided to stand and face Achilles, when Achilles actually approaches, Hektor is overwhelmed by fear and runs always. So once again we see Hektor as so extremely, understandably human; making up his mind—"I have to face this even though I don't want to; I have got to stand and face Achilles"—but then when it actually comes to the moment, not being able to, turning tail and running.

Hektor runs from Achilles as though they are running a foot-race, the bard says, and yet they are running not for some prize but rather for the life of Hektor. Hektor feels—as he runs from Achilles, in Book Twenty-Two—he feels as though he is caught in a nightmare, another wonderful simile that the bard gives us. He says that Hektor's feelings, as he runs from Achilles, are like one of those dreadful dreams where you are trying to run but your feet can't move, and you can't get anywhere, and you can't get away from the person you are running from; this is how Hektor feels as he runs from Achilles. In contrast, Achilles—in this scene when Hektor debates whether to stand and face him, panics, runs away—Achilles is described as looking like the lord of battles; that is, looking like the god Ares himself. And once again, Achilles' armor is blazing. So Hektor is running with extraordinarily understandable human emotion; Hektor is running from someone who is portrayed as looking more than human, as looking like the god of war himself.

As Achilles pursues Hektor in Book Twenty-Two, the two of them run past the springs where the Trojan women used to wash clothes in the days of peace. This is a lovely little detail that gives us a glimpse of Trojan society at peace, as Homer says, before the sons of the Achaians came to Troy. Hektor and Achilles run four times past the washing springs, the wells where the Trojan women used to wash clothes, and this is, in effect, a way of reminding us once again what it is that the Trojans have lost. They have lost not just their lives, not just their hope for defeating the Greeks, but in effect they have lost domesticity, they have lost their family lives—they have lost their community. Think of what is symbolized, what is summed up in the little vignette of the place where Trojan wives used to come out in the days of peace and wash the laundry. It is about as plain, as banal, if you like, as domestic a detail as you can get, washing the clothes;

and yet here it stands for so much. It stands for a time when the women could come out of the city. It stands for a time when marriages could continue and children could grow up, before Paris and Helen wrecked everything through their violation of marriage. It stands for what Hektor and all the other Trojans have irrevocably lost, and it is I think an extremely gripping narrative detail that Hektor and Achilles race past these springs, where the Trojan women used to wash the clothes, as they are running around the walls of Troy, as Achilles is pursuing Hektor.

When Hektor finally stops running—when he realizes he is not going to escape Achilles, he stops and decides to stand and fight—he proposes to Achilles that each of them should promise to return the other's body to his people; that is, if Hektor kills Achilles he will give Achilles' body back to the Greeks, if Achilles kills Hektor he will give Hektor's body back to Hektor's family. This is an absolutely appropriate thing to suggest; this is what civilized warriors, what decent warriors, what honorable warriors ought to do for one another. Achilles absolutely refuses. He says, "Absolutely not; I will throw your body to the dogs, and I will not give it back to your parents." So, once again, Hektor makes an appropriate suggestion, a suggestion that the mores of human society approve of. Achilles reacts inappropriately, by saying "Absolutely not, I will not do this for you."

The two of them meet in battle, after this suggestion that Hektor makes, and Hektor is wounded by Achilles. As always, the gods are there; the action is going on with divine motivation as well as with human motivation. Apollo helps and strengthens Hektor, until an extremely vivid scene in which Zeus actually weighs the fate of Hektor and the fate of Achilles in a golden scale, and Hektor's fate goes down, meaning that he must die. I will come back to that scene at the end of the lecture. But at the instant when Zeus weighs the fates of Hektor and Achilles, Apollo abandons Hektor, stops helping him, and stops strengthening him. Meanwhile, Athena is helping Achilles to overcome Hektor. So the gods are there behind the action, the gods are motivating, as is almost always the case in the *Iliad*.

Achilles wounds Hektor and as he is wounded, as he is dying, Hektor begs Achilles not to defile his body. Achilles responds to him not just negatively, but in fact very, very brutally. When Hektor begs

Achilles, by Achilles' parents, by Achilles' own life, not to defile his body but to let Priam and Hekabe give a ransom for him, this is how Achilles responds. He says to Hektor:

> No more entreating of me, you dog, by knees or parents,
> I wish only that my spirit and fury would drive me
> to hack your meat away and eat it raw for the things that
> you have done to me. So, there is no one who can hold the dogs off
> from your head.

Now, let's think for a moment about what Achilles has just said there. Quite aside from the threat of cannibalism, which is horrifying enough in itself, he says "I would wish that I could do this to you for the things that you have done to me." What exactly has Hektor done to Achilles? Hektor has killed Patroklos, yes; but as I already said, this is normal in warfare. If you send your best friend into battle, you have, at some level, to realize that he may be killed. What has Achilles done to Hektor? Achilles has killed a large number of Hektor's brothers. If anyone should be able to say to the other in this scene, "I cannot forgive you; I wish that I could eat you raw and throw what is left of you to the dogs for what you have done to me," it would make more sense for the man who has seen many of his younger brothers killed by one individual to say that than for Achilles, who has lost one friend to Hektor, to say that. Once again, Achilles' reading of the scene, Achilles' understanding of what is going on, of what it means to be human, is skewed, is out of kilter, is not appropriate. Yes, he loved Patroklos; but Hektor has not inflicted any unusual or extraordinary or grievously heinous wound on Achilles, more than anyone else inflicts on a warrior in battle. Achilles cannot see this, however, and certainly he cannot offer any pity or any mercy to Hektor whatsoever.

And Achilles not only refuses to return Hektor's body to his parents; he does worse than that. He actively and calculatedly defiles Hektor's body. This, of course, is one of the most famous images from the *Iliad* that has permeated Western culture and Western literature ever since the *Iliad* was written—the image of Achilles fastening Hektor's body to his chariot and dragging it through the dust around the walls of Troy. When Achilles does this, he is doing more than simply defiling the body of his dead enemy. What he does would be dreadful in any culture; none of us would find it anything other than horrifying to see the body of some one we had loved treated that way. But in the culture portrayed in the *Iliad*, and in the culture portrayed in later Greek literature as well, what Achilles is doing is even worse than it might appear at first sight; because there is a strong belief in this culture, in the Homeric epics and in later Greek literature, that if a body is unburied the soul, the *psyche* of that person, cannot enter the underworld.

Now, as I mentioned earlier in this series, the underworld is a pretty gloomy place, and the life that a *psyche* lives there is certainly not appealing or attractive; and yet it is very clearly shown us, both in the *Iliad* and in other works of literature, that even worse than being a *psyche* in Hades is to be a *psyche* that was unable to get into Hades. To be a soul whose body is unburied condemns a person to a kind of everlasting Neverneverland, a kind of intermediate state where you are certainly no longer alive but you are not really one of the dead yet, because you are not in Hades. This is a terrifying and horrifying prospect.

So, by refusing to return Hektor's body for burial, Achilles is condemning Hektor to a kind of eternal limbo, a kind of existence in which Hektor is neither truly alive nor truly dead. The parallel with what Achilles is inadvertently doing to Patroklos is obvious. Achilles is refusing to bury Patroklos, because he cannot bear to let him go; and yet he is—whether he sees it this way or not—inflicting exactly the same horror on Patroklos as he inflicts intentionally on Hektor. And, in fact, Patroklos' ghost appears to Achilles in Book Twenty-Three of the *Iliad* and says, "Please give me a funeral so that I can go to Hades." But from the point of view of Hektor's family, when Priam and Hekabe look down from the walls of Troy and see their son's body being dragged behind Achilles' chariot-wheels, they are seeing not just the horror that any of us would see, of their beloved son's body being so hideously mistreated; they are also seeing the horror of their beloved son's soul being prevented from entering the underworld, unless they can get his body back.

Priam and Hekabe watch from the walls as Achilles drags Hektor's body behind his chariot; Andromache also learns of Hektor's death by seeing his body being dragged behind Achilles' chariot. Andromache is portrayed very vividly in this section of the *Iliad*. We are told that, while Hektor and Achilles were fighting, Andromache was inside the palace in her chambers, and—another one of these beautifully-drawn little details that adds so much poignancy to the narrative—Andromache has just told her maids to draw a warm bath for Hektor, to heat water so that when Hektor returns from the fighting he can have a warm bath. Then she hears the sound of mourning and lamentation outside in the city, and she is struck with fear that perhaps the mourning is for Hektor. She runs like a mad woman through the streets of Troy, looks down from the walls, and sees Hektor's body being dragged behind Achilles' chariot—at which point Andromache faints.

Now, as she faints, her headdress and veil fall from her head onto the stones of the street, as she faints dead away. There is a marvelous—I don't want to call it a pun; a "play on words," I suppose would be a better way of putting it—going on here, that is totally untranslatable into English, or I suppose into any other language; because the word that Homer uses for Andromache's headdress is *kredemna*. *Kredemna* means a woman's headdress and veil, but it also is the word that means the battlements of a city, the ramparts and battlements of a city. And when you throw down the *kredemna* of a city, that means that you have sacked the city, that the enemy has taken the city. So, when Homer says that Andromache fainted and she threw down her *kredemna*, he is using a term that brings up irresistibly, in his audience's mind, the idea of the *kredemna* of Troy, the battlements of Troy, being thrown down and destroyed at the same time. And so Andromache's faint and Andromache's loss of her headdress, loss of her *kredemna* prefigures, almost embodies, the sack of Troy which will be caused, ultimately, by the death of Hektor. As I say, this is something that cannot be gotten into a translation, but is very definitely there in the Greek.

There is one more little detail about Andromache's headdress that is very important here. The headdress and veil are the emblem of a married woman. The goddess Hera, for instance, who is the goddess of marriage, is always shown with a veil; very frequently with her hand holding her veil to draw attention to it. When a city is conquered, the women are taken into slavery; and as we have seen with Briseis and Chryseis earlier in the *Iliad*, slavery for a woman in this society means sexual slavery, means providing sexual services to her new master. One way of visually representing the violation of a woman, the violation of a woman's marriage, the taking of her into slavery, is to represent her with her veil being violently torn away from her. So, when Andromache faints and her veil falls from her head, yet another strand of imagery there is a reminder of what Hektor himself foretold in Book Six would happen to Andromache, that when Troy falls she will be taken into slavery, she will become the slave of a Greek master.

So we see all of these things encapsulated in Hektor's death, and in his family's reaction to his death. We see Achilles in no way placated in his grief for Patroklos by having killed Hektor. He is bent on vengeance; he kills Hektor; and he finds that having killed Hektor really does him no good. It hasn't appeased Achilles' desire for vengeance at all, so he moves on to violating Hektor's body. And the contrast of these two characters, the conflict and contrast of these two characters, Hektor and Achilles, will prove to be crucial for the final resolution of the *Iliad*, since it's only through this act of killing and defiling Hektor that Achilles finally, odd though it may seem, finds a way to reintegrate himself into society and to reintegrate himself into humanity. The importance of this conflict between Hektor and Achilles is highlighted by the scene I already referred to, in which—at the high point of their pursuit, of their chase around the walls of Troy, when Hektor turns to face Achilles—Zeus holds out a golden scale and puts two *moirai*, two fates, in the two pans of the scale—the fate of Hektor, the fate of Achilles—weighs them, and Hektor's fate is heavier and goes down.

Now, in closing, let me just say I think this is not meant to indicate that Zeus is in any way determining their fate. Their fate is already set, and I think it simply an extremely vivid visual representation of the fact that their fate is already set. Zeus himself holds the scale; Hektor is fated to die; the pan with Hektor's fate goes down—and at that moment, Apollo abandons Hektor, and Hektor is left to Achilles to kill. So the two characters, Hektor and Achilles, encounter one another, clash with one another, Hektor is killed, and it is through killing Hektor that Achilles will find a way back into full humanity, as we'll discuss in the next lecture.

Lecture Twelve

Enemies' Tears—Achilles and Priam

Scope:

This lecture focuses on the meeting of Achilles and Priam, and the final resolution of the *Iliad*. Even after he kills Hektor, Achilles still is unreconciled to Patroklos' death; at the request of Patroklos' ghost, Achilles gives him a funeral, but remains unconsoled and isolated from humanity. Only the visit of Priam to ransom Hektor's body can reintegrate Achilles into the human community. We look closely at the meeting between these two enemies, Achilles and Priam, and discuss the impact of their encounter for our understanding of the nature of mortality, the underlying theme of the *Iliad*.

Outline

I. After he has killed Hektor, Achilles still cannot reconcile himself to Patroklos' death.

- **A.** Patroklos' ghost appears to Achilles, and asks him to bury Patroklos' body, so that the ghost may pass into the Underworld.
- **B.** Achilles complies with the ghost's request and holds an elaborate funeral for Patroklos (Book XXIII). However, even after the funeral Achilles continues to fast, to refrain from bathing, and to drag Hektor's corpse around Patroklos' tomb.

II. Finally the gods decide to intervene.

- **A.** Apollo addresses the other gods and says that it is time to force Achilles to give Hektor's body back to his family.
- **B.** Zeus agrees. He sends Thetis to speak to Achilles, and Iris to urge Priam to visit Achilles and ransom Hektor's body.
    1. Thetis informs Achilles of Zeus' will. Achilles accepts this information with indifference.
    2. Iris takes Zeus' message to Priam. Despite Hekabe's objections, Priam decides to go.

III. Priam visits Achilles and offers ransom for Hektor's body.

- **A.** At Hekabe's urging, Priam prays to Zeus for success and safe return, and Zeus sends him a favorable omen, the sacred eagle of Zeus.

- **B.** Zeus sends Hermes to guide Priam to Achilles' tent. Hermes appears in disguise, but reveals his identity to Priam just before leaving him.
- **C.** Priam enters Achilles' tent and asks for Hektor's body back. He beseeches Achilles, in his father Peleus' name, to pity him and return Hektor's body, and kisses Achilles' hands.

IV. Achilles reacts with wonder, compassion, and grief to Priam's request, and agrees to return Hektor's body.

- **A.** The two enemies weep together, Priam for Hektor and Achilles for Patroklos.
- **B.** Achilles comforts Priam by referring to the mixed good and evil that Zeus bestows on all humans, and telling him that he too must bear adversity.
- **C.** Priam reminds Achilles of his request for Hektor's body, and Achilles tells him that he has already agreed to give Hektor back, at Zeus' command.
  - **1.** Despite the compassion Achilles feels for Priam, they are still enemies and Achilles' anger is just under the surface. He warns Priam not to make him angry.
  - **2.** Achilles orders his slave women to wash Hektor's body. He does this specifically so that Priam will not become angry when he sees the body's degradation and Achilles, in turn, become enraged and kill Priam.
- **D.** Achilles himself carries Hektor's body to Priam's wagon.

V. Through his encounter with Priam, Achilles accepts mortality, and reassumes his humanity.

- **A.** After taking Hektor's body to the wagon, Achilles tells Priam that it is time to eat.
  - **1.** Achilles cites the example of Niobe, who managed to eat even after all twelve of her children had been killed.
  - **2.** This is precisely what Thetis and others have been telling Achilles, but he has not been able to accept it.
  - **3.** Somehow seeing his enemy's grief moves Achilles to recognize that he too must accept death.
  - **4.** Part of Homer's genius is that he does not explain how this happens; he simply shows us that it does.

B. Achilles himself kills a sheep, roasts it, and serves a meal to Priam. After they eat, Achilles promises a truce of eleven days so the Trojans can give Hektor a proper funeral.

C. Achilles has a bed prepared for Priam. He himself sleeps beside Briseis; this is the last time we see Achilles in the *Iliad*. Now that he has been reintegrated into humanity, he can die (although his death is not shown in the *Iliad*).

VI. Priam returns to Troy with Hektor's body, and the *Iliad* ends with Hektor's funeral.

A. Hermes comes to Priam and urges him not to sleep in the Greeks' camp, but to go back to Troy immediately.

B. Andromache, Hekabe, and Helen each lament over Hektor's body in turn.

C. The last line of the *Iliad* is "so they buried Hektor, tamer of horses."

Essential Reading:

Iliad, Books XXIII–XXIV.

Supplementary Reading:

Mark W. Edwards, *Poet of the Iliad*, Chapter 30.

Gregory Nagy, *Greek Mythology and Poetics*, Chapter 4.

Richard Seaford, *Reciprocity and Ritual*, Chapter 5, Sections C–E (pp. 159–180).

Charles Segal, *Mutilation of the Corpse.*

Oliver Taplin, *Homeric Soundings*, Chapter 9.

Questions to Consider:

1. Is it psychologically credible that Priam's grief should move Achilles to acceptance of mortality and reintegration into humanity? Why or why not?
2. Does the final book of the *Iliad* provide a resolution for the issues raised in the earlier part of the work? What is the role of *kleos* here? Is any implicit answer ever given to the objections Achilles raises in Book IX?

Lecture Twelve—Transcript
Enemies' Tears—Achilles and Priam

Hello, and welcome to Lecture Twelve. In our last lecture we discussed the essential opposition between Hektor and Achilles, and mentioned that it is only through killing his opposite, Hektor, that Achilles finds a way to reintegrate himself into full humanity. In this last lecture on the *Iliad*, we will examine the aftermath of Hektor's killing, focusing especially on the meeting between Achilles and Priam, and the impact of their encounter for our understanding of the nature of mortality, the underlying theme of the *Iliad*.

After Achilles has killed Hektor, he still cannot reconcile himself to Patroklos' death. Killing Hektor, in fact, does no good whatsoever for Achilles. He has been motivated, from Book Eighteen on, by a burning desire for vengeance, a desire to slaughter Hektor to avenge Patroklos. But once he has slaughtered Hektor, his desire for vengeance is in no way slaked; his grief for Patroklos is in no way eased. In fact, the problem, of course, is that what Achilles wants is not really to destroy Hektor, but to have Patroklos back; and of course destroying Hektor does not address that desire at all. Patroklos is still dead; Achilles is still incapable of coming to terms with Patroklos' death, even after the death of Hektor.

Achilles moves his desire for vengeance over from killing Hektor to defiling Hektor's body, as we saw in the last lecture, and yet that brings him no ease of mind or spirit either. In Book Twenty-Three, as we move on into the last two books of the *Iliad*, Achilles is still grieving for Patroklos, still refusing to eat, still refusing to bathe, all of these things, and continuing to drag Hektor's corpse behind his chariot. Eventually, Patroklos' ghost appears to Achilles and asks him, says to him, "Please bury me so that I can go into the underworld." Patroklos' ghost itself appears and begs Achilles for a decent funeral, so that the ghost can come to rest and can pass over into Hades. Achilles complies with the ghost's request and holds an elaborate funeral for Patroklos; in fact the description of the funeral of apt encompasses most of Book Twenty-Three of the *Iliad*. Achilles holds a series of elaborate and magnificent athletic "funeral games," so-called, in honor of Patroklos; contests of chariot racing, of foot-racing, of all kinds of military prowess, all of this done to honor the dead Patroklos. And, as Achilles had promised Patroklos' dead body in Book Nineteen, he does indeed kill twelve Trojan youths on Patroklos' funeral pyre.

And yet even this, even the holding of an elaborate funeral, does not in any way ease Achilles' grief or move him towards a position of being able to accept with equanimity the death of Patroklos and the fact that Patroklos is gone. After the funeral Achilles still fasts, still will not bathe, and still drags Hektor's corpse behind his chariot; the only difference is that now he drags the corpse of Hektor around the tomb of Patroklos, rather than around the walls of Troy. Achilles is kept alive during this prolonged period of fasting, throughout this section of the *Iliad*, by the gods; specifically Athena, who instills nectar and ambrosia into Achilles' chest—directly into his chest—to keep him from dying of starvation. Once again, there is a very clear parallel between Achilles and the dead Patroklos there; just as Patroklos' body was kept from corruption, and Hektor's body also was kept from corruption by the gods anointing them with ambrosia, so Achilles is kept form dying and corruption by Athena instilling ambrosia into his chest. Also, this once again reiterates that Achilles is somehow almost, in a sense, already dead, or already treated as though he were dead; he is getting the same special treatment from the gods that the dead Patroklos and the dead Hektor are receiving.

Finally, the gods decide that they have to intervene and force Achilles to return Hektor's body to his parents. Achilles apparently is stuck at this point; he is never going to progress. Even now that he has held a funeral for Patroklos and has buried him, he still cannot overcome his own great grief, and he is still defiling and mistreating the body of Hektor. And as this continues, Apollo is the god who steps forward and speaks to the other gods, near the beginning of Book Twenty-Four, and says the gods simply must take a very active role in this situation and force Achilles to return Hektor's body to his parents. Apollo starts by reminding his fellow gods that Hektor had been a very pious and reverent man, had offered sacrifices to them, had done everything he should do, and now the gods need to recompense him for his acts of piety in his life by seeing to it that his body can be buried. And then Apollo says specifically about Achilles:

> Achilleus has destroyed pity and there is not in him
> any shame; which does much harm to men but profits them also.

For a man must some day lose one who was even closer
than this, a brother from the same womb, or a son. And yet
he weeps for him, and sorrows for him, and then it is over,
for the Destinies put in mortal men the heart of endurance.
But this man, now he has torn the heart of life from great Hektor,
ties him to his horses and drags him around his beloved companion's
tomb and nothing is gained thereby for his good or his honour.
Great as he is, let him take care not to make us angry;
for see, he does dishonour to the dumb earth in his fury.

Apollo's words are important in various respects. First of all, this is the clearest delineation we have seen of the normal approach towards human grief in the *Iliad*. A man loses someone who is very dear, a brother or a son; he sorrows for him; he grieves for him, and then it is over, Apollo says, because humans are made that way. They have a "heart of endurance," they are able to accept the loss of even the dearest individuals and continue to live themselves after it. But not Achilles; Achilles cannot accept the loss of Patroklos.

Also, Apollo's words about Achilles dishonoring the dumb earth are worth a little bit of consideration. I think it is no coincidence that it is specifically Apollo who steps forward at this point in the *Iliad* and says, "Something must be done; we must return Hektor's body to his family." And I say that not just because Apollo has—throughout the *Iliad*, from the moment when Agamemnon refused to return Chryseis to her father—Apollo has been on the side of the Trojans, but I think Apollo is the appropriate god to articulate this idea here for another reason as well. As I mentioned in my lecture on the opening of the *Iliad*, Apollo is the god of medicine and healing, but he is also the god of plague; those are two sides of the same coin. As so often in Greek theology, the same god controls these two opposites—medicine or healing; plague. And of course, one of the main reasons why, in any human culture that has ever existed, rituals and ceremonies for disposing of the dead have developed is because if you leave unburied dead bodies lying around in your city, what happens? You develop plague. Apollo, as the god of plague and of medicine, is a god who is particularly concerned with the proper disposal of dead bodies.

Now Hektor is not decaying; Hektor is not doing what dead bodies normally do, because the gods have intervened to see that he will not. And yet there is a sense in which the refusal to bury Hektor is an affront, particularly and specifically, to Apollo in his role as the god of medicine and the god of plague. Of course, people in the ancient world did not know how plague was caused; and yet, as a matter of observation, it would become clear that if you left dead bodies lying around in the city you would get a great deal of sickness; that would be interpreted as something that was displeasing to the god who controlled sickness, namely Apollo. So when Apollo says, "This is outrageous; Achilles is acting beyond all measure here," and when Apollo says "Achilles is dishonoring the dumb earth," Apollo is the appropriate god to say this.

I think the idea in dishonoring the dumb earth ties in again with the idea of the earth as the giver of life, the bearer of life. Remember that phrase that the poet uses when he describes Helen's brothers in Book Six [sic Three], when Helen says she does not see her brothers and the poet says that the *phusizoos aia*, the "life-bearing earth," covers Helen's brothers back home in Sparta. The earth is quintessentially the giver of life, and Achilles is dishonoring the earth because he is refusing to let a dead body be treated properly, be put under the earth, be returned to the earth. He is outraging the earth and, in a sense, insulting the earth by dragging a dead body on her surface—and of course the earth in Greek is a "she." So Apollo says, "We have got to intervene for all of these reasons; we have got to put a stop to this outrageous behavior on Achilles' part." Zeus agrees, and Zeus sends Thetis to speak to Achilles and tell him, "You must return Hektor's body to his parents"; and Zeus also sends Iris the messenger to urge Priam to go visit Achilles and ransom Hektor's body.

When Thetis comes to Achilles to inform him of Zeus' will, she tells him that the gods have decreed, Zeus has decreed, that Achilles must give Hektor's body back; that it is time now for Hektor to be returned to his parents. Achilles, surprisingly enough, accepts this information with almost complete indifference. Thetis has said, "Zeus will be angry at you if you do not return Hektor's body to his parents; you must return the body"—all Achilles says in response is, "So be it. He can bring the ransom"—"he" being Priam; of course; "he can bring the ransom and take off the body, / if the Olympian himself so urgently bids it." At this point, Achilles seems fairly indifferent to the fate of Hektor's body. I think he has realized, by this point, that the outraging of Hektor's body, the mistreatment of Hektor's body, is not helping him. It is doing nothing for Achilles; it is not assuaging his grief, it is not giving him that sense of vengeance that he had hoped for. So at this point, Achilles is sunk into pretty much complete indifference—"fine, let Priam take the body." But this is very, very far from being acceptance of the kind that we need to see Achilles reach before we can have a satisfactory close to the *Iliad*.

So Achilles is told "you must return Hektor's body," and accepts this news with almost complete indifference. Simultaneously, Iris goes to Priam and tells him that he is to go to Achilles' tent and ransom Hektor's body. Despite the objections of Hekabe, who is afraid that she will lose her husband as well as her son—she very understandably thinks that a man like Achilles, who would treat Hektor's body as he has treated it, is not going to respect Priam or feel any mercy towards Priam's old age—but despite Hekabe's objections, Priam decides to go. And as we move on in Book Twenty-Four, in the last book of the *Iliad*, Priam does indeed visit Achilles and offer ransom for Hektor's body. At Hekabe's urging—when Priam is determined to go, Hekabe urges him to pray to Zeus for protection and Priam does indeed do this. He prays to Zeus that he will be successful and will be granted a safe return, and Zeus sends him a favorable omen; an eagle, the sacred bird of Zeus, flies by on the right hand, which is the good omen side in Greek augury, and so Priam and Hekabe have some reason to hope for the success of Priam's mission.

Zeus does more than just send an eagle to give Priam hope that he will be successful. Zeus also sends the god Hermes, the guide and messenger god, to guide Priam to Achilles' tent. Hermes appears to Priam as Priam is driving towards the Greek camp; he has a wagon drawn by mules so that he can bring Hektor's body back. Hermes approaches the wagon disguised as a young man—as so often in the *Iliad*, a god appears to a human in disguise—but after he has led Priam to the Greek camp, Hermes identifies himself just before he leaves Priam. He tells him who he is—he tells him that he is in fact the god Hermes—and he advises Priam to approach Achilles and beseech him in the name of his own father, Peleus, to have mercy and give up Hektor's body. So as Priam enters Achilles' tent he does what Hermes has suggested; he beseeches Achilles, he kneels down before him and in his father Peleus' name, Priam beseeches Achilles to pity him and return Hektor's body.

Priam's speech to Achilles is extraordinarily moving, and culminates in some of the most memorable lines of the *Iliad*. Priam starts out by saying to Achilles that he had been a very fortunate man before the Greeks came to Troy; that he had had fifty sons, nineteen of them born of Hekabe, the others born of other mothers, and that Achilles had killed most of them but one was left, Hektor, Priam and Hekabe's one main hope—apparently at this point, Paris is negligible; Priam makes no mention of him whatsoever—but that Hektor was left, as Priam and Hekabe's one main hope, but now Achilles has killed Hektor as well. And Priam ends his great speech by saying—after calling on Peleus' name, he says,

> Honour then the gods, Achilleus, and take pity upon me
> remembering your father, yet I am still more pitiful;
> I have gone through what no other mortal on earth has gone through;
> I put my lips to the hands of the man who has killed my children.

—as he has kissed Achilles' hands as he beseeches him for Hektor's body.

Now, Achilles reacts to this extremely moving speech with wonder, compassion, and grief. He gently sits Priam down beside him, and the two of them weep together. Achilles does not speak at first; they begin, these two enemies, by weeping together. The poet tells us that Priam is weeping for Hektor and Achilles is weeping sometimes for his father, Peleus, whom he knows he will never see again, sometimes for Patroklos. After they have wept for a while, then Achilles comforts Priam, and he comforts Priam by referring to the mixture of good and evil that Zeus bestows on all human beings. So, Achilles himself, who has been unable to come to terms with his grief for Patroklos, who has been unable to accept the admixture of evil in human life, Achilles, confronted with the grief of his enemy Priam, is able to say to him that human beings must not grieve excessively, but must accept that there is a mixture of good and evil in any human life.

Speaking to Priam, Achilles begins by marveling that Priam can dare to come alone to the enemy camp. And then he says that there is no advantage to be gained from excessive lamentation; they should stop grieving, they should stop weeping. And he gives a little parable, or a little description of human life; again it is one of the most famous passages of the *Iliad.* I keep saying that, but this last book is absolutely filled with very, very memorable scenes and memorable passages. Achilles, speaking to Priam says that:

> Such is the way the gods spun life for unfortunate mortals,
> that we live in unhappiness, but the gods themselves have no sorrows.
> There are two urns that stand on the doorsill of Zeus. They are unlike
> for the gifts they bestow: an urn of evils, an urn of blessings.
> If Zeus who delights in thunder mingles these and bestows them
> on a man he shifts and moves now in evil, again in good fortune.
> But when Zeus bestows from the urn of sorrows, he makes a failure
> of man, and the evil hunger drives him. . .

Achilles then goes on to say, "And we have heard how fortunate you were before we came here; and Peleus my own father was very fortunate as a young man, but now hard old age is upon him."

So, in this speech to Priam, Achilles recognizes that human beings have two possibilities in their life, a wholly evil life or a life that is a mixture of good and evil. Only the gods get the third possibility, a life that is only good; that simply does not happen for human beings. In this description of the two urns, the two jars out of which Zeus bestows good and evil, Achilles says to Priam that "you too, Priam, must bear adversity." Very much the kinds of things that people have been saying to Achilles for several books now, but he has been unable to hear.

Sometimes when I teach this passage in classes, some of my students say that this is terribly pessimistic, this idea that the best humans can hope for is a mixture of good and evil. I have never seen it as pessimistic; I see it as realistic. Unmixed good does not happen in human life. That is simply true; maybe my undergraduates are too young to have realized that yet, but unmixed good simply does not happen. What Achilles is saying here, in a very metaphorical and poetic way, obviously, is simply a truism of human life. The best we can hope for is a mixture of good and evil. On any one else's lips, in any other context, it could sound like a truism; when Achilles says it to Priam in this context it is extremely moving and extremely significant.

After this speech in which Achilles reminds Priam that he too must bear adversity, Priam asks again for the return of Hektor's body; and Achilles tells Priam that he is already agreed, at Zeus' command, to give Hektor back. But there is a great deal of delicacy in the way they talk to one another, and a great deal of tension underlying the surface here. Despite their compassion for one another, despite the fact that they weep together at the beginning of this scene, Achilles and Priam are still enemies, and Achilles' anger is just under the surface. When Priam says in effect, "Yes, fine, that is all very well, an urn of good fortune, an urn of evil fortune; but please give me Hektor back," Achilles says, "Don't push me. I have already decided to do that but do not push me; do not make me angry." I don't want to over-sentimentalize this scene; these two men are definitely still enemies. There is a kind of marvelous compassion between enemies going on here, but Achilles realizes that he could, at the drop of a hat, become very angry at Priam, and he warns Priam not to enrage him, not to bring his anger to the surface.

Similarly, Achilles orders his own slavewomen to wash Hektor's body before he returns the body to Priam. Why? Because although the gods have been keeping Hektor's body from decay and from corruption by rubbing it with ambrosia, nevertheless Hektor is still covered with blood, with gore, with dirt. Achilles does not want Priam to see Hektor in that state, specifically because Achilles is afraid if Priam does see his son's body unwashed and uncared for, Priam will become angry, which will in turn anger Achilles, and Achilles will kill Priam. So the killing rage, the rage of these two enemies, is just barely under the surface, and is held in check by both of them intentionally holding it in check, throughout this scene.

After Hektor's body is washed, Achilles himself lifts it and carries it to Priam's wagon; he then comes back inside his tent and has another conversation with Priam in which, I think, we can see Achilles actually, finally, accepting mortality and reassuming his humanity—and with his humanity, of course, his impending death, because those two go hand-in-hand; we, as audience members, know that Achilles is the next important person to die after Hektor. When he returns from taking Hektor's body to the wagon, Achilles tells Priam that it is time to eat. Achilles who has been fasting, Achilles who has refused to eat, who has had to be sustained by ambrosia, says to Priam, "You and I must eat a meal now." And more than that, Achilles cites a paradigm from antiquity—from *his* antiquity—just as Phoinix did to him in Book Nine, talking about Meleagros, unsuccessfully citing a parallel from antiquity to try to persuade Achilles to set aside his anger. Now Achilles cites for Priam a paradigm from antiquity, an example of how humans can and must bear up under even the worst grief that can possibly come upon them. Achilles cites the example of Niobe, a woman who managed to eat, managed to continue her own life, even after all twelve of her children had been killed on a single day.

Niobe had angered Leto, the mother of Apollo and Artemis, by saying that she herself was worthy of more worship than Leto became she had twelve children and Leto had only two. Leto's two children, Apollo and Artemis, killed all of Niobe's children for her presumption in comparing herself to a goddess. But Achilles says, "Even Niobe ate; and so, Priam, you too must eat." And Achilles himself sits Priam down, and serves a meal to him. Now this is precisely what Thetis, and others, had been telling Achilles for some time now—"you must eat; other people have borne the loss of even dearer individuals than your loss of Patroklos; other people have been through even more than you have been through' you must eat." This is what other people have been saying to Achilles, but he has not been able to accept it.

Up until this point, Achilles has been in the position of any person who, when faced with overwhelming grief, at first simply reacts by saying, "No; I cannot accept that this particular person is dead." In that kind of overwhelming grief the sort of comfort that is so often offered, even today, of saying, "This happens to everyone; everyone goes through this; you have got to put up with it because everyone else does." There is a stage in grief when that can seem worse than no comfort at all; it can seem, in fact, insulting. When I think of Achilles going through this stage of grief for Patroklos, I am always reminded of some lines from Tennyson's famous poem *In Memoriam*, in which he talks about his own grief for his beloved dead friend, and Tennyson says:

> One writes, that "Other friends remain,"
> that "Loss is common to the race"—
> and common is the commonplace,

> and vacant chaff well meant for grain.
>
> That loss is common would not make
> my own less bitter, rather more:
> too common! Never morning wore
> to evening, but some heart did break.

In the very different idiom of Tennyson and of Homer, I think, this is the stage that Achilles has been in—"that loss is common would not make / my own less bitter." Achilles has been unable to hear words such as Apollo said, and that I read earlier in this lecture, about how a man loses some one even dearer than this, a brother or a son; he grieves for him, he mourns for him, and then it is over. Somehow, seeing his enemy's grief, seeing Priam's grief, gets through to Achilles, moves Achilles, motivates him to acceptance of what it means to be human, i.e. acceptance of the death—not of ourselves; that is easy in comparison—but the death of those we love. Somehow, Achilles is brought to this through seeing his enemy's grief, rather than through the words of his friends, or even the words of his own mother. And part of the genius of the *Iliad*, I think, is that, unlike what I am doing in this lecture, Homer does not make very heavy weather of this. He does not try to tell us how it happens; he simply shows us that it does happen. He simply gives us the portrait of Achilles being brought to acceptance, being brought to resolution, being brought to recognition of what is necessary, by seeing Priam going through the same kind of grief. Not a friend, but an enemy.

Achilles himself kills a sheep, roasts it, and serves a meal to Priam; and after they eat, Achilles promises a truce of eleven days so that the Trojans can give Hektor a proper funeral. He then has a bed prepared for Priam and he himself, Achilles himself, retires to sleep beside Briseis. This is the last time we see Achilles in the *Iliad*, and we have come full circle. He is back with Briseis now; he is fully reintegrated into the human condition; he is eating, he is sleeping, he is having sex, he is washing, he is doing all of the things that humans ought to do—and as I said before, the irony, the paradox of this is that now he too can die. He has once again become fully alive, and that means that next he can be killed, he can die.

Priam returns to Troy with Hektor's body and the *Iliad* ends with the funeral of Hektor. Achilles has made up a bed for Priam, but Hermes comes to Priam again and advises him not to remain in the Greek camp over night. Once again, the enmity is just under the surface;

better for Priam to take Hektor's body, which Achilles has put in the wagon, and return home now. Priam does this, takes Hektor's body and goes back to Troy immediately, where we see Andromache, Hekabe, and Helen each lamenting in turn over Hektor's body. The last to lament is Helen, and once again there is a kind of coming full circle. Helen, who started the Trojan War, through her abduction—or seduction, depending on whom you ask—by Paris, now speaks the last lament over Hektor's body, and says that Hektor was always kind to her, that Hektor was the kindest of Paris' brothers. So Helen is allowed to say the last words that are said over Hektor, and that gives a kind of closing element to the *Iliad*, since Helen's abduction was the beginning of the whole war.

The last line of the *Iliad* is, "so they buried Hektor, the tamer of horses." In effect the *Iliad* ends *in medias res* just as it begins *in medias res*. Another bard, in another performance, could have gone on from here: "So they buried Hektor, the tamer of horses, but Achilles strode out of his tent and went back to the battle," or some such following line. And yet, while another bard could continue the performance, it seems to me that the *Iliad* is in fact remarkably and beautifully complete. We have seen Achilles withdraw into isolation, return to humanity, and do so only to meet his own death soon after. What possible better place could there be for the poet to end this meditation on death and mortality, on the human condition and what it means to be human, on the necessity of accepting death, even of the dearest and most beloved? What better place to end this meditation on humanity than with the burial of Hektor, that most human of all heroes?

Timeline

c. 3000–c. 1000 B.C.	Successive cities occupy Hisarlik; one of them may have been "Homer's Troy."
c. 1600–c. 1100	Mycenaean civilization flourishes in Greece.
c. 1270	Destruction of Troy VI; Dörpfeld thought this was Homer's Troy.
c.1300–1200	Hittite documents mention Ahhiyawa and Wilusa, which may be references to Achaia and Ilion, and imply a war between the two.
c. 1190	Destruction of Troy VIIa; Blegen identified this as Homer's Troy.
1184	The most commonly accepted traditional date for the Fall of Troy.
c. 800?–780?	The alphabet introduced into Greece.
c. 750?–700	The *Iliad* and *Odyssey* are perhaps transcribed into writing.
c. 530	Peisistratos, tyrant of Athens, perhaps orders a "recension" or standardization of the Homeric epics.
334 B.C.	Alexander the Great visits the site of Troy, and offers sacrifices to Achilles.
c. 3rd–2nd c. B.C.	The Alexandrian scholars edit the epics, writing copious marginal notes or "scholia" on them. The epics are probably divided into their standard book-divisions at this time.
48 B.C.	Julius Caesar visits the site of Troy.
29?–19 B.C.	Virgil writes the *Aeneid*, modeled on the Homeric epics but taking the

	viewpoint of the Trojans (whom the Romans considered their ancestors). Book II of the *Aeneid* gives the fullest extant account of the Sack of Troy. The *Aeneid* was left incomplete when Virgil died in 19 B.C.
1054 A.D.	Permanent break between Roman Catholic and Greek Orthodox churches leads to rapid loss of knowledge concerning Greek language and literature in the West.
c. 1170	*Le Roman de Troie* by Bevoit de Saint-Maure brings the Trojan War story into the troubadour tradition.
c. 1313–1321	Dante writes *The Divine Comedy.*
1396	Manuel Chrysoloras offers classes in Greek in Florence. This begins the revival of interest in Greek literature in Europe.
1450	The Vatican Library is founded: it had acquired nine copies of the *Iliad* and four of the *Odyssey* by 1475.
1453	The Sack of Constantinople by the Ottomans. At this point, a great many Greek scholars flee to Italy, bringing manuscripts with them. This is when the study of Greek becomes important in Europe.
1495	Aldus Manutius founds the Aldine Press in Venice and begins printing editions of Greek classics.
1498	Erasmus begins teaching Greek at Oxford. He becomes professor of Greek at Cambridge in 1511.
1508	Girolamo Aleandro begins courses in Greek in Paris.

1795 .... F. A. Wolf publishes *Prolegomena to Homer*.

1822 .... Charles McLaren suggests that Hisarlik is the site of Troy.

1865 .... Frank Calvert does trial excavations at Hisarlik.

1870–1873 .... Heinrich Schliemann conducts his first excavations at Hisarlik. He finds the "Treasure of Priam" in 1873.

1874–1878 .... Schliemann conducts excavations at Orchomenos, Mycenae, and Ithaka.

1878 .... Schliemann's second excavation at Troy.

1882–1883 .... Schliemann's third excavation at Troy.

1888–1890 .... Schliemann's final excavation at Troy, which ended with his death.

1928 .... Milman Parry publishes his "oral composition" theory of Homeric verse.

1945 .... The "Treasure of Priam" disappears from Berlin's Museum for Prehistory and Early History, and is presumed destroyed.

1988–present .... Joint German-American excavations carried out at Troy.

1993 .... Official confirmation that the "Treasure of Priam" is in the Pushkin State Museum of Fine Arts in Moscow, as had been reported in 1991.

1996 .... The "Treasure of Priam" goes on exhibition in Moscow.

Glossary

ambrosia: The food of the gods. In the *Iliad* the gods anoint the dead bodies of Patroklos and Hektor with ambrosia to protect them from corruption. See also *nektar*.

Analysts (or Separatists): In Homeric studies, scholars who argue that the *Iliad* and the *Odyssey* are compilations of many separate, shorter poems.

aristeia: A "type scene" in which a particular hero fights with exceptional valor. An *aristeia* may be only a few lines long (for instance, Agamemnon's in *Il.* XII) or may extend for several books (for instance, Achilles' in *Il.* XIX–XXII).

athanatoi: "Deathless ones." A term used to refer to the gods, particularly as contrasted to mortals, or *thnêtoi*.

bard: The singer of epic poetry. In a preliterate culture, a bard recreates his song in each performance, using traditional formulas and type scenes as building blocks of his poetry.

dactylic hexameter: The meter of epic. It is constructed of six "feet," each consisting of *either* a dactyl (one long syllable followed by two short syllables) or a spondee (two long syllables). The resulting line is flexible and varied in Greek, though it tends to sound pedestrian in English.

Epic Cycle: A series of epics, no longer extant, which told the story of those episodes of the Trojan War not contained in the *Iliad* and the *Odyssey*.

epithet: An adjective or group of adjectives closely associated with a character's name. Examples include "Hektor *of the shining helmet*," "*swift-footed* Achilles," and so on.

formula: In Parry's definition, "a group of words which is regularly employed under the same metrical conditions to express a given essential idea."

geras: A "prize of honor"; a particularly valuable or esteemed token of distinction conferred on a warrior by his peers. Chryseis is Agamemnon's *geras*; Briseis is Achilles'.

guzlar: A South Slavic bard, such as those studied by Milman Parry and Albert Lord. The *guzlar* chants his songs to the accompaniment of a stringed instrument called a *guzle*.

Hittites: Indo-European people whose kingdom flourished in Anatolia from c. 1650–c.1200 B.C. Some scholars believe that Hittite documents mention Greece (Achaia) and Troy (Ilion), and even imply a war between the two.

"The Homeric Question": The great scholarly question of whether the Homeric epics were written by a single author (or perhaps by two authors) or are compilations of various shorter, traditional poems. See also *Analysts* and *Unitarians*.

in medias res: "In the middle of the subject." This phrase describes the typical opening of an epic.

Indo-European: The prehistoric parent language of Greek, Latin, Sanskrit, most modern languages of Europe, and many modern languages of India. Indo-European was never written down, but scholars have made hypothetical reconstructions of some of its words and forms by comparative study of the languages which descended from it. The people who spoke this language are referred to as "Indo-Europeans."

Hisarlik or Hissarlik: The flat-topped hill in the Troad where Schliemann located the prehistoric ruins of Troy.

Ithaka: Odysseus' home island.

kleos*, pl. *klea: Glory or fame; that which others say about one, particularly after one's death. *Kleos* is what epic conveys upon its heroes. The phrase *kleos aphthiton*, "imperishable glory," exactly parallels the Sanskrit *sravas aksitam* and may reflect an original Indo-European poetic phrase for imperishable glory.

mênis: Wrath; the first word of the *Iliad*, where it refers especially to Achilles' anger. Elsewhere in Homer, the word is used only in association with gods.

mêtis: Wisdom, skill, cunning, craftiness. Odysseus' most common epithet is *polumêtis*, "of much *mêtis*."

Mycenaean culture: The name given by archaeologists to the prehistoric Bronze Age culture discovered by 19th-century archaeologists.

Myrmidons: Soldiers under the command of Achilles.

nektar: The drink of the gods. See also *ambrosia*.

Nekuia: Odysseus' visit to the Underworld, *Od*. XI. The scene that opens *Od*. XXIV, which shows the souls of the suitors arriving in Hades, is often called "the second *Nekuia*."

nostos: Return or homecoming. Throughout the *Odyssey*, Odysseus strives for his own *nostos* and the *nostos* of his companions. Some scholars think that *nostos*-poetry was a whole subcategory of epic, to which the *Odyssey* belonged. One poem of the Epic Cycle was entitled *Nostoi*, or returns. The English word *nostalgia* literally means "longing for return/homecoming."

Ogygia: The island of the nymph Kalypso, where Odysseus was held captive for seven years.

polutropos: "Of many turns." This ambiguous epithet, used to identify Odysseus in the first line of the *Odyssey*, refers both to his wanderings and to his cleverness.

proem: The opening lines of an epic, which introduce the main theme of the poem.

psyche: Often translated as "soul," this word originally seems to have meant "breath." It is what leaves the body at death. Though it survives in some sense in Hades, its existence there is vague and shadowy.

Scheria: The island of the Phaiakians, where Odysseus is treated with marvelous *xenia*.

Telemachy: The first four books of the *Odyssey*, which concentrate on Odysseus' son Telemachos.

thnêtoi: "The dying ones." A term used to refer to human beings, particularly as contrasted to the immortal gods, or *athanatoi*.

thrift: In discussing Homeric verse, this refers to the fact that different phrases used to describe one character will occupy different metrical positions in the line. Sometimes also called "economy."

timê: Honor, especially the external, visible tokens of honor bestowed on a warrior by his peers. See also *geras*.

type scenes: Standardized scenes that are repeated with minimal variation in the epics. They include short, fixed descriptions of feasting, of setting sail, etc., as well as longer and more flexible accounts of battle. See also *aristeia*.

xenia: "The guest/host relationship." Our term "hospitality" does not adequately convey the seriousness of the concept. *Xenia* was protected by Zeus, and covers the whole range of obligations that guests and hosts (*xenoi*, see next entry) have to one another. Violations of these obligations bring dire consequences: Paris' theft of Helen was, among other things, a violation of *xenia*, as are the suitors' actions throughout the *Odyssey*.

xenos: A guest, host, friend, stranger, or foreigner (cf. *xenophobia*). The range of this word's meanings reflects the essential nature of *xenia* (see previous entry), which does not depend upon prior acquaintance but operates between strangers. Once two men have entered into a relationship of *xenia* by one of them staying in the other's house, they are "guest-friends" and have obligations to one another.

Unitarians: Scholars who believe that the Homeric epics were composed in their present form by one poet, not assembled from various much shorter poems.

Biographical Notes

I. Real People

Blegen, Carl (1887–1971). American archaeologist, who directed the University of Cincinnati's excavations at Troy (Hisarlik) from 1932 to 1938. He argued strongly that Troy VIIa, from c. 1250 B.C., should be identified as Homer's Troy.

Calvert, Frank (1928–1980). A British citizen who lived in the Troad (and worked as American consul). His family owned part of Hisarlik, and Calvert probably directed Schliemann's attention to it as the most likely site of Troy. Calvert had done some trial excavating in 1865, before Schliemann arrived in Turkey, and perhaps should be recognized as the actual discoverer of Troy.

Dörpfeld, Wilhelm (1853–1940). Schliemann's successor as excavator of Troy and Mycenae. He thought that Homer's Troy should be identified with Troy VI (c. 1300).

Homer (c. 700 B.C.E.?). The name traditionally given to the bard of the *Iliad* and the *Odyssey*. But there is little to no agreement about when or where such a person lived, or even if it is reasonable to refer to one bard for the epics at all.

Lord, Albert (1912–1991). A student and colleague of Milman Parry who carried on Parry's Yugoslavian fieldwork after Parry's tragically early death.

McLaren, Charles (1782–1866). Scottish journalist and editor of the 6th edition of the *Encyclopedia Britannica*. He suggested, in 1822, that the ruins of ancient Troy must be at Hisarlik.

Parry, Milman (1902–1935). An American scholar whose 1928 doctoral dissertation for the University of Paris was the first clear demonstration of the importance of formulas and oral compositional techniques in the Homeric epics. Just before his early death, he was engaged in fieldwork on oral poetics in Yugoslavia, where he traveled in 1933 and 1934–1935.

Schliemann, Heinrich (1822–1890). German archaeologist; the "discoverer of Troy" and excavator of Mycenae. He began excavations at Hisarlik in 1871 and discovered the "Treasure of Priam" in 1873. From 1874–1876 he ran excavations in Greece, notably at Mycenae and Orchomenos, and returned to Troy in April

1876. Though he did not understand the complexity or age of the ruins he excavated, misidentifying Troy II (c. 2200 B.C.) as Homer's Troy, Schliemann deserves great credit for his pioneering work.

Wolf, Friedrich August (1759–1824). Author of *Prolegomena to Homer* (1795), which gave rise to the 19th-century controversy over "the Homeric Question."

II. Epic Characters: Humans, Monsters, and Gods

(Note on transliteration of names: With one exception, I have followed the transliteration used in Richmond Lattimore's translations, since those are the versions I recommend that students buy. The one exception is the name **Achilles.** While "Achilleus" is certainly more correct, "Achilles" has become the standard English spelling to such a degree that I find it hard to adjust to any other.)

Achilles. Greatest Greek warrior. His withdrawal from battle because Agamemnon takes his concubine Briseis, and his subsequent return to avenge the death of his friend Patroklos, form the framework of the *Iliad.*

Agamemnon. Commander-in-chief of the Greek forces. Brother of Menelaos; husband of Klytaimestra. In the *Iliad*, his initial refusal to surrender his concubine Chryseis and subsequent appropriation of Achilles' concubine Briseis motivate Achilles' withdrawal from battle. In the *Odyssey*, the story of his murder by Aigisthos and Klytaimestra, and the vengeance taken by his son Orestes, is frequently cited as a parallel to Odysseus' family situation.

Aigisthos. Cousin of Agamemnon and Menelaos, who seduces Klytaimestra while Agamemnon is away at war. He murders Agamemnon upon his return from Troy, and is himself killed by Agamemnon's son Orestes. This story is frequently cited in the *Odyssey* as a parallel to Odysseus' family situation.

Aiolos. The "king of the winds." He gives Odysseus a bag with all the contrary winds in it, but unfortunately the companions open the bag just before they reach Ithaka.

Aias the Greater. Son of Telamon; the greatest Greek warrior after Achilles. He figures prominently in the *Iliad.* According to the Epic Cycle, he committed suicide out of shame after the Greeks voted to ward the dead Achilles' armor to Odysseus rather than to him. His ghost is still angry over this slight when it appears in *Od.* XI and refuses to speak to Odysseus. (His name may be more familiar in the Latinized form Ajax.)

Aias the Lesser. Son of Oïleus. He raped Kassandra in Athena's temple during the Sack of Troy, thus bringing down Athena's anger on all the Greeks. Menelaos recounts how he was drowned by Poseidon (*Od.* IV).

Alexandros. See Paris.

Alkinoos. King of the Phaiakians, husband of Arete, father of Nausikaa.

Andromache. Wife of Hektor, mother of Astyanax. She appears several times in the *Iliad*, most notably in her conversation with Hektor (*Il.* VI) and her lament over his corpse (*Il.* XXIV).

Antikleia. Odysseus' mother, whose ghost he sees in the *Nekuia*.

Antinoos. With Eurymachos, one of the two ringleaders of the suitors. The first suitor to be killed by Odysseus (*Od.* XXII).

Aphrodite. Daughter of Zeus and Dione; wife of Hephaistos (in the *Odyssey*, though not in the *Iliad*); mother (by the mortal Anchises) of the Trojan Aeneas; lover of Ares. Goddess of sexual passion. She motivates Paris' abduction of Helen. Favors the Trojans.

Apollo. Son of Zeus and Leto, twin brother of Artemis. In the *Iliad*, he appears mainly as the god of prophecy and as the bringer of plague and sudden death. Later authors would stress his association with reason, healing, and music. His identification with the sun is much later than Homer.

Ares. Son of Zeus and Hera; god of war; particularly associated with the physical, bloody, distressing aspects of war (cf. Athena).

Arete. Phaiakian queen, wife of Alkinoos, mother of Nausikaa (*Od.* VII–VIII).

Argos. 1) Agamemnon's city. 2) Odysseus' old dog, who dies upon seeing his master (*Od.* XVII).

Artemis. Daughter of Zeus and Leto; twin sister of Apollo. A virgin goddess. She is the patron of hunters, of wild animals, and girls before their marriage. She brings sudden death to women. Her identification with the moon is later than Homer.

Astyanax. Baby son of Hektor and Andromache; appears with his parents in *Il.* VI. During the Sack of Troy, he is thrown from the walls of the city and killed.

Athena. Daughter of Zeus, who sprang from his brow fully grown and wearing armor. She is the goddess of warfare in its nobler aspects (cf. Ares). A virgin goddess, she is associated with wisdom, cleverness, and weaving. In the *Odyssey*, she appears as Odysseus' special patron. Usually favors the Greeks, but becomes enraged with them during the Sack of Troy.

Briseis. Achilles' concubine and *geras*. Agamemnon's taking her motivates Achilles' withdrawal from battle in *Il.* I.

Charybdis. A very dangerous whirlpool, personified as a female entity. Odysseus has to sail between her and Skylla.

Chryses. An old priest of Apollo. Agamemnon's refusal to return his daughter Chryseis motivates the opening episode of the *Iliad*.

Chryseis. Daughter of Chryses; concubine and *geras* of Agamemnon. His refusal to return her to her father motivates the opening episode of the *Iliad*.

Circe (Kirke). Goddess, daughter of Helios the sun-god, enchantress. She turns half of Odysseus' companions into swine. Odysseus spends one year with her as her lover.

Demodokos. The bard of the Phaiakians, who sings three songs in *Od.* VIII.

Diomedes. A Greek warrior, who wounds Ares and Aphrodite during his *aristeia* in *Iliad* V. Exchanges armor as a token of *xenia* with Glaukos (*Il.* VI).

Eumaios. Odysseus' swineherd, who remains loyal to his master. The disguised Odysseus goes to his hut and receives *xenia* from him in *Od.* XIV. Eumaios fights with Odysseus and Telemachos to defeat the suitors.

Euryalos. A young Phaiakian, son of Alkinoos, who insults Odysseus by saying he does not look like an athlete.

Eurykleia. Odysseus' and Telemachos' old nurse. She recognizes Odysseus by the scar on his thigh (*Od.* XIX).

Eurylochos. Odysseus' second-in-command; often opposes or argues against Odysseus' commands. Encourages his companions to kill and eat Helios' cattle (*Od.* XII).

Eurymachos. With Antinoos, one of the two ringleaders of the suitors; his words to the seer Halitherses in *Od.* II illustrate the suitors' rejections of their society's most important mores.

Eurynome. Odysseus' and Penelope's housekeeper.

Glaukos. Trojan ally, close friend of Sarpedon. Exchanges armor with Diomedes as a token of *xenia* (*Il.* VI).

Hades. Brother of Zeus, husband of Persephone. Ruler of the Underworld (Tartaros), which comes to be called Hades after him.

Halitherses. Ithakan seer, who tries to reason with the suitors in *Od.* II.

Hekabe. Queen of Troy, wife of Priam, mother of Hektor, Paris, and Kassandra. (May be more familiar in the Latinized spelling of her name, "Hecuba.")

Hektor. Crown prince of Troy, son of Priam and Hekabe, husband of Andromache, father of Astyanax. He kills Patroklos and is killed by Achilles.

Helen. Daughter of Zeus and Leda, sister of Klytaimestra, wife of Menelaos; the most beautiful woman in the world. Her seduction (or kidnapping?) by Paris is the cause of the Trojan War.

Helios. The sun god. Father of Circe. Owner of the cattle on the island Thrinakia, which Odysseus' companions eat although they have been warned not to do so.

Hephaistos. Son of Zeus and Hera, or perhaps of Hera alone. In the *Iliad*, he is married to Charis; in the *Odyssey*, to Aphrodite. He is lame and ugly. The smith-god, who forges Achilles' new armor in *Iliad* XVIII and to some extent represents fire itself.

Hera. Wife and sister of Zeus, mother of Hephaistos and Ares. She is the patron goddess of marriage and married women. In the *Iliad*, hates the Trojans and favors the Greeks.

Herakles. Greatest Greek hero, son of Zeus and the mortal woman Alkmene. He lived (probably) two generations before the Trojan War. He is cited as a paradigm of the hero throughout both epics; Odysseus speaks to his spirit in the Underworld (*Od.* XI).

Kalchas. Seer/soothsayer for Agamemnon and the entire Greek army.

Kalypso. Nymph (or minor goddess) who keeps Odysseus captive on her island Ogygia for seven years.

Kassandra. Daughter of Priam and Hekabe; sister of Hektor and Paris. During the Sack of Troy, Aias the Lesser rapes her in the temple of Athena. This outrage motivates the goddess' anger at the Greeks.

Klytaimestra. Wife of Agamemnon, mother of Orestes, half-sister of Helen. She takes Aigisthos as her lover while Agamemnon is away at Troy, and assists Aigisthos in murdering him upon his return. This story is frequently cited in the *Odyssey* as a parallel to Odysseus' family situation.

Laertes. Father of Odysseus, father-in-law of Penelope, grandfather of Telemachos. Appears in *Od.* XXIV.

Laistrygones. Monstrous cannibals who destroy eleven of Odysseus' twelve ships (*Od.* X).

Leodes. Young suitor, the first to try to string Odysseus' bow.

Lykaon. Young son of Priam; half-brother of Paris and Hektor. He fruitlessly begs Achilles for mercy in *Il.* XXI.

Medon. Odysseus' herald, who served the suitors unwillingly. Odysseus spares his life at Telemachos' request.

Melanthios. Odysseus' goatherd, who is disloyal to his master; brother of Melantho. He brings armor and weapons to the suitors in *Od.* XXII.

Melantho. One of Odysseus' slavewomen, disloyal to her master; lover of Eurymachos; sister of Melanthios.

Menelaos. Brother of Agamemnon, husband of Helen. Prominent figure in the *Iliad*; appears briefly in *Od.* IV.

Nausikaa. Young Phaiakian princess who befriends Odysseus when he washes up on the shores of Scheria (*Od.* VI).

Nestor. Oldest and wisest of the Greeks; appears in both the *Iliad* and (briefly) in *Od.* III.

Odysseus. Husband of Penelope, father of Telemachos, son of Laertes and Antikleia. Cleverest and craftiest of the Greeks; an important character in the *Iliad*, where he takes part in the Embassy to Achilles (*Il.* IX). Main character of the *Odyssey*.

Orestes. Son of Agamemnon and Klytaimestra. He avenges his father's murder by killing Aigisthos and Klytaimestra. This story is frequently cited in the *Odyssey* as a parallel to Odysseus' family situation.

Outis. "Nobody," or "Noman," the name by which Odysseus identifies himself to the Cyclops Polyphemos.

Paris (also called Alexandros). Son of Priam and Hekabe, brother of Hektor; prince of Troy. His abduction or perhaps seduction of Helen from her husband Menelaos motivates the Trojan War.

Patroklos. Achilles' dearest friend, who goes into battle wearing Achilles' armor and is killed by Hektor.

Peleus. Achilles' father; husband of Thetis. He does not appear in the *Iliad*, but is alluded to very frequently.

Penelope. Wife of Odysseus, mother of Telemachos. One of the main themes of the *Odyssey* is her courting by 108 suitors and the difficulties this causes her. The question of whether or not she will remain faithful to Odysseus permeates the epic.

Persephone. Wife of Hades, queen of the Underworld.

Phemios. Odysseus' bard, who served the suitors unwillingly. Odysseus spares his life at Telemachos' request.

Philoktetes. The greatest Greek archer in the Trojan War. Odysseus says that he himself was "second only to Philoktetes" as an archer (*Od.* VIII).

Philoitios. Odysseus' cowherd, who is loyal to his master. He fights with Odysseus and Telemachos to defeat the suitors in *Od.* XXII.

Phoinix. Achilles' old "foster-father," takes part in the Embassy to Achilles in *Il.* IX.

Polyphemos. Cyclops, son of the god Poseidon (*Od.* IX). His curse of Odysseus, who blinded him, motivates most of Odysseus' troubles in the *Odyssey*.

Poseidon. Brother of Zeus, god of the sea. In the *Iliad* he favors the Greeks; in the *Odyssey* he hates Odysseus for blinding his son, the Cyclops Polyphemos.

Priam. King of Troy, father of Hektor and Paris, husband of Hekabe. He visits Achilles in *Il.* XXIV to ransom Hektor's body.

Sarpedon. Trojan ally from Lykia, son of Zeus. Close friend of Glaukos. He is killed by Patroklos in *Il.* XVI.

Skamandros. A river of Troy; personified, it battles Achilles in *Il.* XXI.

Skylla. A six-headed, human-devouring monster. Odysseus has to sail between her and Charybdis.

Teiresias. The great Theban seer whose spirit Odysseus consults in the Underworld (*Od.* IX).

Telemachos. Son of Odysseus and Penelope. The first four books of the *Odyssey* (the *Telemachy*) focus on him. In Books XVI–XXIV, he helps his father defeat the suitors.

Thetis. Sea-goddess; mother of Achilles; wife of Peleus.

Xanthos. 1) One of Achilles' immortal horses, who speaks to him in a human voice at the end of *Il.* XIX. 2) Another name for Skamandros.

Zeus. The ruler of the Olympian gods. Brother and husband of Hera; brother of Hades and Poseidon; father of Aphrodite, Apollo, Ares, Artemis, Athena, and perhaps Hephaistos. Originally a sky-god, he controls thunder and lightning. The patron of justice, suppliants, and *xenia*.

Bibliography

I. Essential Readings: A Selection of Translations of the Homeric Epics

Lattimore, Richmond, trans. *The Iliad of Homer*. Chicago and London: The University of Chicago Press, 1951; *The Odyssey of Homer*. New York: Harper Perennial, 1991. These are my preferred translations for several reasons. First, Lattimore translates the Greek line by line; thus, line references to the original make sense for this translation as well. This is very helpful to the student who is reading supplementary materials that include line references. Second, Lattimore preserves Homer's formulas in his translation; whenever Homer repeats precisely the same words, Lattimore repeats precisely the same words. This goes a long way toward preserving the "feel" of Homer in English. Third, Lattimore's language is somewhat archaic and difficult sounding. Again, this is truer to the original than a more idiomatic rendering would be, since the dialect of the epics is itself an artificial, poetic dialect. Fourth, Lattimore's meter consistently gives as adequate a sense of Homer's hexameters as can well be done in English, and at times is magnificent.

Acknowledgment: Quotes in these lectures from *The Iliad of Homer*, translated by Richmond Lattimore, copyright 1951 by The University of Chicago, were used with permission by arrangement with The University of Chicago Press.

Fitzgerald, Robert. *The Iliad*. New York: Anchor Press, 1989; *The Odyssey*. New York: Vintage Books, 1990. Many people prefer these translations for their readability. They are very good modern English poetry; however, in my estimation they do not accurately convey the feeling of Homer's style. Fitzgerald's meter does not even attempt to convey the hexameter, and he does not preserve the formulas.

Fagles, Robert. *The Iliad*. New York: Penguin USA, 1998; *The Odyssey*. New York, Penguin USA, 1997. These new translations received a great deal of critical attention when they appeared, most of it very favorable. Although I prefer them to Fitzgerald's versions, in my view they are marred by excessive use of colloquial language (e.g., phrases such as "cramping my style"). Similarly, Fagles' meter does not capture the feeling of the Homeric hexameter.

II. Supplementary Readings

(Note: The amount of scholarly writing on Homer is staggering; hundreds of books have appeared in the past ten years alone. In fact, it is a common lament among classicists that no one individual could possibly be familiar with everything that has been written about Homer. Faced with this vast amount of scholarship, I have tried to winnow out a representative selection of useful and interesting studies. I have avoided books that assume knowledge either of Greek or of complicated modern theoretical approaches. I have also included several works that disagree, at least to some extent, with my own view of some of the issues raised by the epics, so that students may gain some sense of the range of possible interpretations that the epics elicit. Finally, I have tried to pick works that have good bibliographies, to aid those students who wish to continue their journey through the thickets of Homeric scholarship.)

Allen, Susan Hueck. *Finding the Walls of Troy: Frank Calvert and Heinrich Schliemann at Hisarlik.* Berkeley and Los Angeles: The University of California Press, 1999. A fascinating, well-written, and meticulously documented account of the work and interactions of these two archaeologists, which argues that Calvert deserves credit as the actual discoverer of Troy.

Austin, Norman. *Archery at the Dark of the Moon: Poetic Problems in Homer's Odyssey.* Berkeley, Los Angeles, London: University of California Press, 1975. A well-written, detailed analysis of several key themes in the *Odyssey.* Particularly interesting discussion of Odysseus' and Penelope's interactions before and after the slaughter of the suitors.

———. *Helen of Troy and Her Shameless Phantom.* Ithaca and London: Cornell University Press, 1994. Discusses Helen's role in Homer and other Greek authors, including the version of her story that said only a phantom went to Troy. Explores Helen's fundamental dual nature as both woman and goddess.

Clay, Jenny Strauss. *The Wrath of Athena: Gods and Men in the Odyssey.* Princeton: Princeton University Press, 1983. A very well-written, clear discussion, focusing on Odysseus' relationship with Athena but covering many important critical issues.

Cohen, Beth, ed. *The Distaff Side*: *Representing the Female in Homer's Odyssey.* New York, Oxford: Oxford University Press,

1995. A collection of important essays spanning the disciplines of classics, history, and art history.

Doherty, Lillian Eileen. "Sirens, Muses, and Female Narrators in the *Odyssey*," in Cohen, *Distaff Side*, pp. 81–89. A thought-provoking examination of the importance of the Sirens in the epic.

Edwards, Mark W. *Homer: Poet of the Iliad*. Baltimore and London: The Johns Hopkins University Press, 1987. A well-written discussion of some of the major themes and issues of the *Iliad*. Includes detailed commentaries on several key books.

Fitton, J. Lesley. *The Discovery of the Greek Bronze Age*. Cambridge: Harvard University Press, 1996. A readable and entertaining account of the pioneering archaeologists who excavated the most important Bronze Age sites.

Gantz, Timothy. *Early Greek Myth: A Guide to Literary and Artistic Sources*. 2 vols. Baltimore, London: Johns Hopkins University Press, 1993. An extremely detailed survey of all the sources of traditional Greek myths. The materials on the Trojan War are in Vol. 2.

Griffin, Jasper. *Homer on Life and Death*. Oxford: Clarendon Press, 1980. An elegant, beautifully written discussion of Homer's presentation of mortality.

Hölscher, Uvo. "Penelope and the Suitors," in Schein, *Reading the Odyssey*, pp. 133–140. An examination of Penelope's motivations for coming down to see the suitors in *Odyssey* XVIII.

Kirk, Geoffrey. *The Songs of Homer*. Cambridge: Cambridge University Press, 1962. A discussion of the nature, genesis, and quality of the Homeric epics, which pays detailed attention to historical background and the Parry-Lord theory of oral composition. Clearly written and well worth reading, even if somewhat dated.

Lord, Albert Bates. *The Singer of Tales*. New York: Atheneum, 1978. Uses the fieldwork Lord and Parry did in the former Yugoslavia as a basis for theorizing about the formation of Homeric verse. Fascinating reading for anyone at all interested in oral poetry and how it works.

Lowenstam, Steven. *The Scepter and the Spear: Studies on Forms of Repetition in the Homeric Poems*. Lanham, MD: Rowman & Littlefield Publishers, Inc., 1993. A reassessment of the forms and significance of repetition in the Homeric epics, in light of the discoveries of Parry and Lord. Several intriguing interpretations, well-written, and all Greek quotations are translated.

Murnaghan, Sheila. "The Plan of Athena," in Cohen, *The Distaff Side*, pp. 61–80. Examines Athena's role throughout the *Odyssey*, with special attention to Book XIII.

Morrison, James V. *Homeric Misdirection: False Predictions in the Iliad.* Ann Arbor: University of Michigan Press, 1992. As the title indicates, this book examines false or misleading predictions in the *Iliad* and argues that they are a method for building suspense among an audience that already knows the basic outlines of the traditional story.

Nagler, Michael N. "Dread Goddess Revisited." In Schein, *Reading the Odyssey*, pp. 141–161. An interesting analysis of Circe, Kalypso, and Penelope, with detailed discussion of the import of Odysseus and Penelope's bed.

Nagy, Gregory. *The Best of the Achaeans: Concepts of the Hero in Archaic Greek Poetry*. Baltimore, London: Johns Hopkins University Press, 1979. Very densely written, technical examination of several key words in Homer, focusing especially on *kleos*. Recommended for those with an interest in the workings of the Greek language (all Greek is transliterated).

———. *Greek Mythology and Poetics*. Ithaca and London: Cornell University Press, 1990. A collection of essays on a wide range of subjects, which examines Greek poetry and mythology in its wider Indo-European context, particularly through comparison with Indic mythology and poetics. Chapters 2 (Formula and Meter) and 4 (Patroklos, Concepts of Afterlife, and the Indic Triple Fire) are particularly relevant for this course.

Olson, S. Douglas. *Blood and Iron: Stories and Storytelling in Homer's Odyssey.* Leiden, New York, Köln: E. J. Brill, 1995. A well-written and thought-provoking discussion of several of the major critical issues in the *Odyssey*. Interesting reading.

The Oxford Classical Dictionary. 3rd ed. Eds. Simon Hornblower and Anthony Spawforth. Oxford and New York: Oxford University Press, 1996. The standard one-volume reference work on Greek and Roman antiquity.

Parry, Milman. *The Making of Homeric Verse: The Collected Papers of Milman Parry*. Ed. Adam Parry. Oxford: The Clarendon Press, 1971. All of Parry's published and unpublished writings on Homer, collected by his son. Parry's arguments are highly detailed and assume knowledge of Greek, but will make fascinating reading for any student who wants to learn more about Parry's insights on the epics' composition.

Powell, Barry. *Homer and the Origin of the Greek Alphabet*. Cambridge: Cambridge University Press, 1991. A highly controversial work, which argues that the alphabet's adaptation for the Greek language was motivated by the desire to record the Homeric epics. This argument has not found wide acceptance among scholars, but the book is thought-provoking and lucidly written. It also provides a great deal of information about early non-alphabetic writing systems.

Schein, Seth L. *The Mortal Hero: An Introduction to Homer's Iliad*. Berkeley, Los Angeles, London: University of California Press, 1984. An excellent, lucid, informative introduction to several of the major themes of the *Iliad*. This book had a profound influence on my own understanding of the *Iliad*, though I have come to disagree with Schein on several points.

———, ed. *Reading the Odyssey: Selected Interpretative Essays*. Princeton: Princeton University Press, 1996. Collects several important essays on specific aspects of the *Odyssey*.

Seaford, Richard. *Reciprocity and Ritual: Homer and Tragedy in the Developing City-State*. Oxford: Clarendon Press, 1994. As the title indicates, Homer is only part of this book's subject matter. However, there are several chapters on the Homeric epics that are thought-provoking and useful.

Segal, Charles. *The Theme of the Mutilation of the Corpse in the Iliad*. Mnemosyne Suppl. 17. Leiden: E. J. Brill, 1971. Traces the theme of mistreated corpses throughout the *Iliad*, with special discussion of Achilles' treatment of Hektor. Clearly written, readable, and interesting; unfortunately, Greek quotations are usually not translated.

Shapiro, H. A. "Coming of Age in Phaiakia: The Meeting of Odysseus and Nausikaa," in Cohen, *Distaff Side*, pp. 155–164. Compares Homer's description of the Odysseus-Nausikaa scene with its representations in Athenian art of the 5th century B.C.E., and concludes that an implicit threat of rape was very much part of the 5th-century audience's understanding of the scene.

Shay, Jonathan. *Achilles in Vietnam: Combat Trauma and the Undoing of Character*. New York: Athenaeum, 1994. A fascinating and deeply disturbing book. Dr. Shay, a psychiatrist who treats

Vietnam veterans suffering from post-traumatic stress disorder, reads the *Iliad* against the background of those veterans' experiences. The book contains a great deal of profanity (in quotations of veterans' statements to Dr. Shay) and some extremely graphic descriptions of combat violence, and so may not be appropriate for all students. But those who can stomach its uncompromising portrait of the reality of war will find it intensely thought-provoking.

Slatkin, Laura M. "Composition by Theme and the Mêtis of the *Odyssey*," in Schein, *Reading the Odyssey*, pp. 223–237. Discusses the importance of the concept of *mêtis* for the narrative and thematic structure of the *Odyssey*.

———. *The Power of Thetis: Allusion and Interpretation in the Iliad.* Berkeley: University of California Press, 1992. An elegant little (122 pp.) book which examines Thetis' role in the *Iliad* and the poet's use and adaptation of myths not recounted within the epic itself.

Vernant, Jean-Pierre. "Death with Two Faces," in Schein, *Reading the Odyssey*, pp. 55–61. A discussion of Homer's depiction of death, with close attention to Achilles' words to Odysseus in *Odyssey* XI.

———. "The Refusal of Odysseus," in Schein, *Reading the Odyssey*, pp. 185–189. A detailed discussion of Odysseus' refusal to become immortal and stay with Kalypso.

Wolf, F. A. *Prolegomena to Homer: 1795*. Trans. Anthony Grafton, Glenn W. Most, and James E. G. Zetzel. Princeton: Princeton University Press, 1985. A clear, readable translation of this groundbreaking work, with detailed and helpful notes.

Wood, Michael. *In Search of the Trojan War*. A fascinating, well-written, and well-documented examination of the evidence for the historicity of the Trojan War. Includes many illustrations, maps, etc.

Woodford, Susan. *The Trojan War in Ancient Art*. Ithaca: Cornell University Press, 1993. A useful summary of the mythical background to the Trojan War, with illustrations from ancient art.

Zeitlin, Froma I. "Figuring Fidelity in Homer's *Odyssey*," in Cohen, *Distaff Side*, pp. 117–152. An extremely detailed examination of the depiction of female fidelity in the *Odyssey*, focusing primarily on Odysseus' and Penelope's bed and its connections with the rest of the epic.

Notes

Notes